SIMPLY THE BEST

Adrian McGregor is a writer with wide experience on
Australian newspapers as well as on Fleet Street. He
has worked for the *Sydney Morning Herald*, the *Australian* and the *Courier-Mail*, and for five years he was
Queensland Bureau Chief of the *National Times*. He has
a BA from the University of Queensland where he tu-
tored in journalism for many years. He has won several journalism prizes, including a National Press Club
award for best sporting feature. His trail blazing
bestseller *King Wally* created a new readership for
rugby league books. It was followed by the popular
Wally and the Broncos (1989). His biography of Greg
Chappell (new edition 1990) has been acclaimed as one
of the finest contemporary contributions to the history
of cricket.

By the same author

King Wally
Wally and the Broncos
Greg Chappell: Cricket's Incomparable Artist

SIMPLY THE BEST

THE 1990 KANGAROOS

ADRIAN McGREGOR

University of Queensland Press

First published 1991 by the University of Queensland Press
Box 42, St Lucia, Queensland 4067 Australia

Typeset by University of Queensland Press
Printed in Australia by The Book Printer, Victoria

Distributed in the USA and Canada by
International Specialized Book Services, Inc.,
5602 N.E. Hassalo Street, Portland, Oregon 97213-3640

Cataloguing in Publication Data
National Library of Australia

McGregor, Adrian.
  Simply the best, the 1990 Kangaroos.

  1. Kangaroos (Rugby Team). 2. Rugby League football
  — Tournaments — Australia. 3. Rugby League football
  — Tournaments — Great Britain. I. Title (Series :
  UQP sports).

796. 3338

ISBN 0 7022 2370 0

To Helen

PREFACE

Like the Olympic and Commonwealth Games, Kangaroo tours
of England occur only once every four years and in the world of
Australian rugby league nothing exceeds the excitement of an
approaching tour. I grew up reading about Kangaroo tours, listening to broadcasts of them, watching telecasts and eventually
I wrote about them in the course of my biographies of Wally
Lewis. It seemed only natural then that I should eventually follow one — the 1990 Kangaroos — and write a book about it. To
do this I left Australia three months before the Roos, settled in
an old wool-weaving village outside Manchester and began re-
searching the English club scene. To my surprise I found rugby
league no minor sport pottering away in the forgotten north of
England. I encountered a confident, wealthy, expanding sporting industry, the full impact of which Australia's Test team was
soon to feel. That led me to delve into the history of the North
and the nature of the people who produced such a fierce, excit-
ing, game. I didn't have to go down a coal mine, freeze on the
moors or dice with death on the M62 to watch the Roos, but unless you know the true North, you can't know rugby league in
England.

That I wrote this book I must thank, in rough order of priority, John Alexander editor-in-chief of the *Sydney Morning Herald*
for employing me, the University of Queensland Press, particularly Craig Munro for his good-humoured support — and the
Toshiba. The infectious enthusiasm of Steve Ricketts of the

Courier-Mail bore me forth and to him I owe my bus ride from York and my introduction to Ray Fletcher of the *Yorkshire Post*. To Ray I am especially indebted for making me so welcome in Leeds and then not flinching when I eventually asked him to speed-read this manuscript for me. Needless to say I eventually qualified for my librarian's card in how to use his and David Howes' prodigious *Rothmans Rugby League Yearbook*. It was sheer luck that my visit also coincided with the publication of Ian Proctor and Andrew Varley's invaluable *Stones Bitter Rugby League Directory*. Andrew provided most of the photographs for this book, as well as a friendly smile whenever we met, which was often. The extra photographs are from Queensland Newspapers, several by staffer Steve Moorhouse, who snapped the back cover shot of me. Two photographs, as identified, are courtesy of the *Yorkshire Post*, and for Peter O'Halloran's series from the video of Mal Meninga's stunning second Test try, I'm obliged to Channel 10 in Brisbane.

I am grateful to the Australian media corps for their professional acceptance of me and I especially thank the Queensland editor of *Rugby League Week*, Tony Durkin, and Channel 10's David Morrow for their friendliness towards a blow-in comrade.

In England I gladly acknowledge the assistance of Trevor Delaney and his book, *The Roots of Rugby League*, and for pointing me towards Code 13. Other authors whose rugby league research I found valuable include Geoffrey Moorhouse, Robert Gate and Andrew Hardcastle. Chris Aspin's readers on cotton and wool mills were educational. On the technical front I hope to have converted to rugby league Mike Grey, of Software Systems, Oldham.

I have tried to be consistent in using Great Britain or Britain when referring to the Test team and England when writing about the clubs. Some English pounds sterling I have not changed to Australian dollars because time has made currency conversions meaningless. Likewise the Poms have not all converted to metric in height and weight.

The Kangaroos played their last match in England on November 24, 1990. To produce this book in time for the 1991 Australian football season would have been impossible without the professional assistance and generous support of Helen King.

The Heartland of Rugby League in England

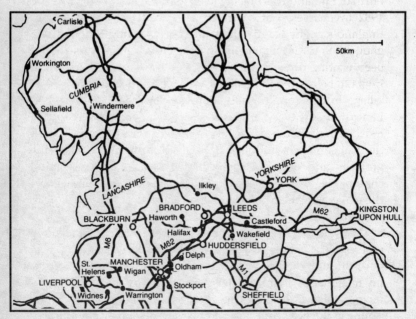

1 SAINTS FALL EASY

Sunday, match day, bloomed as blue as a backdrop to Bondi Beach, the sun a little weak maybe and the air a might nippy, but by far the brightest morning since the Kangaroos arrived six days earlier. Their tour bus was parked outside the entrance to the Ramada Renaissance Hotel in the centre of Manchester and I was waiting to tail them to their showdown with St Helens. It was October 7, first match for the 1990 Kangaroos and the north of England was bracing itself for what had been, since the 1982 Invincibles, not so much a football tour, as a lesson. England's rugby league clubs had been waiting four years to gauge their improvement against the world champions and I'd been waiting three months to witness the contest. I arrived in England before the football season began and settled in a small village in the Pennine hills, halfway between Yorkshire and Lancashire, the two counties where the Kangaroos were to play most of their matches. In three months I visited every club on the Kangaroos' schedule, spoke to the officials, walked the grounds and admired their photographic galleries of past champions. I steeped myself in the tradition and the history, the reality and the romance, the fall and rise of rugby league in England.

I sat and daydreamed in the George Hotel, Huddersfield where rugby league was born in 1895, and I wandered for an hour through the Rugby League Hall of Fame near Castleford, my imagination cast back nearly a century by the exhibition of memorabilia. But I didn't need to visit museums to see rugby league in the north of England, it was so obviously alive and vibrant, elbowing for circulation in new magazines and beaming through new satellite television channels. And since Australians identify rugby league with the North itself, I saw it down every narrow street, peeping from behind curtains and ingrained in the faces of workers. When I hired a television set from a store in Oldham, 16 kms from Manchester, the cashier said her husband watched Winfield Cup replays — available from most video shops. The engineer who installed my satellite aerial was an avid St Helens fan and my neighbour confided his boss was a director of Salford RLFC.

To east coast Australians, Yorkshire and Lancashire towns are more relevant to their education than the Tower of London. England and Australia have cricket in common but nobody pretends that singular game, by its very nature, possesses the camaraderie of rugby league. It may sound naive to refer to an international brotherhood of rugby league, yet hundreds of Australians have come to England to play, many to stay. I found that, in the North, to be Australian was to be welcomed, to be an Australian on the rugby league trail ensured a hospitality bred of an intangible bond. My accent helped me and I enjoyed translating theirs. Pubs were "poobs", road was "rord" and honey was "hoon-air". Good morning became "How are't gorn?" and if a shop was out of stock it was, "Arven't got nowt!" One day in a coffee shop the waitress repeated my order, "Woon coosted par" and when she departed I practised the accent softly to myself, "Thar's moosted in me coosted par." At which a passing waitress whirled and advised me sympathetically, "Well mairk them give yew a frairsh 'n loov!"

The more I travelled and learned about English rugby league the more I realised what an important heritage the North possessed and what a responsibility it had to preserve in good health the game they bequeathed Australia. I spent my childhood years in Gundagai, not too far from where the dog still sits on the tucker box five miles from the town, but we followed a different animal, the Gundagai Tigers. On weekends, as the evening train steamed through the gullies beside the Murrumbidgee River bound for Cootamundra, it gave three blasts on its whistle if the Tigers had won that afternoon, none if they lost. So the news was brought to the properties.

Occasionally a country lad would make good, go to the big smoke and become a Kangaroo, just like Laurie Daley from Junee and Cliff Lyons who actually played for the mighty Tigers — Gundagai, not Balmain. As a boy I thumbed the newspapers and knew Wigan meant Billy Boston and Leeds the unerring boot of Welsh wizard Lewis Jones. In 1962 I sat dumbstruck at the Sydney Cricket Ground as the British Lions, inspired by Alex Murphy, destroyed mighty St George — Gasnier, Raper, Provan and all. Such was the wonderful sense of competition engendered, such was the experience of generations of Australian youth. Imagine then my wonder at walking into The Griffin Hotel in Wigan and tackling a pint of lager with the bete noir of my youth, Billy Boston. From Gundagai to The Griffin, that for me was rugby league's legacy.

As the day of the Kangaroos' arrival neared I felt the same sense of excitement that must have been overtaking thousands of Australians as they prepared for their whistle-stop Kangaroo supporters' tours, over-nighting around England and Europe before driving North to catch up with the Roos. Yet I knew their fleeting visit would merely whet their interest, for in my three months I had not satisfied all my curiosity about the North. I talk not of Emily and Charlotte Bronte's home in Haworth in the Pennines, nor of Wordsworth's scenic wilderness in The Lakes district. I speak of Thrum Hall, The Watersheddings and Wilderspool, rugby league club grounds so redolent with mystery I might as well have stepped through Alice's looking glass.

Now I was about to visit these clubs again — this time as a member of the Australian rugby league writers contingent following the Kangaroos — and we were beginning with St Helens at prosaic Knowsley Road, the first step on the road to the first Test at Wembley. The Kangaroos are aware of the importance of stamping their authority on the tour but, as well as the tension of the opening match, competition for Test spots is about to begin. It has been reported in the British media that Peter Sterling considers Allan Langer, on form, to be the fifth best halfback in Australia behind tour threesome, Ricky Stuart, Des Hasler and Greg Alexander, plus Manly's schoolboy-faced Geoff Toovey. Similarly Kerrod Walters knows only his very best will stay the challenge of tour vice-captain, Benny Elias.

At 1.25 pm the driver guns the diesel and the team's tour bus, plastered with huge KANGAROOS 90 signs, motors out of Manchester towards St Helens whipping up swirls of amber and rust-red autumn leaves from the roadside. This is their first view of the English countryside — green fields, stone fences and stone farm houses with slate roofs. Bales of green hay, fermenting under the sun, waft a sweet rotting smell. Occasionally, in the distance, row upon row of cramped terrace houses climb the bald hillside of an old mining village, unchanged for a century. Maybe the players don't even notice. We are travelling only to arrive, all thoughts cast far ahead. Passing cars regularly toot at the bus and at traffic lights a pedestrian gives the bus the thumbs up. We all settle back for the journey that has now begun and will only end 13 matches and two months later.

The week's preparation has made the team's recent arrival seem an age ago. At Manchester airport the boys staggered forth, in their green and gold blazers and Greg Norman stetsons, like a gaggle of jet-lagged cowboys. All except Mal Meninga who looked like a Mouseketeer, decked out in a gaudy yellow Fourex baseball cap with built-in radio and antenna earphones. The chief executive of the English Rugby Football League, David Oxley, with his Oxford educated voice, stepped forward to welcome tour manager Keith Barnes, a Balmain stalwart whose accent betrays his Welsh childhood. Bobby Fulton, his face creased by sleep, gallantly tackled a media conference. He had a stronger squad — not better Test team — than either the 1982 or 1986 teams, he said. "Those two sides did divide into two levels," he reminded us. "I've got 28 players and every one can play at Test level. Honestly, you've got to see them to believe it." This was Fulton's third tour — the first two were in 1973 and 1978 as a Kangaroo — but some Warrington well-wishers remember him from even earlier.

"He played a season with us in 1969," they enthused. "Turned a rubbishy team into a top side."

As the Kangaroos' luggage arrived Keith Barnes handed David Oxley a hat-box sized, fire-engine red, padlocked metal box. "We've got our hands on the Ashes at last," said Oxley laughing. Barnes quipped back, "You haven't seen it for a while so I thought you'd like a loan." The Ashes trophy, whatever its meltdown value, is so obviously a symbol it is almost superfluous. Each side will know who has won and lost, who triumphed, who tumbled. But for Great Britain the old silver cup inside the red box has assumed the significance of a treasured chalice which will restore to them their rugby league dignity, lost on tour in Australia in 1979 and only glimpsed fleetingly since.

The Roos' second day brought a photo-call and press conference at Manchester United soccer club's splendid stadium at Old Trafford, venue for the second Test. In the centre of the field stood a three-metre high plastic sculpture of a coal miner, arms akimbo, feet astride, wearing safety hat and lamp and Great Britain tracksuit. Glenn Lazarus wrestled the miner to the ground for a photograph and later stood him up, but with his tracksuit pants around his ankles. Meninga introduced the players individually . . . "Mark Carroll, Mark Geyer, Mark Sargent — few Marks in this team — Mark Gillespie," and David Gillespie's rough visage broke into a wry grin. Aussie humour in England is like a burst of sunlight. When Fulton, in answer to a question, began expansively, but seriously, "Well, I remember when I played at Wembley in 1973 . . ." the players erupted laughing as though Fulton was big-noting himself. The British were mystified but Fulton was laughing as hard as his players. It was half larrikin, half egalitarian, wholly harmless. It could never happen to Malcolm Reilly.

After questions ended there was a moment's silence until a light-hearted query emanated from the ranks of the players, "Can we win without Wally?" Meninga's loud reply, "Yes!" was almost drowned in the ensuing laughter. The shadow of Wally Lewis still hung over the tour and Meninga, admired and uncomplicated, had not yet imposed his personality upon the team. As captain of the Canberra Raiders he admitted there was not a lot to the leader's role. But on tour the captain becomes a figurehead and as the only surviving member of the 1982 and 1986 heroes he was the natural governor. He showed with that one exclamation — ''Yes!''— he wanted success to work its own catharsis on recent controversy.

Day three, Wednesday morning, I drove to Wigan where Great Britain coach Malcolm Reilly was announcing his Test training squad. The contrast to the Aussie turnout the previous day was dramatic. At a small table sat Reilly, Great Britain captain Ellery Hanley, RFL chairman Bob Ashby and Test team manager, Wigan chief Maurice Lindsay. All four were sombre, almost apologetic. Reilly, usually so competitive, was asked to comment on Fulton's claim that these Kangaroos were the strongest ever to leave Australia. ''Yeah, Bobby's probably right,'' he said. ''There is tremendous strength in depth. I don't think they'll miss the Lewises and Sterlings. The standard of the game over there is such that if any one of these lads had come over six years ago they would have been stars because their standard of fitness and commitment is so high.'' I was astounded. Fulton couldn't have said better himself. Ellery Hanley was no better. Given a Dorothy Dix question by an English journalist — did he think he could win the Ashes? — he replied in that soft whisper of his, ''It's a good possibility but I wouldn't like to pre-judge that.'' Was this the knight Britain hoped would champion its league? It is not everyone's style to project unwarranted confidence, but Reilly and Hanley seemed twin poles of negativism.

Senior rugby league writer for the *Yorkshire Post*, Raymond Fletcher, explained the dichotomy in English rugby league. ''We've been living and breathing for this day, we've had summer camps and squads — the obsession to beat Australia has gone overboard,'' he said. Fletcher agreed it would be good for the game if Britain won, but apart from the golden years after the war, when attendances at all sport were up, rugby league was enjoying its best era ever. ''Yet up until that last win in

1988 we'd lost 15 Tests in a row, so fans aren't worrying too much," he said. "You might say rugby league here's been riding the crest of defeat."

But talk of Tests was premature and back at the Ramada, Nick Potter, liaison officer for Castlemaine, sponsors of the Australians, was stocking the hotel cold room with 100 two-dozen cases of Fourex cans — 2,400 cans for the team and friends, just for starters. The team had discovered the YMCA-owned Castlefield Hotel 10 minutes jog from the Ramada. Open only three months, the Castlefield incorporates Manchester's largest sports complex — squash courts, a 25-metre pool, basketball court, a 100-metre indoor running track and, of most interest to the Roos, a weights gym. The remarkable upper body strength of the Australians and why they are seen to push opponents off, begins with barbells.

That Wednesday afternoon Fulton took the squad to train at Swinton, scene of Australia's record 50-12 defeat of Great Britain in 1963. I can remember listening in the early hours of the morning, static scratching the commentary, as Ken Irvine ran in three tries and Reg Gasnier, Ken Thornett and Graeme Langlands two each. Would they get to 50 points? I wondered, and they did. If the victory was historic, Swinton is merely archaic. Like most English stadiums it consists of a covered stand with seats along one touchline, and the other three sides given over to standing-room-only concrete terraces with anti-crush barriers spaced at intervals. Peering over the touchline opposite the grandstand was a row of terrace houses whose back windows provided armchair views of play. Keith Barnes said the ground had deteriorated dramatically since he played a Test there in 1959. Yet considering the 1990 Kangaroos were scheduled to play Tests in three of the finest football stadiums in England — of any code — international rugby league has come a long way in 30 years.

Thursday, day four, gale winds and rain gusted over Manchester. Fulton ran the players in wet weather tracksuits while the media retreated to the players' bus to drink hot chocolate prepared by the driver, Tony Gibbons, a veteran of four Kangaroo tours. The bus interior was strewn with football magazines, cards and tracksuit tops. Music was blasting forth from the sound system and overhead was a television screen which Fulton used for match vidoes en route to games. When we returned to the hotel, Fulton and Keith Barnes instituted a daily 6 pm conference for the dozen or so travelling Australian sportswriters. Senior *Daily Mirror* reporter, Peter Frilingos, remarked rhetorically of Fulton's affable mood, "This is good, but wait until he loses his first match!" Fulton laughed and shot back, "I won't be here, you'll have to ask Keith."

Roos medico Dr Nathan Gibbs had pinned a large weight sheet on the wall of a treatment room to spot anyone's weight ballooning and Friday morning found 111 kg Martin Bella dismayed by a 3 kgs weight gain in just five days. To his relief a check revealed faulty scales, which a week later collapsed. Gibbs also conducted caliper tests for weight-fat ratios which showed Greg Alexander was the least likely candidate for obesity. On a calipers test his ratio was 3 per cent, about as low as it is healthy to go. Only body builders, aiming for ultimate muscle definition the day before a contest, would have less. Des Hasler was just over 3 per cent as was Andrew Ettingshausen. All as lean as greyhounds.

Saturday, match eve, Fulton announced, "We're goin' t'see Alux," imitating the accents of Leigh coach Alex Murphy, the greatest post-war halfback of any nation. The bus headed out of town but the approach to Leigh was via a series of narrow back streets which forced driver Gibbons to back and fill, eventually calling owners from their homes to shift their parked cars. The residents of Glebe and Prescott Streets, Leigh, stood in the doorways of their small terrace houses and gazed in wonder at the massive, gold emblazoned Kangaroos coach on their doorsteps — an encounter of a new kind.

First man to welcome Fulton was Murphy as a crowd of children and fans who had heard the news gazed in awe. Though from different eras Murphy remembers Fulton's first match with Warrington, the only time they were opposed. "I gave him a bit of stick all night," said Murphy. "But in the last minute he scored the winning try and as he passed me he said, 'There, pick the bones out of that.' Aye, Bobby's a winner all right.'' High praise from the high priest, for as fleet of foot was Fulton, Alex Murphy was like Mercury.

He won Wembley cups in 1961 and 1966 with St Helens, in 1971 with Leigh and finally in 1974 with Warrington. He was equally devastating at the Sydney Cricket Ground. Though only 19 he toured with the 1958 Lions and in his biography said of the deciding Test at the SCG, ''They told me Johnny Raper, the Australian loose forward, had never been passed down the blindside from a scrum. I passed him before he got his head out of the scrum.'' Modesty was never one of Alex's strong suits. He toured again with the victorious 1962 Lions who then accepted a challenge from St George, the champions of the Sydney club competition. The Lions took apart proud Saints 33-5 and I walked home from the SCG to wait for the day Murphy retired to let Australia up off the mat. In those days the Lions roared long and loud. Younger generations of Australians who consider the Kangaroos to be born to rule should remember also that though Australia has now held the Ashes for 20 years, England, as they were then known (not Great Britain), once held them for 30 years from 1920 to 1950 and that when we finally won, it was considered the greatest day in Australian rugby league history.

Murphy's signing with St Helens in 1955 was almost a caricature of the exploitative old English club scene. A junior star, he was wanted by St Helens but could not sign a contract until he turned 16. On the eve of his birthday he played in a junior cup final at Knowsley Road, St Helens' home ground. Agents for other clubs were lurking so, after the match, the immortal Jim Sullivan, then St Helens' coach, guided Murphy down the back stairs and drove him to the home of the club chairman, Harry Cook. There they plied him with interminable glasses of orange juice, biscuits and games of snooker until, on the stroke of midnight, they signed him for 80 pounds. Other clubs had been willing to offer 1500 pounds.

At Leigh the Roos warmed up and began practising moves.

Murphy, his face as sharp as a tomahawk, watched for a minute and then interpreted the plays. "Bobby's getting them to counter attack from defensive positions," he said and began a commentary. "The reserves will hit it up three times and then Fulton will chip behind the line. See?" Ettingshausen cleaned up, played the ball and suddenly it was spinning through fingertips out along the backline. The players yelled code words and Murphy called the plays before they occurred. "All thinking for themselves, all talking, oh nice," he said admiringly. I asked who had the toughest job? "Daley," said Alex. "He's got the crown off the king hasn't he? And him," he said pointing at Allan Langer. "He has to clear the traffic jam." And who was the class? "Him," he said, pointing at Gary Belcher.

And so to Sunday and the Kangaroos coach nears the town named after the 14th century Chapel of St Eleyns, 65 kms west of Manchester. St Helens is actually closer to Liverpool than to Manchester but belongs to neither. When Australians read about English football towns they conjure up images of Australian towns like Junee in the Riverina, population 3,720, Maryborough in Queensland, 20,177 or even Wagga's whopping 35,577. St Helens has 190,000, Warrington 200,000 and Wigan 310,000. Throw in Widnes-Runcorn and there, 30 minutes drive west of Manchester, supporting just four first division clubs, dwells a rugby league population of nearly a million people.

Except for Fulham, in London, rugby league is played professionally only in the north of England and even there not in the heavily populated Liverpool-Merseyside metropolis. With 1100 teams nationally, mostly amateur, rugby league is a minority sport compared with soccer's 40,000 teams and rugby union's 1800 teams. Nor can the English RFL match Australia's 6,700 rugby league teams.

But rugby league is played throughout Lancashire, Greater Manchester, Cumbria, North, South and West Yorkshire and Humberside — a total population base of over 10 million, more than the combined populations of N.S.W. and Queensland. The rugby league counties support only six of England's 44 first and second division soccer teams. In the north, rugby union runs a distant third behind soccer and rugby league in popularity. And despite its regional base, rugby league ranks ahead of rugby union and county cricket in the table of England's most popular spectator sports. Rugby league is a minority sport in England, but it is by no means a small sport.

The bus approaches St Helens town centre and, within sight of Pilkingtons glassworks, turns up Knowsley Road beside a stream of fans, all got up in red and white, walking towards the nearby ground. Pilkingtons, St Helens and rugby are synonomous. Pilkingtons are the world's largest producers of flat and safety glass; Anthony Pilkington, with a family fortune of $450 million, ranks 47th in Britain's list of the 50 richest people. Lady Mavis Pilkington is St Helens club president, but the Pilkington Cup is also the knockout trophy for which English first division rugby union clubs play. In 1989 St Helens made the Challenge Cup final which was coincidentally held on the same day as the Pilkington Cup final. Faced with the choice of union at Twickenham or league at Wembley, Lady Mavis chose . . . Wembley.

Though fallen from their glamorous Murphy years, St Helens finished fifth in the league in 1989-90 and turned over the touring Kiwis. Because it is the club's centenary, St Helens has been awarded the Roos' first match and Knowsley Road is like a fairground with hospitality tents, stalls selling football souvenirs and a radio station pumping out rock. I glance in one tent and there is St Helens and Great Britain centre and goalkicker, Paul Loughlin, leaning on crutches having twisted an ankle at training the previous day. It is axiomatic that Great Britain must field its very best side to defeat Australia. Grim news for Malcolm Reilly, sad news for the series. Discussion begins among the media of a Test replacement. A certain name is proposed. "He thinks tackle is something you take when you go fishing," quips Tony Durkin, Queensland editor of *Rugby League Week*.

A rousing cheer attracts me to the marquee entrance to see Mal Meninga, last out of the team bus, receiving a rapturous welcome from St Helens fans. He played for the Saints in 1984-85 and became a legend in a season, more famous even than Wally Lewis at Wakefield Trinity or Peter Sterling at Hull. With Meninga aboard, St Helens won the Lancashire Cup and the Premiership final in which, according to St Helens secretary Geoff Sutcliffe, "Mal scored two long range tries — two interceptions — just brought the house down." When Canberra arrived for the world club challenge against Widnes in 1989, St Helens invited the Raiders to watch the Saints take on New Zealand. Introduced on the pitch Meninga could scarcely leave for the crush of fans. Even stellar signings like Michael O'Connor and Paul Vautin suffered through joining St Helens post-Meninga. "Everyone was compared with Mal and never measured up," said Sutcliffe. "He was impossible to live up to."

Past St Helens champions are introduced to the crowd of nearly 16,000 before the match. Cheers greet Alex Murphy but roars meet Vince Karalius who terrorised Australia with the Lions in 1958. Australia dubbed him the "Wild Bull" yet with his cruel face and curly black locks and the way he stuck it to Australia, he could just as easily have been the matador. Vinty was in the 1956 St Helens side which demolished Australia 44-2 at this very ground. Even more revered than Karalius is a solid, crew-cut gentleman named Tom Van Vollenhoven whose name still makes the top 10 in British club try scoring records. He skirts the touchline, down which he once pounded, in an easy, rolling gait. It is said he had it all — acceleration, speed, swerve, strength and a fend, yet because he was South African, and not eligible for Britain, Australia never saw one of his 392 tries.

Clubs scheduled to play the Kangaroos are influenced by two opposing views — the first that it is an honour, and a famous opportunity, to bump against the Australians who have not lost a club match in England for 12 years. This is adopted by Saints coach, Kiwi Mike McClennan. Some weeks earlier I suggested to him his team was on a hiding to nothing, plus the risk of injuries, such as someone doing a kneecap. Mike was swinging a golf wood outside his office at the time. He smiled. "What we're going to do is break their kneecaps," he replied and whipped the evil clubhead through. "You've got to realise that every sporting nation and every sporting person wants to beat the Australians," he said. "I'm sorry about that. It's inbred in the British and New Zealanders." But Saints captain, Shane Cooper, also a Kiwi, leant to the other view. "To me it's prestigious but not the ultimate game," he said. "We don't get two points and we don't get to Wembley playing the Kangaroos."

The excitement which greets the opening of a Kangaroo tour is akin to an Olympic Games — four years between tours, time for new talent to surface, old hands to lose it, idols to grow larger than life, standards to change — the Roos might have been a pre-war team disembarked from an ocean liner so great is the crowd anticipation. Not a person in that 16,000, nor in the millions watching it televised in England and Australia, knows how the 1990 Kangaroos will fare. We're about to find out.

Under a rinsed blue sky in soft autumn sunlight, Meninga leads out basically the team which trounced New Zealand two months earlier. Saints begin as though the McClennan theory of kneecapping has prevailed over the Cooper pragmatism. Four Saints hit Laurie Daley simultaneously, penalty Australia. The crowd protests. It's on! Perfect pitch, crowd singing, sport transcends all troubles.

After four minutes St Helens make their first mistake, only two players chase a downtown to Belcher. Not enough. He's used to four, splits the Saints pair and dashes to halfway. Quick ruck, Ettingshausen to Langer — in my mind I hear Alex Murphy calling the names — a half-volley to Daley to Meninga now hurtling through like an accelerating express. Captain Cooper, cover defending, chooses to shadow Michael Hancock on the wing — well someone had to do it. That leaves young Saints fullback, Gary Connolly, 19, as the last defender. Meninga may be safely tackled from behind or side-on, but head-on at top speed is akin to inviting him to leap into your arms from a roof gutter. His weight times velocity equals crushing impact. Meninga preserves Connolly's honour with a classical out-and-in, swerving clear to score untouched. It is all so quick, so precise, so inexorable, the crowd falls silent. I feel a twinge in my own heart. I had watched the Yorkshire and Lancashire Cup finals and had begun to believe in the integrity and strength of the English game, but I'd forgotten about this.

Belcher initiates the next try as well, stepping unpredictably with that high, Carl Lewis-like knee action of his, down to the Saints quarterline. Fast passing and Ettingshausen slides over in the corner. Yet midway through the first half it is only 8-0 and the Aussie machine is not exactly humming. Hancock so stutters and stammers that Bob Lindner holds up a hand like a traffic cop to direct Mick forwards. Meninga misdirects a pass over the sideline, Daley is lucky to escape the sinbin for a high tackle. After the 33rd minute Kerrod Walters and Hancock touch down for tries as does Steve Roach, showing an intuitive combination with Balmain team-mate Paul Sironen worthy of, say, Ella and Ella. By half-time the Roos lead 22-0.

St Helens manage an excellent second half try but the Australians' tally of tries climbs to eight and the score to 34-4, despite Meninga kicking only one goal from six attempts. It is Australia's highest ever score against St Helens but more important is what the team has learned. English referees let tackled players stagger about for many seconds without calling "Held", providing specialist ball thieves like Langer and Daley time to rip into their art. Australia will also have to rethink a crossing move, commonly used in Sydney, because the referee penalises it as obstruction.

At full-time the media descend upon the dressingrooms, producing a wholly avoidable melee of television lights, cameramen, photographers, tapes, mikes and notepads, glistening torsos, towels, bandages and beer. The players, tubbing in two huge all-in baths in one room, find they can't re-enter the main room to dress. "This is bloody ridiculous," exclaims Steve Roach steaming from hot bathwater and anger. But if you want to speak to Bobby Fulton that's where he is. His grin says it all. Considering many of the guys haven't played for six to seven

weeks, yeah he's pleased. Mal's solution to the goalkicking :
"I'll tell the guys to score a few more closer to the posts."

I fight my way upstairs to the traditional post-match reception — a bunfight second only to the change rooms bout — and
run into Tom Van Vollenhoven. "I just said to Mal Meninga I
don't think you're going to have any problems this tour," he
says in clipped South African accents. "You're a beautiful running and handling side. My impression was you could score
tries whenever you wanted, from any position. I haven't seen
backs running so strong and hard and handling so good. I'm
very impressed with you." I feel flattered by the embrace of
Tom's pronouns.

Meninga is replying to a presentation of half a dozen locally
made wine glasses to each player. Few can hear his speech but
it's conclusion is that he couldn't have wished for a better start,
"just a pity it had to be at St Helens' expense." At 5.45 pm
Allan Langer stands on the top stair of the bus tossing tiny Kangaroo lapel badges like confetti to a crowd of children. As the
bus departs the players toast the crowd with cans of beer. It re-
minds me of a 16th century description of glass I read while visiting Pilkington's splendid glass museum. It went:

> A drinking glass fill'd in part with water,
> being rub'd on the brim with the finger witted,
> yields Musical notes . . .
> and makes the liquor frisk and leap.

Castlemaine's Nick Potter had loaded five large buckets of
ice into the tour bus and emptied 10 dozen cans of beer into
them for post-match celebrations. Having bettered both the
1982 and 1986 Kangaroos' scores against St Helens, the 1990
mob had good reason to "wit" their lips and make their liquor
frisk and leap.

2 WAKEFIELD'S UNHOLY TRINITY

At his Old Trafford press conference the day after arriving in England, Bobby Fulton had delivered a calculated message to the referees of England by virtually advocating the illegal second-row feed for the side putting the ball into scrums. At the start of the English season the RFL Controller of Referees, Fred Lindop, had circulated instructions to referees that "Blatant second-row or loose forward feeding will be penalised". Fulton was suggesting English referees turn a blind eye as they did in Australia. "If you know you're going to win the scrum you adopt an attacking line," he said. "Each side knows who's attacking and who's defending. If the ball's put in the middle neither side knows who's getting possession so they both stand up flat, just about shaking hands, and you don't get attack from scrums."

Question: Doesn't that do away with the theory that a scrum gives fairly equal chance to both packs? Fulton: "It does. But if you've got the feed and the head you've deserved it so you deserve to get the ball. It stops referees being seen to be biased towards one side. It eliminates the cheating theory. The secret is for the halfback to move close to the scrum so you don't accentuate the angle of put in."

Fulton's concern about scrums might seem unnecessary given the reduced role of the scrum since the 1983 hand-over rule which exchanges possession after six tackles. In the 1948 Wembley Challenge Cup final played under unlimited tackle rules, Bradford Northern and Halifax packed down in 54 scrums. Today referees whistle up, on average, less than 20 a match. Yet the scrum remains a vital potential source of possession for both sides as shown when, the day before the Roos landed, referee Robin Whitfield sent off Wigan's Ellery Hanley for chatting him over contentious scrum rulings. Penalties from rugby league's unstable scrums — which often resemble a dog-fight under a blanket — have long been a blot on the game. But as Bobby Fulton said, "Old fashioned people might say what's the use of having scrums. But scrums have been with us for years and will be until we're all in wooden caskets."

The scrum itself is such a throwback to the very earliest be-ginnings of rugby its continuing existence is like coming upon a dinosaur in a zoo. In Elizabethan times folk games were free-for-alls with upward of 200 players scrimmaging for hours for possession of a solid leather ball. These games had not changed much by 1846 when, at Rugby school, the laws decreed "that all matches are drawn after five days or after three if no goal has been kicked."

Before the Kangaroos arrived I drove down to the town of Rugby, in the midlands of England, on the usual tourist's pil-grimage and immersed myself in the fantasy of the town's name — Rugby Theatre could be a playhouse devoted to foot-ball drama, Rugby Library full of footy books and Rugby Cen-tre must be the game's headquarters — not a shopping mall. Rugby is a town dominated by the ancient slate steeples and sandstone towers of its school. Founded in 1567, the school brought Rugby international fame some 250 years later when one of its students broke the rules. I walked around the school's high, castellated walls, through the Queen's Gates and into the Close to the scene of the offence — two rugby fields. Facing them was a long brick wall and set into it, in a plaque of pink and grey marble, was etched:

This stone commemorates the exploits of William Webb Ellis who, with a fine disregard of the rules of football as played in his time, first took the ball in his arms and ran with it thus originating the dis-tinctive feature of the rugby game. A.D. 1823.

This plaque was erected in 1895, the year that 21 clubs in the north of England split from the English Rugby Union over pro-fessionalism, thus taking the first steps towards the game of rugby league. The plaque is now thought to have had as much to do with the politics of cementing ownership of the game of rugby as with Ellis' feat, if indeed it was Ellis. Whatever the case Rugby was the school and I spent a pleasurable few moments imagining the chaos in Ellis' day — 150 or more schoolboys screaming, hacking and hoofing at the ball in a mass scrimmage, literally trying to drive it through their opponents legs. While the ball was on the ground it was fair game for flying boots. The boys were not allowed to pick the ball up or handle it unless it squirted clear from the scrimmage and was caught on the full or on the bound (bouncing). All play then stopped, rather like the modern rugby union mark, while the catcher, if within kicking distance of the posts, either attempted a kick at goal — place or drop kick — or punted it down field to gain ground.

It is now accepted that Ellis' transgression was not to pick the ball up, but that having caught it on the bounce he ran forward with it instead of kicking it. The hue and cry that greeted this must have been great indeed for in general play, while the ball was on the ground, it was only shins being damaged in the savage kicking. But a schoolboy being chased by 150 excited players invited homicide from one side or the other because of the fierce kicking which would ensue once he was run down. Indeed Ellis' running game is said not to have gained fashion for some years until teams were reduced to safer numbers and dangerous hacking outlawed.

Between 1840 and 1860 there were two broad categories of football being played at England's top private schools — the dribbling game of Eton, Harrow, Westminister and Charterhouse and the handling game of Rugby, Marlborough and Cheltenham. However when graduates met at Cambridge University, Old Etonians were incensed that Old Rugbeians kept handling the ball — though not necessarily running with it — in the middle of the game. In 1846 a Cambridge meeting dominated by old Etonians published the Cambridge Rules which basically banned handling. These same rules were adopted in

1863 by the Football Association and soccer was launched in England.

Eight years later, in London in 1871, clubs playing the handling game formed the English Rugby Union and published a set of rules. Scoring continued to be by goals with the additional feature of "running in" whereby some players stood off from the mass mauls in the hope of running with the ball past the opposition's goal line. This won no points but permitted the scoring side to "try" a kick at goal — thus evolving the exclamation, "A try!" A player was now permitted to pick the ball up at any time but could not pass it. When tackled he was obliged to call "down" and release the ball, whereupon a scrimmage formed around him. Each pack then sought to drive the ball with their feet towards the opponent's line. But with teams of 25 players a side these scrimmages did not always move. An early historian wrote, "A quarter of a hundred of heavyweights appeared to be leaning up against each other for periods of five minutes while occasionally the ball became accidentally disentangled . . ."

The game became faster in 1875 when English universities reduced teams to 15-a-side, and faster again in 1880 when passing the ball was made legal. This in turn encouraged forwards to heel the ball back rather than toe it forward. In set scrums halfbacks began following the ball through to their opponent's side to cut off this new passing game. A general offside law was introduced in 1882 but up to this stage matches were refereed by consensus between the opposing captains. Even gentlemen have trouble agreeing on offside and referees were introduced in combination with two umpires who appealed to the referee on behalf of each team. Inevitably came the day — Batley versus Halifax, Yorkshire Cup, 1885 — when the referee saw an offence by Batley, attacking, and blew his whistle without any umpire appeal from Halifax, defending. Hearing no umpire appeal Batley played on, scored and claimed victory. Halifax protested they had stopped at the whistle. The dispute went to the English Rugby Union judiciary in London, Halifax's appeal was upheld and "play the whistle" entered the English vocabulary as an axiom for complying with a referee's ruling, right or wrong.

Thus the evolution of rugby union proceeded and about the same time that rugby union reached Australia (1875), the earliest rugby clubs were being founded in the north of England. Among those on the Kangaroos schedule, Hull was formed in 1865, Halifax, Widnes and Wakefield Trinity 1873, St Helens 1874, Warrington 1875, Wigan 1879 and Leeds 1890. When the northern clubs withdrew from the English Rugby Union in 1895, these Yorkshire and Lancashire clubs — who formed the Northern Union — did not suddenly lose the rich traditions of their beginnings. The history of rugby's early rules is as relevant today to the league of rugby clubs who formed their own competition in the north, as it is to the union of rugby clubs in the south. Though rugby league in England celebrates its centenary in 1995 it still shares rugby's heritage. No one disputes that rugby union is true heir to the game begun at Rugby school but this should not ignore the fine pedigrees of those clubs, now playing rugby league, whose foundations preceded the break away.

In the south of England an extensive middle class supported rugby against the rapid spread of soccer. In the working class north both rugbies came under pressure from the growing challenge of soccer's round ball, simple rules, fast play and easy exchange of possession. The Northern Union, now professional, had to look to its crowd appeal and, in 1897, dropped its first rugby union feature, the line-out. But not until 1906 was the matter of the sideline fully resolved with a direct kick into touch on the full resulting in the familiar "ball-back" — a scrum from whence the ball was kicked. Set scrums were still in their infancy and in 1903 teams were not above packing every forward in the front row to permit quick heeling of the ball. Referees quickly scotched such absurdities but it took the Northern Union, proceeding cautiously, until 1907 to decide that more than three up front was against the spirit of the rules.

To open up play, Northern Union halfbacks were compelled to stay their side of the scrum and not follow the ball through as is still permitted in rugby union. That was decided in December 1895, yet even earlier, in October — just two months after the split from the English RU — Halifax and Manningham had experimented with 13-a-side and a soccer ball. It was agreed that "true Rugbeians cannot accept the round ball" but they could accept the reduced numbers. The grand change, proposed by Leigh and seconded by Warrington for 13-a-side, was introduced by the N.U. for the 1906-7 season. The elimination of rugby union's scrum flankers released Northern Union backlines from the shackles of swarming defences. But the question which still vexed the new game was how to restart play when players were caught with the ball. American Football had resolved this in 1882 by totally stopping play at every tackle with a "down" — the original rugby union shout when tackled. Professionalism has now reduced American football to plays lasting less than 10 seconds. Rugby union persisted with untidy rucks and mauls which still kill play and remain a major source of penalties.

In 1899 the Northern Union decided that if a tackled player was not held he could drop the ball at his feet, and "play the ball" though he could not propel it forward. The crucial change came in 1906, the N.U. ruling that the tackled player be permitted to regain his feet before so "playing the ball". Later that season the N.U. confirmed that the ball could be played in any direction, "including heeling out behind the tackled player". This rule, once mastered, exchanged rugby union's glorious uncertainty of possession after a tackle for a tidier, faster game in which the crowd saw the ball more often. Rugby league's continuing appeal as a spectator sport rests upon statistics which show the ball is in play for 50 minutes in a modern rugby league match compared with 25 minutes for rugby union.

By 1906 therefore the Northern Union was playing the game which, within two years, was to take root in Australia where it acquired its lasting name, rugby league. At the turn of the century Northern Union matches featured up to 120 scrums and modern All Black forwards would have admired the skill of these forward packs in push-over tries, wheeling scrums and dribbling the ball at their toes in fearsome forward rushes. This latter skill puzzled me given the unpredictable bounce of the rugby ball and my intrigue deepened after a visit one day to the Rugby League Hall of Fame in the Bentley Arms Hotel near Castleford. On a wall poster Harold Wagstaff, Great Britain captain in the famous ''Rorke's Drift'' Test at the Sydney Cricket Ground in 1914, told how the Lions, though reduced to 10 men, were leading 9-3 with 20 minutes to go. He wrote:-

I managed to make a cut through, I went to the wing on which was Johnson, and when I gave Chick the ball there was only the full-back in front of him. Chick went away with it but then none of us dreamt we would witness the scoring of as wonderful a try as Test football ever will produce. A few yards from Hallett, the Australian fullback, Chick put the ball on the ground and began a dribble, he had half the length of the field to go but he went every inch of the distance, and the ball never left his toes. It might have been tied to his feet — a ball on the end of a piece of string — so perfectly did he control it. No international Football Association player could have dribbled the ball better than Johnson did that afternoon on the SCG. Man after man he beat until finally he tapped the ball over the line and dived for the touch. Alf Wood kicked the gaol and there we were 14-3. Victory was ours.

How on earth did Chick Johnson so cleverly control a rugby league ball? The answer came that day I visited Rugby. A Ricky Stuart-length punt from the school is the James Gilbert rugby museum, a small building packed with sepia photographs, old velvet caps and rust-marked, red rose and white sweaters of past England players. I was drawn to a glass case in which sat a fat leather football, made by the Gilbert family in 1851. Rugby union footballs have retained the same length circumference for over a century — 30-31 inches. The curator Jane Chance un-locked the case and we put a tape around the 1851 model's width circumference — 27.5 inches. But it was only half in-flated. Pumped hard it would have blown out to nearly 29 inches. In other words, though made of four stitched oval pan-els the old ball was nearly as round as it was long, halfway be-tween a soccer ball and a modern rugby ball. I retired to the nearby William Webb Ellis pub to ponder these statistics. The old ball was ideal for goal kicking — the principal form of scoring 150 years ago — and for dribbling at the toe. In 1892 the width around was reduced to 26 inches, narrower, but still of sufficently reliable bounce for Chick Johnson's 1914 ''Rorke's Drift'' dribble. Reduced once more, to 25 inches, in 1931 the dribble lost reliability and popularity. Today rugby union balls are bigger than rugby league balls — half an inch wider (23-24.5 inches) and 1.25 inches longer (30-31 inches). And that is why when rugby union kickers take a shot at goal you may as well go and have a pie, because with the larger and slightly rounder ball, they rarely miss.

The practice of a game always precedes the rulemakers and rugby league, its laws and interpretations — even the type of ball — have constantly altered, not just between eras, but season to season, nation to nation, even city to city. Bobby Fulton's scrum theories recognised this and were intended to nip potential refereeing problems in the bud before the tour began. The 20-12 penalty count against them at St Helens had not been a good start.

The Kangaroos' first mid-week match, against Wakefield Trinity, took the team out of Lancashire across the Pennine mountains into Yorkshire. The Pennine chain starts on the Scottish border and runs some 200 kms south, like a raised spine down northern England, dividing the counties of Yorkshire and Lancashire. Though less than 1000 metres high the Pennines, snow-clad in harsh winters, were a major barrier between the two counties until, in the 1970s, the M62 motorway provided a quick crossing. The two counties have historically opposed each other in everything from great 15th century houses warring for the throne of England to the modern equivalent in county cricket. But what they have in common against the rest of England is rugby league.

Wakefield is only 13 kms from the city of Leeds and in fierce competition with it. Wakefield Borough, a huge conurbation of over 300,000 people, embraces the rugby league towns of Castleford (50,000) and Featherstone (15,000). Wakefield itself is a white collar town, its streets milling with lawyers, civil servants and administrators and a growing business class as the area metamorphoses from wool and mining into a thriving European manufacturing centre. The town is the British headquarters for Dunlop and Coca Cola, and defeated Barcelona to become the European headquarters for Pioneer CD and laser disk production. Wakefield, not Leeds, is the historic capital of West Yorkshire and still boasts the county police, county courts and county hall, all splendid stone Victorian buildings. Known in medieval times as the "Merrie City", Wakefield celebrated its 900th anniversary in 1990 and a tourist guide proudly showed me its 14th century cathedral, Opera House and an art gallery building dating back to 1590. But I noted that the star turn of their outdoor sculpture park, reputedly Europe's finest, is Henry Moore and he is a son of nearby Castleford.

Wakefield Trinity rugby league team has not had the same success in transcending its recent past. Leeds, Bramley and Keighley rugby league clubs all sprang from church teams and Wakefield was begun in 1873 by the local Holy Trinity Church. It was at Wakefield's home ground that David Storey's epic rugby league novel, *This Sporting Life*, was filmed, starring a young Richard Harris. Irishman Harris, wild drinker, was an instant success with the players during filming and became a staunch fan. When Wakefield beat Huddersfield in the 1962 Challenge Cup Final at Wembley, Harris swapped his sheepskin coat for a team jumper and leapt fully-clothed into the bath with the team.

Wakefield's ground is named Belle Vue but ironically the view is of a nearby power station's smokestack and massive concrete cooling towers. The club directors who exploited Harris in that film were later mirrored in real life because by the 1980s, despite no opposing soccer club, Wakefield was bankrupt. The council had taken over Belle Vue, a brewery bought the clubhouse and the team had sunk into second division. Wally Lewis's 10 matches with them in 1983-84 was their sole bright spot and supporters joyfully named their 1990 club fanzine "Wally Lewis Is Coming", as we all thought he was. Instead Wakefield got an Australian general manager, Neil

Cadigan, a bargain buy considering he came equipped with a player Wally always admired, Penrith's redoubtable Chris Mortimer.

The coach who dragged Wakefield out of second division in 1987 was a nippy little ex-Great Britain five-eighth named David Topliss. He captained Hull against the 1982 Roos and Oldham against the 1986 Roos and in each case lost by only six points, results of which he is justifiably proud. But Toppo wasn't making foolhardy predictions. "We're second favourites, about 100 to 1," he joked. "I told the lads it would be the fastest game they'd ever play. That the Aussies would move up that much faster and think that much faster. I said it was a once-in-a-lifetime chance for them." I tempted him to a prediction on the Test series — "Me hand on me heart says Great Britain, but me head says Australia. But if we could win that first Test, ahh, that would be, that would be . . ." and words could not describe such impossible joy.

On match night, Wednesday, October 10, steady rain drifted down and Andrew Ettingshausen drew a ribbing from his team-mates when he paraded in front of the grandstand in an elegant, ankle-length Drizabone; Balmain's irrepressible Laurie Nicholls drew gasps from the crowd when he turned up with his chest covered only by his usual green and gold singlet. Fulton had taken his concern about rulings a step further and, together with Topliss, visited referee Kevin Allatt before the match. Fulton said later that after the meeting Topliss had remarked ominously, "We're going to have trouble here tonight with interpretations."

After 18 minutes Australia's non-Test side, led by Benny Elias, were held to 8-8, with similar barging tries by Newcastle's Mark Sargent and South Africa's Nick du Toit. Topliss had told his team that, having not played for five weeks, the Australians' timing would be off. And so it was until Ricky Stuart put up one of his bombs, performing a ballet-like scissors kick with both feet off the ground. The ball, from toe to turf, hung six seconds in the air, rising out of sight from my stand, from the television cameras and apparently out of sight of Wakefield because when it landed over their line Chris Johns casually touched down for a 14-8 lead.

Referee Allatt made his intentions known when a scrum erupted in a melee and Mark Carroll and Wakefield hooker John Thompson were sent off as scapegoats. Peter Wilson, of *The Daily Star*, explained, ''They won't muck around with sin-binning, these referees. They hate unsightly brawls. They'll only use the sin-bin for technical breaches and minor offences.'' With only 12 men apiece and holes aplenty Australia raced to 24-8 by half-time.

Bobby Fulton had been invited by referee Allatt to see him at half-time if he wished and Fulton did wish. How's the game going? Fulton inquired. ''Pretty well,'' said Allatt, ''I've got a terrific rapport with your players.'' Fulton replied, ''Well the stats sheet doesn't show that,'' but decided against pursuing the penalty count complaint. Instead he said, ''Just do us a favour will you? Give us a couple of penalties.'' Allatt blinked at this brazen request and asked why, what for? ''So we can practice our taps,'' cracked Fulton and Allatt and his linesmen roared laughing.

But by the last quarter the penalty count was no laughing matter, 18-6 against Australia including the sin-binning of Des Hasler. Two of the penalties were against Ricky Stuart for second-row scrum feeds and though Stuart had been warned by Fulton not to query the referee this was too much. He asked Allatt politely, ''What's the story? I've been feeding the scrums the same all game.'' No you haven't, said Allatt, his body language revealing his intense irritation. The last 10 minutes were a farce. First Wakefield scrum half Billy Conway and Dale Shearer were sin-binned — down to an 11-a-side game. Both teams were weary from playing short for so long on a heavy, slippery ground and with the result beyond doubt at 36-18 , most were listening for the siren. With two minutes left Stuart was sent off for an alleged high tackle which, from Allatt's motion, would have done justice to Mike Tyson. Allatt seemed incensed, excited and expended and his final act, having blown full-time, was to dismiss David Gillespie for words allegedly spoken as the players trooped off. So Australia won the game but lost the penalty count 26-7 and Wakefield won the surviving players count, 11 players to Australia's 9. It was a sorry ending as the floodlights dimmed and rain fell like a curtain of soft white light across the emptying stands.

One of the first media people to reach Fulton was BBC radio reporter Harry Gration whose three minute interview wound up with him asking whether Fulton was unhappy with the referee.

Fulton: No I'm not unhappy with him. I think he should be unhappy with his own performance. I mean I'm not going to criticise referees. The guy is obviously a man that shouldn't be out in the middle.

Gration: The one thing the Australians have done over the last 12 years is play good rugby, didn't you feel at the end of your performance today that that disintegrated a bit?

Fulton: Well that's your opinion, we didn't instigate the two incidents, they were instigated by the English players from Wakefield Trinity but the fact of the matter is we will not take a backward step. The penalties today . . . probably you don't know much about rugby league, I don't know, I've never met you before but the point is . . .

Gration: What right have you got to say that?

Fulton: Well I don't even know who you are.

Gration: I am asking you, I'm an interviewer.

Fulton: Well who are you? Do you understand the way the game is played, that's all I'm saying.

Gration: Yes I do.

Fulton: Well that's fine, well OK, if you understand the way the game is played it's your opinion as a commentator. When you ask me a question I'll answer it. Now don't you attack me for the way I answer questions if you want to interview me, if you don't want to, turn the tape off.

Gration: Thank you.

Fulton: Thank you.

It was perhaps 10 minutes before the Australian media contingent spoke to Fulton in a club room. He again began by saying he would not complain about Allatt but then doused him with acid humour. "It was like Fawlty Towers out there," he said. "I expected John Cleese to appear at any time. He told me before the game he was 48 years of age — maybe he should be at home with a cup of hot chocolate in front of a nice log fire. He reckoned he refereed me when I was at Warrington, I must have given him a gobful or something. This is my third trip over here and that's the worst penalty count against any side I've been involved with in England."

This was my first view of Fulton in full critical flight and it was a performance to behold. He said the Kangaroos' conduct was sensational under the circumstances, "a real Gallipoli-type effort". He continued, "There were very few scrum penalties and all of a sudden there were three or four in a row when we had a three-man pack. Just ludicrous." The Gillespie dismissal was a joke. "It wasn't him, it was someone else," said Fulton. "We know who said it, but we aren't saying." As I moved amongst the players in the post-match reception it became apparent Fulton was reflecting their disgust as well as his own. Did the referee lose control? Ricky Stuart, never before sent off, looked cautious. "Am I allowed to say yes? " he asked. "He certainly did, especially late in the game. He just started sending people off."

I'm not going to analyse Fulton — to use a favourite Fulton preamble — but his post-match comments have to be examined on two levels. The first is that of an emotional, highly strung coach whose team had nearly been whistled off the park. His clash with Gration was a product of Fulton's intense sensitivity whenever the Kangaroos received criticism — even as mild as Gration's. After 16 years reporting sport, 10 as BBC radio rugby league correspondent, Gration justifiably took exception to Fulton's insult that he probably knew nothing about league. He had also met Fulton several times before. But similarly, considering Australia had played the last 25 minutes with an average of 11 men, and were penalised 10-1 in the last 15 minutes, Gration's comment-question that Australia had disintegrated towards the end teetered between the obvious and the provocative.

It requires no great insight to observe, as I had at the start of the tour, that taking Fulton head on is tantamount to prodding the Minotaur. Softly, softly trod the Australian media because no single interviewer, nor indeed the entire media corps, was going to change Fulton's prickly personality on tour. Fulton deals with the media as he once played football — unpredictably, aggressively, close to offside and whenever possible, doing it to others in case they were thinking of doing it to him. When provoked, as by referee Allatt, Fulton operates on a controlled burn, a Whitlamesque maintained rage, in which a facade of cool and critical reason masks a deep anger. In such a state he is upset, flails at shadows, upsets himself more — as by the Gration incident — but ploughs on because bluff and bravado, taking the bastards on, is his way. And he's fearless.

That is Fulton the spontaneous, but underneath there is a second level, Fulton the premeditated. Some weeks earlier I had met Allan Pearman who was secretary of Wakefield Trinity for 15 years. "They'll deny it, but having left the game I can say it," he told me. "There's a number of referees around who, if you have any sort of Australian twang, then you're going to be penalised and first chance you get you're off. One particular referee would come into my office before the game and ask me to point out the Australians on the teamsheet." With the Kangaroos a teamsheet wasn't necessary. So that while Fulton was cranking up the hyperbole and the emotional barometer, he was also pursuing calculated policy and long-term goals. Referee Allatt had unwittingly dealt Fulton the opportunity to legitimately broadcast his case against biased or unsympathetic referees. British rugby league writers rarely record penalty counts even though in this case it was fundamental to understanding the Kangaroos' frustration. But Fulton's comments were widely reported and it was clear that Allatt's exaggerated penalty count had given the Australian management a loaded gun to point at the English RFL and at every subsequent referee scheduled for the Kangaroos' matches. And so it proved with a special three-man judiciary, of whom one was Keith Barnes, exonerating Stuart of his high tackle and ruling that being sent off was sufficient punishment for Carroll and Gillespie.

While Fulton was happy to up the ante, there was a price to pay and rugby league bore the cost. More British people would have heard of the Kangaroos through that unpleasant clash with Gration than the RFL would have liked. It was the worst kind of publicity. Gration's interview became celebrated throughout British radio waves, being replayed on four out of five BBC radio channels, the regional networks and even the world service. The BBC received hundreds of phone calls supporting Gration, Fulton received a pasting in *Rugby League Week*. Editor Norman Tasker wrote that Fulton's comments were ''crass'' and that Fulton had revived memories of the ''Ugly Australians'' reputation of past cricket teams. As soon as he read the column Fulton rang Tasker in Australia, protesting fulsomely. As Tasker himself had written, to Fulton, rugby league was no game, it was almost war.

3 THE ROAD TO WIGAN

Of the starry dreams which two childhood friends employed to clamber out of the dockside streets of Tiger Bay in Cardiff, Billy Boston's seemed more modest than Shirley Bassey's. Billy's dream was to pull on the blood-red jumper of Wales for an international at Cardiff Arms Park and thrill to the anthem of his nation. He would have too. He scored 126 tries in his last rugby union season for the Army's Royal Signals, averaging four a match. But the old axiom applied — neither the prophet nor the genius is recognised in his own valley, not soon enough anyway. In 1953 Wigan appeared on Boston's doorstep and signed him for 3000 pounds. He was only 19. Billy bought a house in Wigan with half the money and left Wales for the life of a professional footballer in northern England.

The very next season, after only six games of rugby league, he toured Australia with Great Britain, and for eight years bullied Australia's wingmen — first Noel Pidding, Ian Moir and Don "Bandy" Adams and then Eddie Lumsden, Peter Dimond and Brian Carlson. Not until 1962 did Australia produce the speed of Mike Cleary and Ken Irvine to thwart the powerhouse winger and even then Great Britain retained the Ashes.

I felt a sense of humility at confronting the nemesis of my childhood heroes as, late one Wigan afternoon, I knocked on the door of Boston's pub, The Griffin, a block from Central Park. The man who greeted me could have stepped out of the SCG program — big, wide jovial face, tight black curly hair still receding from his forehead, powerful body filling out a blue t-shirt. He has such a presence he reminded me of a West Indian version of Arthur Beetson. I jogged his memory of Mike Cle-

ary. "Cleary! By gees he could run," he said. "I never had to
mark him, we were both right wingers. But he caught me three
times — NSW against Great Britain at the SCG. He came across
from the other wing. I knocked him off three times and he kept
catching me." Billy hobbled back from the bar carrying two
pints of lager. The pub was empty, before opening time. Team
football photographs covered the walls of the bar, the lounge,
the snooker room, every niche and corner.

Wingers were an endangered species today, he was saying.
With two crook knees bowing under the weight of his large
frame I feared he might be including himself on the list. "Oh
aye," he said, catching my gaze. "I can 'ardly walk across the
road. It's them 'ard Aussie grounds. Every tarm I coom back
off tour they was damaged and needed op'rations." He patted
his girth, "I blame Australia. When I left with the 1954 Lions I
weighed 13 st 7 lbs and when I got back I was nearly 15 stone,"
he said. "I'd never seen them strawberry milkshakes before
and I was 'avin' 'em for breakfast dinner and tea. And I never
took that weight off." But I had sidetracked him about wingers. "Look at Australia, playing O'Connor, Shearer and
Ettingshausen, three good centres, as wingers," he said.
"Great Britain has Offiah, but name another? They've had Joe
Lydon, a centre, and Jonathan Davies, he's a stand-off."

He lit up a smoke, sipped his pint and waited. I shrugged.
What's the reason? "Modern game," he answered. "I scored
50 tries in a season in 1961 and it took them 23 years to do it
again. That was Hanley. He's done it twice and Offiah's done
it once. We used to do it regular. Brian Bevan got 70 odd,
Tommy Van Vollenhoven 60 odd, got 60 myself in 1957. My
point is — Hanley's a stand-off. I'll bet his wingers never
scored 50 tries the season he did. In my day the inside backs
made the play and we'd do the scorin'." And score Billy did,
571 tries in 16 seasons with Wigan, second only to Brian
Bevan's 796 on the all-time career scoring list. He notched his
first 100 tries for Wigan in just 68 matches, still the league record. Even the modern wonder Martin Offiah took 80 matches
to reach his century.

Boston's still only 56 — retired in 1968 — his knees painfully arthritic, but no one scarred Boston more than his own country. Twice, after tours of Australia, he was left behind in Sydney when the Lions continued their tour to South Africa. "I could have gone, but I'd have stayed in different hotels to the team and not played a match," he said. "What was the point? I told the team officials I wasn't bothered about not going. Australia was no bad place to be left. Then they sort of blamed me, because I withdrew." To this day Billy wishes Great Britain had backed him and declined to tour. His melancholy lifted suddenly. "If they didn't accept black players now Great Britain wouldn't have a team, eh!"

From his hotel Boston has seen the great transformation in modern football, from the 1982 Roos on. Brett Kenny — he said the name reverently — one of the finest players he'd ever seen. "The season he played at Wigan his wingers scored 85 tries between them. He always moved the ball," said Billy, slipping imaginary passes using his smokes as a ball. In pride of place on the lounge wall is Brett, framed, finishing his electrifying solo Wembley try that stole the heart and the 1985 Challenge Cup from Hull. "The following year Zip Zip (Steve Ella) came and he scored plenty — but not his wingers," said Billy. Yet he won't genuflect before the undefeated records of the 1982 and 1986 tourists. "How many matches do they play?" he asked rhetorically, because he knew. Thirteen this tour, I said obediently. "We played 30 matches in Australia, sometimes three a week," he said. "I played 19 meself. When you play 30 and you're unbeaten, then you can tap y' chest." The same went for the clean sweeps of three Tests. He pulled us another pint and made an astounding allegation, that Great Britain had once been cheated out of a Test.

"In 1962 we were two Tests up on Australia and leading 17-13 in the third at the SCG," he said. "No team had ever won three Tests on tour in Australia. Then Irvine scored from a pass that was five yards forward and I told the ref, Darcy Lawler. I said, 'That were five bluidy . . .' And he said, 'I know it was and I'd have given it if it was 10 yards forward.' I said, 'Y'what!' And he said, 'If I hadn't I'd have set Australian football back 50 years.' I said 'Who cares about Australian football?' and he said, 'I do.' '' Bill eyed me a moment. A loyal show of sympathy for outclassed Australia, I suggested? ''Oh aye!'' Bill exploded. ''But Rascagneres never showed any mercy in 1986 when he gave a penalty try against us in the third Test at Wigan. He never worried about setting back British football. I was there, Central Park.''

At opening time The Griffin filled with members of the Griffin Dragons, an amateur side of which Bill is patron. The Dragons held their general meeting upstairs, about 20 players signing, paying fees, joking and boasting to me how they'd once won 27 matches straight. The team coach Billy Ashton, a wry little character, warned the players, ''Don't forget, we need a phone number for your wife or girlfriend if you get knocked unconscious.'' Boston laughed, ''There's a few withdrawn their names now.'' No matches on Test Saturdays and who wanted seats on a coach for Wembley? ''You're a bad lot, I'm not going to Wembley with you,'' said Bill. His wife Joan nudged me, ''He remembers what he used to get up to.'' Coach Ashton eyed me over a pint and favoured me with a trade secret. ''Get y' field goal in fust,'' he said. ''Five charges oop t' middle then drop it. Dorn't wairt until the end. Remember thart.'' I said I would.

The meeting broke up and before I departed I asked Boston if he ever saw Shirley Bassey after he left Tiger Bay. He nodded, yuh, once. She was singing in a chorus line at the local Hippodrome. Then fame lifted her out of reach. And Cardiff Arms Park? ''About five years ago I went in a celebrity party to watch Wales play England in rugby union,'' he said. ''But during lunch in a pub it began to blow and squall and sleet and then the match cooms on television, right there in t' bar. They all went but I give me ticket away and watched it on telly, warm and comfortable. It was only across road from the game, but you know . . . soom'ow it had escaped me.''

We shook hands and I hit the M62, the six-lane motorway which links Leeds with Liverpool via a Manchester orbital. It has two speeds, stuck fast or bloody fast. Near the centre of Manchester, where traffic is always backed up, a hoarding advertises a pint of beer with the words, "Pity the M62 isn't as clear." The day before the Kangaroos' match against St Helens a live telecast of the match-of-the-day was delayed 45 minutes because Castleford were trapped on the M62 on their way to Widnes. If it's not stop it's go — flat tack. The left-hand lane is choked with semi-trailers labouring at a mere 65 mph, the centre lane attracts the majority travelling between 70-80 mph and then there's the right-hand lane. It's meant for overtaking but in practice doubles as a Grand Prix circuit.

The official British speed limit of 70 mph is observed only by those who can't exceed it. Even Princess Anne was booked at 90 mph. New cars are regularly advertised that you can push them to 130 mph-plus, "on your own private road" or "on the autostrada". In The Times Motoring Supplement only 16 of the 93 types of car tested had a top speed of less than 110 mph. For some weeks I'd declined to join these ranks of would-be Formula One drivers, but ex-All Black John Gallagher, who had a Ford Sierra 1.6 like mine, told me the car was quick. So that evening, after leaving the Griffin, I accelerated to 85 mph, switched to the fast lane to overtake and lingered there winding the Sierra's needle around. Suddenly I was flashed from behind by powerful high-beam headlights. In the rear-vision mirror I saw a car bearing down so quickly I thought I would be rammed. I squeezed back into the centre lane and looked across in time to see a Mercedes driver clapping his hands at my evasive action. I flicked a glance at my speedo, 98 mph, looked up and the Mercedes was already drawing away. I stayed in the centre lane to home. For me, driving on the M62 gave new meaning to the phrase, life in the fast lane.

When I returned to Wigan for the Kangaroos' third tour match on Sunday, October 14, I took the A580 — a far more sedate four-lane highway — and followed the signs to The Three Sisters, the Pennington Flash and Wigan Pier, three names which tell Wigan's story. The sisters are three 50-metre-high coal mine slag heaps — "the Wigan Alps" — and the Flash is a flooded 100-year-old mining subsidence. Both have been successfully reclaimed from dereliction and converted into popular water and motor sport parks. But they are tourism tyros compared with Wigan Pier. In 1936 George Orwell spent several weeks in Wigan and wrote *The Road to Wigan Pier*, a haunting description of working class life in Wigan in the depths of the depression. He wrote, ''There are over 2000 houses standing which have been condemned for years and whole sections of the town would be condemned en bloc if there were any hope of other houses being built to replace them.'' People, he wrote, ''will put up with anything — any hole and corner slum, any misery of bugs and rotting floors and cracking walls, any extortion of skinflint landlords and blackmailing agents — simply to get a roof over their heads.''

Orwell's book made Wigan a metaphor for the whole decaying post-industrial revolution North and the town has never forgiven him for the international opprobrium he brought upon them. Even today London companies wishing to open branches in the North make video films of modern Wigan to convince employees' spouses they are not being sent to a hellhole. Wigan Borough Council still owns a quarter of the housing in the district but the slums of Orwell's visit were bulldozed after the war — no houses without baths or backdoors, few back-to-back terraces where families in the front half walked around the terrace block and down the rear lane — sometimes as much as 200 metres — to reach the toilet in the backyard. Near the turn of the century the ground beneath Wigan was a swiss cheese of mine shafts and tunnels — 1000 pitheads within five miles of the town centre, employing 30,000 miners. Today there are no working mines in Wigan and King Coal's legacy is a vast area of shallow mineworkings, a wasteland which Wigan spends \$2.5 million a year regenerating.

Wigan townscape has been so rebuilt that when I sought to follow a heritage trail for George Formby — the town's ukelele-playing pre-war songster — I was told many of his old haunts had disappeared. In the city centre the new pride is a shopping mall, The Galleries, in which the date of construction, 1989, is carved into stone as proudly as if it had been medieval. An arcade of glass ceilings and slender steel arches, full of expensive stores, it is indistinguishable from any Australian suburban shoppingtown. Over the public sound system came the slick rhythms of Dire Straits. ''Hey Romeo!'' two passing schoolgirls chorused. ''Hey Juliette!'', I called after them. ''Who's Ellery Hanley?'' They wheeled and giggled, ''Roogby player, the bairst!''

The joke about Wigan Pier — instead of Brighton and Blackpool's huge seaside amusement piers, Wigan boasted only small coal wharfs for loading canal barges — predated Orwell. But Orwell's Parthian shot was to assert on radio, ''I am afraid I must tell you, Wigan Pier doesn't exist.'' The saying goes, ''Kick a Wiganer and they all limp'' but exactly half a century later Wigan had the last laugh. In 1986 the Queen opened Wigan Pier — canalside warehouses transformed into a heritage centre — which has since won every English tourism Oscar imaginable. And the ultimate irony — it features the George Orwell pub. I couldn't resist calling in but the bar area paid no tribute to Orwell. I walked upstairs to the restaurant and told the cashier it was lamentable that the hotel should so ignore its namesake. She smiled and pointed to the sign above the door to her office, ''Room 101'', the notorious torture room from Orwell's *1984*.

Wigan is built on a hill and from the bustling, friendly marketplace you can see, a few blocks away, the floodlights of Central Park, home of England's rugby league club par excellence. During the Wigan Sevens pre-season competition, in the clubhouse window for all to admire or envy, were three cups won the previous season: the huge Challenge and Championship Cups — the knockout and league cup double — and the Regal Trophy, another knockout cup. Sitting nonchalantly beside this brood was Wigan and former Parramatta coach John Monie — 1989-90 English Coach-of-the-Year. When the silver tableau caught the eye of visiting Leeds coach David Ward he stopped his pre-match harangue and pointed upwards to his players. ''See tha' big bastad oop thar, tha's Challenge Coop,'' he said. "Took tha' to bed wi' me for week when ah farnally won it."

Yet 10 years ago Wigan were in second division, struggling to stay afloat until acquired in 1982, for $250,000, by a consortium led by one of the most powerful men in English rugby league, Wigan chairman Maurice Lindsay. I arranged to meet Lindsay in the club's upstairs executive suite. Wigan's colours are cherry and white and so was this overripe room — cherry red carpet, chair and stool coverings, and curtains in cherry red velvet, wall paper in raised cherry red and white velvet vertical stripes, and ceiling rotting-rust cherries.

The new consortium initiated a sustained program of buying the best players and the proof is in photographs adorning the walls, beginning in 1984-85 with Brett Kenny and John Ferguson. Winning Wembley is said to be worth $650,000 to a club and with that cash flow Wigan awoke. The list of stars lured to Central Park eventually read like an international Who's Who: Ellery Hanley, Joe Lydon, Andy Goodway, Andy Platt, Andy Gregory; Australians Steve Ella, Greg Dowling and Ian Roberts; and from New Zealand Kevin Iro, Dean Bell and that very season, All Black Frano Botica. Wigan juniors Shaun Edwards, Bobby Goulding and Martin Dermott — all Lions — were saved from the hands of poachers. Wigan now has a wage bill the equal of a major soccer club and the cream of their players are fully professional with annual football incomes of $200,000. Contracts of between $100,000 and $125,000 for the rest put them above all but the wealthiest of Australian clubs.

The engineer of all this wealth was Maurice Lindsay, a shortish man with thinning sandy hair, sing-song accent and a disarmingly innocent face. Not until he drew near to shake my hand did I note that whatever his expression was saying, his merry eyes were guardian to clever thoughts. Lindsay, who made his fortune hiring out construction equipment, was Great Britain manager for the coming Test series. He was to be the extroverted, articulate foil for the more introverted inspiration of Malcolm Reilly. Lindsay's record with Wigan had to be reckoned with when sizing up Great Britain's chances.

Apart from players, Lindsay's two great coups were to sign coaches Graham Lowe and John Monie. "We realised there was a depth of knowledge in Australia we didn't have," he said. Lowe, a Brisbane premiership winner, author of the New Zealand Rugby League's coaching manual and former coach of the New Zealand national team, came first. Lowe reformed Wigan, gave them a kicking game, stepped up defence rates and steamrolled to the 1986 league premiership by a record 15 points. "Graham was charismatic," said Lindsay. "His evangelical ability reminded me of Billy Graham. I've heard him talking an hour before a match, showing American football motivational tapes on the big video screen and he had the players in the palm of his hand. It made the hairs stand up on the back of your neck to listen to him."

For all the cups Lowe won for Wigan his biggest scalp came with Wigan's unexpected defeat of Manly in the 1987 world club challenge at Central Park. Lindsay set it up, flying to Sydney to meet with ARL chief Ken Arthurson, ARL general manager Bob Abbott, and NSW general manager John Quayle. They all shook hands over the $50,000 prizemoney put up by Fosters, and Arthurson said, "We'll split the cash." To which Lindsay replied, "No, let the winners keep it."

Maurice Lindsay's eyes grew round as he mimicked the reaction of the Australian trio. "They looked at me as if I was mad or had had too much to drink," he said. "Manly had Mick O'Connor, Fatty Vautin, Dale Shearer and Rambo Gibbs, with Bobby Fulton in charge. They didn't imagine for a moment they'd lose." And what about the Manly argument that the challenge was a letdown so soon after their grand final? "They only use that as an excuse when they lose," grinned Lindsay.

Manly were so impressed they eventually signed Lowe as club coach in 1989. Wigan released him because "He wanted to go," said Maurice, shrugging his shoulders. "We were sorry to lose him, he was a good mate. But if it had been an auction . . . Ken Arthurson said, 'Maurice we've got $6 million'. I said, 'Ken if it came to a fight we'd peck your eyes out.' I mean $6 million is only 2.4 million pounds. We're building a new stand here for 1.3 million pounds and we're not going into debt for that.'' Lindsay searched for more proof. ''Lowe, in his first season with Manly, tried to buy Kevin Iro from us, but Iro stayed. Let's just say Wigan had a little bit more muscle.''

Wigan's replacement for Lowe, John Monie, was like upgrading from business to first class. ''Graham never won the League and the Cup in the same year,'' said Lindsay anticipating my question. ''John is the most competent all-round coach in the world. He's a rugby educationalist. Ellery Hanley and Andy Gregory don't need emotional uplift before a game. Where Graham lifted them on the day, John is the opposite. He intensifies Monday to Saturday, remedies weaknesses, nurses if necessary, and on Sunday he doesn't do anything, he lets them do it themselves.''

The cups, the premiership, world club champions and last year Wigan cleaned up New Zealand — what was left? The match whispered to be the Kangaroos' fourth Test. ''It's our goal this year,'' said Maurice. ''The players are keen. I'm steeped in Sydney football. I knew we couldn't beat Australia last tour. But now . . .''

The broad shoulders of John Monie might have sagged at such bravado from his chairman, but when I ran into Monie at the launch of the Rothmans Rugby League Yearbook he was almost equally gung ho. ''We're going all out,'' he warned. ''When I was in Australia in June I looked at all the Test players and I've got notes on all of them, up-to-date information of their strengths and weaknesses.'' For Monie, victories with Parramatta were memories for the sideboard. He was not distracted by misguided loyalties. ''I'm Australian, makes no difference,'' he said, fingering the knot in his Wigan club tie. ''I hope Australia win the Tests, but I think Wigan can beat Australia.''

So did Wigan fans, 25,000 and hundreds more standing on a Scotsman's hill overlooking the ground. Drinkers overflowed onto the road outside Boston's hotel, on a corner a hawker was selling Aussie team t-shirts, ''Guaranteed not to fade,'' he assured me. ''True, but can you say the same of Wigan,'' I replied. In the Wigan club shop Mark Carroll and Brad Mackay bought Wigan jerseys which cost $82 each. "You should give them a discount," I suggested. The young sales assistant smiled. "Ah woooed!" she purred.

Wigan's history is ancient and their supporters fiercely loyal. The main grandstand was a sea of cherry and white, from scarfs, caps and sweaters to banners and flags and when the Kangaroos came out for a 20-minute warm-up the crowd burst into song.

> Wigan reigns supreme,
> We are the greatest team,
> The world has ever seen,
> Wigan the champions.

and

> We're all part of Monie's army,
> We're all going to Wembley,
> We'll really shake them up,
> When we win the Challenge Cup.

More songs followed, massed voices in wonderful unison but with such accents I enlisted the help of a young supporter behind me to translate. "We're letting you know what we've won," she said excitedly. It was a ritual war chant, the Zulus of Wigan, boasting of past victories to sap the confidence of their adversaries. A series of calls began, "Come on you Re-eds" and, to the tune of the Stars and Stripes Forever, "Here we go, here we go, here we go". My translator listened attentively to the next song and blushed. "That's rude, can't tell you," she said. The Aussies went through their fingertip handling exercises, catching balls like a cricket slips cordon, then ran a few criss-cross, multi-directional passing patterns which were as bewildering as they were impressive. By the time they were running three men with the ball at two touch-tacklers the crowd's enthusiasm had subsided before such effortless artistry.

Then Ellery Hanley led Wigan out in glorious sunshine and the crowd found deafening voice once more. Klaxon horns blasted out "Honk,honk,honk,honk, honkhonkhonkhonk, WIGAN!" and then it was, "Hanley, Hanley, give us a wave Hanley," and Ellery obediently saluted. "There's only one Andy Gregory", sung to the tune of "Guantanamera" brought a nod from Cockrobin with shoulderpads and chest shield. And to take us up to the kick-off the grandstand choir broke into "When the Saints" and "You Are My Sunshine". They generated the most partisan yet joyfilled atmosphere I've ever experienced at a match. It was a mighty crowd, bred from a century of shared suffering and success. And all spontaneous, so different from Australia's scantily clad, American-style pom-pom girls.

Australia ran out the expected Test team — Belcher, Ettingshausen, Meninga, McGaw, Hancock, Daley, Langer, Roach, Kerrod Walters, Bella, Cartwright, Sironen and Lindner, plus substitutes Alexander, Stuart, Lazarus and Mackay. Only Stuart and Alexander had not played Tests. For Wigan — Hampson, Lydon, Edwards, Gregory, Betts and Hanley were in Reilly's Test squad; Goodway, Skerrett, Lucas and Dermott were Lions, and Iro had played for New Zealand. It was the next best thing to a Test and it began like one, with Roach and Bella being pelted backwards and Australia defending grimly. This had become the pattern, club teams fairly hurling themselves like dervishes at Australia early on. Kerrod Walters was the man fated to err under this pressure, risking an overhead pass which he won't treasure on video. The ball flew wide of Langer, and Shaun Edwards of true pace toed at it once, twice, and over Australia's line. Bob Lindner decided Edwards would score and cut him down with a copybook diving tackle, without the ball. He's some competitor, Bob Lindner. Referee Colin Morris was already sprinting for the centre of the posts to award a penalty try to Edwards.

Wigan 6-0, the crowd in full throat, Australia making uncharacteristic errors. Fulton had chatted to Hancock about his St Helen's crabbing and trying to run over the top of players. "He's better off running between players because you know they're arm grabbers over here," said Fulton. So Meninga ran wide and angled Hancock back inside where he made good jinking ground. Hanley replied by rounding Daley with insolent ease. And so it went, nip and tuck for 25 minutes, worthy of any Test, but after a Belcher downtown I noted Wigan players taking two tackles to jog back into line. Hanley twice stopped "Blocker" Roach with rocking, energy sapping, full-frontal body tackles. It meant that when Daley sweetly chip kicked, regathered and sent Ettingshausen swan-diving for the corner, Hanley's cover defence was already expended. Six-all.

In the grandstand the overflow media were cheek by jowl with the vociferous crowd and one Wigan supporter had bayed furiously at every Kangaroo success. Now he positively screamed, "Forward pus! Forward pus! Aw c'mon ref, aw nooooor." Ray Chesterton of the *Daily Telegraph* turned and said, "Mate, I've been listening to you for 20 minutes and you know nothing about the game!" I searched for a likely exit but the fan took it on the chin, as well he might because Wigan's defence was beginning to show all the resistance of a paramour reclining on a cushion. It became apparent that Hanley, Gregory and Iro were less than fully fit and in 12 minutes before half-time a rolling wave of green and gold swept over for three tries, Hancock, 10-6, Belcher 16-6, Ettingshausen 20-6.

The crowd on free hill had a good view of all those tries but they were destined for a barren second half as Australia began scoring at the other end. Four minutes after restart Ettingshausen's wondrous athleticism brought him his third try, a hat-trick to match his St Helen performance — 24-6. The score crept to 34-6 with tries by Langer and Mackay by which time Australia had lost interest. As with St Helens it was Wigan's worst defeat by Australia. Poor Wigan fans first fell silent, went through a phase of half encouraging, half scolding — "Oh c'mon Wigan, c'mooon" and finally lapsed into applause at each Kangaroo try. Even our one-eyed fan behind us was exclaiming, "Ohh super roogby, ohh farn trah." Only Meninga's kicking remained mortal, three goals from seven kicks and if my lip-reading was correct he christened his last miss with one word, "Shit!"

Had Bobby Fulton been worried by Wigan's early pressure? "I'd be a fool if I said otherwise," he admitted. "But we knew that from the way St Helens and Wakefield came at us. And we knew Wigan's intensity would last longer because they're coached by an Australian. And they've got wall-to-wall internationals. But they haven't come up against an organised defence like ours," and here he permitted himself the ghost of a smile. What Fulton didn't need to say was that, with the penalties only 8-7 to Wigan, the matter of English refereeing was now closed.

A few nights later I returned to the Griffin where Ettingshausen, Langer, Daley and McGaw were due to appear in a Fourex promotion. Griffin Dragons coach Billy Ashton had a sorry story to tell. "We're leading St Helens Nutgrove when me stand-off gets sick of playin' tight, runs wahd, florts a long pass to his centre, Nutgrove intercept and score under t' bluidy posts!" We both laughed, you wouldn't read about it eh? One Wigan supporter, Dawn Richardson, whose dedication, she said, extended to wearing cherry and white knickers, was lamenting Wigan's defeat. "I felt like crying," she said. "My son Paul, he's 14, was upset too. When Australia scored their third try I went for a coffee and a chap came in after me. He said, 'They've scored again.' I said 'I know, three tries.' And he said, 'No, four! They've just gone in again!' " Had she ever stopped singing? "No, but we changed our tune," said Dawn. To what? She laughed and whispered, "Aussies are sheep shaggers, and Meninga's a wanker!"

The Aussie quartet arrived about 10 pm in jeans, sneakers and white sponsor's t-shirts, looking more like The Right Stuff than suspect shepherds. "What happened to Wigan?" Daley asked Boston. Billy scowled, "I went to the bar at half-time," he said. "Joost took a glance every now and then. They didn't do themselves justice. It's no' the Wigan I'm used to watchin'. You lads deserved better than that." Daley agreed, "Yeah, we could have done with a good hit out. But a good crowd, eh." Boston smiled self-deprecatingly. "Aye, I'll say this for Wigan fans, no one left except meself and I said I was going to the toilet.''

Later, back at the Ramada, I rode a lift up with Bob Lindner. Good effort against Wigan, I said, they're a good side. He grinned, ''Mate, they WERE a good side.''

4 THE FALL AND RISE OF ENGLAND

Wigan's loss struck hard those in English rugby league who believed that 1990 could be the Year of the Lion. The signs were ominous — Australia were outscoring the '82 Roos by 40 points and were only eight points behind the '86 team despite Meninga kicking just four goals from 13 attempts. But it was the manner of their wins which spread alarums. Lacking the field marshalling of a Lewis or a Sterling, the Kangaroos were calling upon their common soldiering — the drills, discipline and relentless pressure of the Sydney competition. They were worrying English clubs into defeat, and then into abject submission.

Over in their plush new headquarters in Chapeltown Road, Leeds, the RFL executive felt their collective heart miss a beat as they pushed forward with the strategem begun 15 years ago to resuscitate not just the Great Britain team, but rugby league itself in England. Because curiously enough, by the time the 1982 Invincibles stormed through England earning universal praise as the Team of the Year in any sport, English rugby league was no decaying edifice set to crumble at the prod of a Kangaroo paw. Only two years earlier the 1980 Challenge Cup final between Hull and Hull Kingston Rovers, attended by the Queen Mother, sold out Wembley in record time. The shock that reverberated through the north in 1982 was incredulity that Australian standards had so thoroughly outstripped England's. To understand why, we have to return to 1974 when rugby league in England truly was at a low ebb.

Though Britain had regained the Ashes from Australia in 1970, the domestic game was atrophying due to an ageing administration. When English RFL operations chief Geoffrey Keith joined as an office boy in 1973 he was told by an executive, "I don't know why you're taking this job — there'll be no rugby league in two or three years." There can be no denying the valuable role of secretary Bill Fallowfield who was responsible for introducing the four-tackle rule. But after 28 years in control he had lost the will to delegate and dominated an unwieldy, hidebound RFL council of quiescent professional clubs. The game was moribund. Morale was down, crowds diminishing and in the era which displayed on television the tremendous athleticism of Bjorn Borg and Jimmy Connors, rugby league footballers looked to lack both fitness and skills. Crisis enveloped the RFL in 1973 when, for their very survival, the neglected amateur (junior) ranks voted to split from the RFL just as rugby league had split from the ERU 78 years before. The RFL forced a reluctant Fallowfield to retire, aged 60, and replaced him with the least likely candidate imaginable.

David Oxley, then 36, was a public school headmaster with just the blend of accents you would expect of a Hull-bred, Oxford graduate in English literature. Oxley had moved from head of the English Department at St Peters, York — the oldest school in England — to become headmaster of the Duke of York Royal Military school in Dover which was set up originally for the orphans of the Duke of Wellington's Peninsula wars. Oxley, a useful centre, played rugby union at Oxford and though he did not gain a Blue — awarded only to those who play Cambridge — he was a greyhound, which meant he was among the top 30 Oxford players. His future lay in heading some premier English public school but, ever a Yorkshireman, he had been nurtured on rugby league and sought a place in the fabric of northern life. Oxley was shortlisted for the RFL job, drove to Leeds one Sunday night, was put up in a seedy hotel across the road from the RFL, interviewed on Monday and, as Oxley put it, "The next day I was The Man, in a depressing half-decent office, no guidance, just start."

Three months later the RFL employed its first ever public relations officer, David Howes, an energetic 23-year-old general feature writer on the Hull *Daily Mail*. Howes, a schoolboy half-back, like Oxley, watched his career plans plunge off the graph in pursuit of the game he loved. So soured had press relations become under Fallowfield that Howes, the publicity officer, found the media never rang. For the next six months Oxley and Howes — "the ex-teacher and that PRO man"— took to the road to learn the worst and spread the gospel of renewal. "We went out and about five nights a week, made speeches, talked to referees, attended club meetings, listened to everybody and anything," said Oxley. "And we found this paradox — though people talked about a dying game, rugby league was far from dead because too many people cared too much about it."

Said Howes, "We had no pedigree in rugby league adminis-tration, so we were very naive really, but it was our very na-ivety, our enthusiasm to make it work, that gee-ed people up." Oxley the stately centre and Howes the nippy halfback swept through the north, Oxley's square-jawed gentility imparting confidence and Howes's quick-witted manoeuvrings excising opposition. It is not an exaggeration to say that between them they began the long haul of reviving faith in an entire sporting code. I met them often during my six months, Oxley unfail-ingly friendly, Howes, manic, trapped by RFL minutae when a vision of rugby league's future may be the greater priority.

In many ways — with Sunday football, two divisions and the six-tackle rule already in place — Oxley and Howes had today's product to sell. On top of this they made an uneasy peace with the rebel amateurs, stitched up television deals and marketed the game with such zeal that by 1975 they drew nearly 20,000 to a France-Wales international at Swansea. By 1979 the RFL was on course with morale restored, school foot-ball re-emerging, crowds up, media onside and strong Wem-bleys. Admittedly the 1979 Lions to Australia were hammered in three Tests but the alarm bells at home didn't ring — or those within would not hear. Selection policies and players were left to bear the blame. The 1981 season brought a 37-0 Test rout of France at Hull. A 2-19 loss two weeks later at Marseilles was put down to . . . well, France. No one wanted to rock the En-

gland boat, cruising contentedly along, conscious only of its
entertaining domestic scene. Then the 1982 Kangaroos drew
alongside and fired a first Test broadside which still echoes
across the carpets of the RFL. "After a few club games Frank
Stanton realised how poor our fitness and preparation was,"
lamented David Howes. "He changed his tactics completely,
just let his team run, suddenly the Australians were playing a
game at high speed, keeping the ball alive."

David Oxley remembered that Hull Test well. "It was only
10-4 at half-time and we hadn't played too badly," he said.
"But the second half . . . 40-4 in the end wasn't it?" Oxley had
returned to the team hotel shellshocked. "I didn't want to see
anybody, just sit and contemplate, but what surprised me was
that the players seemed normal — maybe they were covering
their embarrassment, but it didn't seem right to me." From the
ashes of those Ashes the RFL suddenly had to resurrect the English game once more. "We'd been selling the domestic game
on its general image and suddenly that drubbing showed it was
not worth its salt internationally," said Howes. "All credit to
the Australians but they set us right bloody back again!"

Six months before Stanton's 1982 Roos landed, Phil Larder,
a schoolmaster and 12 years a centre with Oldham, had been
appointed director of coaching with BARLA, the British amateur association which was still split from the RFL but on better
terms. He had sensed the coming storm and after it struck at
Hull he grasped the true dimensions of the danger. He
thought, "Hell, if we don't do something, fast, Australia is
going to say there's no point in playing Great Britain because
they're too far behind!" He then took an extraordinary step. In
the middle of that Test series he rang Frank Stanton and threw
himself, and the future of English football, at Stanton's mercy.
English training and coaching methods were antiquated, he
told Stanton. Could he come and observe and learn? "Stanton
contacted Australia to ask how much he could reveal," said
Larder. "I was with the enemy, wasn't I?" Back came back the
ARL: If the man's genuine, show him the lot. Stanton invited

Larder into camp for a full week before the second Test at Central Park, Wigan, which Australia won 27-6.

"It was a real eye-opener," recalled Larder. "We hadn't seen tackle shields before. It allowed Stanton to train far more realistically than if unopposed. His ball players were driving into real opposition but the contact was not severe. And when ball-carriers were blocked, they were turning and off-loading. Our players were playing tig and pass which encourages you to stand straight and shallow and doesn't encourage support play. Stanton told me, 'Phil, train tig and pass, play tig and pass.'"

In February 1983, two months after the Kangaroos left England's shattered fields, Larder presented a report of his findings to a conference of 22 English coaches, one of whom was Malcolm Reilly. The report poured out all Larder had learned from a week of Kangaroo cramming — fitness, tactics, ballwork and equipment. Australians were fitter than English players yet trained only three times a week and were not full-time professionals. English players did not train under match conditions for fear of injury, whereas Australians used cushioned shields. Larder detailed how Stanton had collated three months of tackle counts from all Sydney first grade matches and averaged out a tackle count for every position in a theoretical team. This he pasted up in the team room to motivate each Kangaroo to produce a better tackle count than the Sydney average for his position.

The report startled the RFL. Larder was made coaching director of the professional game as well as the amateurs and was dispatched to Australia to learn the full catastrophe of the coaching upheaval which had left England buffeted in its wake. He visited clubs and even sat in with Arthur Beetson and the Queensland State of Origin team but most illuminating of all was his meeting with Jack Gibson. In the 1970s, Gibson had seen how American coaches developed a defence strategy as well as an attack philosophy because in American football a different team defended while the attack sat on the bench. "Jack came back and geared 50 per cent of his training to defence," said Larder. In Australia coaches talked about attack — when you had the ball — and defence, when you repelled the opposition with a static defensive line. "Jack adopted the American terminology by calling it off-fence and dee-fence," said Larder. "And he attacked all the time, he attacked with defenders, nailing their ball-carriers before they could move. Plus he brought back tackle counts, straight from the Los Angeles Rams. That's how Stanton's Kangaroos conceded only seven tries in 15 matches."

Larder's major conviction was that anyone playing rugby league ought to be on a heavy strength weights program. In the 1970s most British players were employed in heavy manual jobs like mining, which built up their torsos and legs. As the mines closed fewer players were in those jobs but the natural strengthening had not been replaced by other means. "In terms of weightlifting, Deryck Fox, the smallest player on the 1990 Lions tour to New Zealand, was stronger than any forward who played for Great Britain in 1982," said Larder. "We've got tests to prove it."

English clubs and coaches were now in an emotional double bind. No one could deny the superiority of Australian methods, but English pride had been deeply wounded. "Between 1982 and 1986 Australia became a dirty word," said Larder. "All I heard was, 'Don't talk to us about Australians, we don't want to copy Australians.'" Senior *Yorkshire Post* rugby league writer, Raymond Fletcher, remembered the arguments well. "The old guard coaches used to say, 'Oh the Aussies are good but they don't have our ball skills.' Ball skills! We had fat, overweight forwards who stood still and offloaded the ball, which Craig Young was doing at full gallop with the Kangaroos." The RFL wisely ignored the anti-Aussie prejudice and decreed that every coach employed by a professional club had to pass a special level of coaching exam. To avoid the possible embarrassment of famous coaches failing, those who had five years experience had to attend the course, but would not be examined afterwards. Larder's final major administrative task was to write a coaching manual, using as a guide the Australian version written by his ARL counterpart Peter Corcoran. To side-step any suggestion of Down Underism, Larder borrowed from the Football Association (soccer) manual for the coaching course's structure and administration.

A key legacy of the 1982 Roos was lifting the ban on Anglo-Australian transfers which had been in force since 1977. A trickle became a flood. By 1984-85 the Leeds dressingroom re-sounded to the antipodean accents of Gavin Jones, Trevor Patterson, Steve Martin, Neil Hunt, Mark Laurie, Tony Currie, Wally Fullerton-Smith, Steve Bleakley, Terry Webb and Eric Grothe. At Halifax around the same period the club was being coached by favourite Canterbury son Chris Anderson and the books listed 13 Australians. A Leeds-Halifax match around this time was said to have fielded 20 Australians. Resentment among English players boiled over when clubs began buying Australians — no better than local lads — simply for their ca-pacity to draw crowds. Little known Aussies on holidays from Goodiwindi or Camooweal became the flavour of the season with spectators, but not with teammates nor, more impor-tantly, with the British Department of Employment which di-rected that such wholesale importing was depriving home players of a chance to earn their living. In 1985 the RFL voted that by 1988-89 each club could have a maximum of only three imports. The Aussie import bubble burst.

By the time Wally Lewis's 1986 Roos toured, the RFL had in place sport conditioning, strength acquisition, fitness testing, sport sciences, video analysis and coaching programs. How-ever, as David Oxley knew — "Four years wasn't long enough and the Australians hadn't stood still, but Rascagneres gave a very harsh penalty try when it was 12-12 in the third Test". And Phil Larder knew too — "I said then we ain't got a prayer, we were still rebuilding, but we had them on the ropes until Lewis beat us with a little bit of magic in the third Test."

When the RFL legislated to limit the import of Australian players, the vacuum of expertise was filled by a wave of Aus-tralian coaches, once more raising the hackles of the endan-gered domestic species. But not Wakefield's David Topliss.

"We've still a lot of old-fashioned coaches who've got their heads buried in the sand," he said. "And that's why the Aussie coaches came over." Of the top eight English clubs in 1989-90, half of them — Wigan, Hull, Castleford and Warrington — were coached by Australians and one, St Helens, by a New Zealander. Of the 19 players selected in Reilly's 1990 Test squad, 11 were from these clubs.

At Warrington, ex-St George fullback Brian Johnson took over in November 1988 after having played there for several seasons. "English football is far less defence orientated," he told me one day at Wilderspool Stadium. "The fans are happy to see a game won 50-48 and the players are happy to play it." Nor were players probability conscious. "In Australia, if you think there's a 50-50 chance of your pass going astray, you hold on to the ball," he said. "Over here if you're a 10 per cent chance you throw it and give it everything you've got." Johnson, as laconic as a fireside stockman, was also amused by a curious legacy from the 1982 and 1986 Roos. "Deep down in every Englishman's heart there's a belief that they still have the skilful players and Australians are just fit and play boring games based on defence," he said. Perversely English players would spare nothing to build maximum fitness but turned their noses up at practising skills — the very schoolboy routines Meninga's men went through for 20 minutes before every match.

Former Brisbane Redcliffe coach, Darryl Van de Velde, joined Castleford in 1988-89, treading warily, testing fitness levels, skills and strength before upping the training regime. Van de Velde, a finance consultant and look-a-like for Telly Savalas, brought with him fitness charts on Redcliffe players. "They covered two mile runs, bench pressing their own body weight 10 times, aerobic and anaerobic analysis," he said. "I found many of these blokes down 10 to 15 per cent compared to Australians. With a few exceptions they used the weights room as a hobby, go there when they felt like it."

Over at Hull, blond-headed Brian Smith, formerly of Illawarra, arrived in 1988-89 and was amazed at how little of

Australia's defence play had rubbed off in England. Smith un-
earthed one player, a 12-year professional, who had never been
shown how to tackle — the target area or where to place his
feet. "So how was I to structure a defensive group of tackles,"
said Smith. But, as Johnson said, fitness was a fetish. One
night after a particularly exhausting session in which not one
Hull player shirked it, Smith's eventual successor as Hull
coach, Noel Cleal, walked over and told him, "You'd be flat
out getting that sort of commitment from any club in Sydney
you know." Another night ex-NSW State of Origin forward
David Boyle seconded the comment. "Mate, the players would
have walked off at Souths if you'd put that on."

In 1987 the English RFL did the next best thing to appointing
an Australian as national coach. They chose to fight fire with
brimstone and put their hopes in as formidable a fellow as ever
pulled a British jersey over his head — Malcolm Reilly. In the
Rugby League Hall of Fame there's a photograph of Reilly entitled "Scourge of the Aussies". That he was, a member of the
1970 Lions to Australia, the last team to win the Ashes for Great
Britain. Reilly was the scourge wherever he played and I don't
think I've ever encountered a harder man. His handshake was
like gripping a stone sculpture. When Laurie Daley met him
later in the tour his response was similar, "Bloody handshake!" I had a drink with Reilly in Chequers, the pub in
Ledsham, Reilly's tiny village just outside Leeds. Two features
of his face are memorable — his cold, steely eyes and the tense
set of his jaw muscles. I got the feeling that if you tinkered care-
lessly with this man, he might just uncoil, like a spring from a
clock, and pieces would fly everywhere.

After his performances in Australia with the 1970 Lions
none questioned Reilly was a champion lock forward, but some
doubted his temperament. First he had been fined by the Lions
tour management after a brawl outside South Sydney Leagues
Club. Then, more seriously, he appeared in the Supreme Court
in Sydney defending a damages claim after a fight at a Brisbane
party. A reveller had shouted at Reilly, "Wait until Beetson
gets you, you Pommie bastard." Perhaps the chap should have

followed his own advice because, as with the Leagues Club altercation, Reilly's antagonists suffered the consequences of baiting a granite-faced, 22-year-old Lion.

According to David Poulter, chairman of Reilly's old club, Castleford, it was no secret that Reilly could be easily wound up off the field. "In his younger days as everybody knows he used to be a bit wild," said Poulter. "Like lots of young lads he was a bit fiery. But he was a gentleman on the field. He was such a strong, aggressive player, but he always played the game fair and clean." But could this be the gentleman who, after he joined Manly in 1971, kept making headlines for being sent off — 1971, head high tackle; 1972, using a forearm to the head of a player not in possession of the ball; 1973, using an elbow and punching; 1974, head butting; 1975, deliberate kicking and using indecent language. In defence of this litany Ken Arthurson, Manly's secretary in those days, protested that Reilly was abused, niggled and goaded in every tackle in every match. Reilly was Manly's hired gun and Sydney footballers were eager to eyeball him. Reilly never blinked and never stepped back.

Armed with this fiercely competitive nature, Reilly took on the unenviable post of Great Britain coach in 1987, defeated France 2-0 that year and then headed for Australia with the 1988 Lions. When they lost to NSW northern division 36-12 in an early tour match — Great Britain's biggest tour defeat by a non-Test side for 38 years — Reilly locked the team in the dressingroom and upbraided them for 20 minutes before the media was permitted to nose the chastened air.

In Chequers pub, Malcolm Reilly bought us both a pint, sat down at a table and recalled the first Test of the 1988 tour, in Sydney. "We came close to winning — very close," he said. "If we could have just controlled our kicking in the second half Australia would have had a struggle to win." And if he had won? "It would have been wide open, yeah. The balance would have changed," he said. "In the second Test we played from our hearts instead of our heads. We wanted to win so badly we did a lot of silly things. It was a bad loss that."

BBC commentator, Ray French, himself a British World Cup forward in 1968, will remember the 1988 third Test for a lifetime. "We were ridiculed, written off by the Sydney papers — don't go to this match, it's a farce, not worth the admission, Brits are a disgrace," he recalled with displeasure. "I'll be quite honest, I had every record for the highest score against us ready for the broadcast. And we won. The first time since I'd taken over commentating from Eddie Waring in 1981." If one glare from Reilly is said to restore order among skylarking players, his menace is not confined to his team. As the Australian media spread through the Great Britain dressingroom after their historic Sydney victory Reilly isolated one writer and commanded icily, "You, out!" Since both morning and afternoon newspapers had given the Poms a torrid time the accused momentarily hesitated. Reilly continued, "You can walk out or be carried out." Few doubted his words, least of all the reporter concerned.

Reilly set a personal example of the standards he knew to be necessary to match Australia. English reporters on the 1990 Lions tour of Papua New Guinea and New Zealand watched a contest between Kelvin Skerrett of Wigan and Hull KR's David Bishop performing sitting curls — semi-situps — which Skerrett won with about 300. The corps aver Reilly took off his sunglasses, rose from his banana lounge and performed close to 400. After another contest, swimming underwater lengths, he again let the players do their best and then outswam them.

Reilly's Test coaching record approaching the 1990 Kangaroos — 10 wins and seven losses — scarcely matched his ambitions, particularly after a disappointing drawn Test series in 1990 against France and Papua New Guinea, teams Australia jousts with more in sympathy than anger. But Reilly's feat in lifting virtually a Second Thirteen Great Britain to defeat the Kiwis in New Zealand in 1990 prompted Bobby Fulton to comment admiringly, "I never thought it possible." Yet what Reilly was up against — as demonstrated by the way the 1990 Kangaroos were overrunning club sides after 30 minutes or so — was the lack of sustained intensity from English club players.

John Monie had pin-pointed it after Wigan's demoralising loss. "Everyone starts keen and eager and then fatigue sets in," he said. "If you can't play out 40 minutes with intensity, and then double it, they'll get you in the end."

It is alleged the British public, be it soccer, cricket or rugby league, love the quick gratification of knockout competitions. "Instant death," said the BBC's Ray French. "They like to go to a match where it's all or nothing." The RFL runs three knockout cup competitions during its long, nine-month season, all more or less parallel with the main league championship. The early season features county cups — the Yorkshire and Lancashire Cups; mid-season brings the Regal Trophy and, towards season's end, the celebrated Challenge Cup at Wembley. John Monie's achievement in winning the league championship and three cups was considered impossible because the more knockout cup games a club wins the more it has to play. Wigan in 1989-90 played 43 matches — including a Charity Shield match and a tour game against New Zealand — compared with 29 by any club which lost in the first round of the three knockout Cups, and didn't make the premiership finals.

Yet the most telling comparison is between Australia and England. Sydney clubs tolerated mid-week knockout competitions but argued they interfered with preparations for the weekend matches. Last year, 1990, the knockout cup went pre-season, extending the season to seven and a half months. But a club which made the Winfield Cup grand final and the final of the knockout cup would still have played only 29 matches, an average of a match every 7.7 days, compared with Wigan's 1989-90 average of a match every 5.8 days. Admittedly Australia's harder grounds take a greater toll on players, however two days is precious grace to a worn and torn footballer. In much the same way that less frequent Sheffield Shield matches better prepare Australian cricketers for Test cricket than England's non-stop county championship, so the Winfield Cup builds more match intensity than England's Stone's Bitter Championship.

England's incessant cups are the bane of Darryl Van de Velde's life at Castleford. "We thrashed Bradford, who held the Yorkshire Cup, and from midweek on the players were all cup this, cup that," said Van de Velde. "I told them to forget about the bloody Yorkshire Cup, we had a championship match to play on Sunday. What happens is, I don't get the best out of them because they don't want to get injured before the next cup round. I have to bring them down to earth, nearly sends me off my brain." Castleford went on to win the Yorkshire Cup but Van de Velde was supremely unimpressed. "It holds no credence with me. The strength is over in Lancashire, with Wigan and Widnes," he said.

County cups give respite to the uninspired coach and the limping club. Win three consecutive matches and you're into the final so club directors have a paragraph to adorn the annual report. National director of coaching Phil Larder has pushed for the county cups and the mid-season cup to be axed, even though the latter attracts national exposure through BBC television. "You can't build up intensity playing 40 or so games a year," he said. "Intensity comes through having four to five days to build up before a game. Our coaches know that if they try to do that twice a week, before every match, it would begin to wash off the players. Anyway, I don't think the players are capable of responding that often. They're struggling now to survive the faster, fitter, stronger collisions Australian training has brought to us."

Larder's major recommendations to the RFL for the past three years have been to reduce the number of games and shorten the season. He argues that fewer matches would be offset by increased crowds and no loss of revenue. Further he says, improving England's international standing would trickle down to the domestic game, boosting popular interest.

Since rugby league is a breakaway movement, carving its own course and creating new traditions, probably no other sport has it's future so intimately tied to the foresight or conservatism of its administrators. How the game is played in Britain depends on how the RFL organises it. Between them in 16 years, the RFL and its servants, Oxley and Howes, have doubled crowds, increased sponsorship exponentially from $25,000 to $2.5 million a year and given the game television coverage across five stations worth $12 million a year. But are Oxley and Howes still needling the RFL, advocating radical surgery on the bloated season schedule, or have they become the great survivors, no longer stimulating change in the self-contented ranks of the influential clubs?

None of their considerable achievements remedies what Brian Smith told me before he left Hull to coach St George in Sydney. He recounted how he always showed videos of Australian matches to his players on the team bus travelling to away games. One day a player pulled him aside and said, ''Tell me, I won't tell anyone else, I promise, because I know how proud you are of Australian football. But those tapes, are they speeded up or not?'' Smith replied,''No mate, that's how it is.'' And that's how it would be for Malcolm Reilly and Great Britain.

5 FAST REACTORS IN CUMBRIA

One week into the tour a group of players sat at a table in the ground floor bar and coffee area of the Ramada relaxing and reading football magazines. Suddenly one of them yelled, "Hey, Cement!" and David Gillespie, who was walking towards the front entrance, stopped in his tracks. So did everyone else in the foyer, startled at such an expressive name. In days to come I saw hotel staff similarly bemused when tall, strapping Mark McGaw readily answered to "Sparkles", though onlookers were less surprised to see Steve Roach respond to "Blocker".

The Kangaroos had the exclusive use of a conference room on the hotel's mezzanine floor and they had installed a snooker table, pin-ball machine, juke-box, television, video and a massive refrigerator stacked with beer. But as often as not they preferred the ground floor bar where they could watch the passing parade of guests through the foyer. They played cards, read newspapers or just chatted with visitors from home. In the sociology of the small group, nicknames are part of the bonding process where code names allow for an intimacy of conversation in public. It also permits bandied abuse between players while averting the potential damage of a genuinely personal insult. To give Bozo a friendly burst to his face was one thing, to abuse coach Bob Fulton was another.

I never heard anyone call Andrew Ettingshausen anything other than ET, or Greg Alexander other than Brandy. Badge Belcher, Rowdy Shearer and Napper Lyons had worn those names for years. Some of their nicknames come from television, such as (Chicken) George Meninga from *Roots*, Alf Langer from *Alien Life Form*, and Eddie Bella from the *Munsters*. Brad Fittler was Freddie because when he was called into the 1990 NSW State of Origin team Jack Gibson forgot his name and called him that. Mark Carroll, identifying his luggage tag, simply printed Spud and Mark Geyer rejoiced in his famous sportscar initials. New boy Ricky Stuart varied between Tricky and Sticky but ex-policeman Mark Sargent was always going to be Sarge.

One player was known as Buttocks, another Heiffer Head and another Brick with Eyes. But these were clearly verbal caricatures rather than nicknames and I never heard anyone use them in training, calling for the ball, which is the true test of a working nickname. Up with ET and Brandy for regular use was "Sherriff" Brian Hollis, Roos trainer since New Zealand in 1989. His nickname comes from his work as a regional manager with the NSW Sherriff's Department and he said he carried a badge to prove it, but you could never trust the Sherriff because from the outset he became the jester in the court of His Majesty Bob Fulton. Hollis was Fulton's trainer at Manly — "God's country" — and on tour he was strapper, ran the line delivering instructions during matches and was first to the side of a downed Kangaroo. "I watch the back play, not the game," said Hollis. "I watch to see who doesn't get up, who's lagging behind. They all train for body impact, they're all champions, but you can't train to be knocked out." Hollis asks groggy players do they know the score or know where they are. "Some say 'Piss off!' and you know they're all right," Hollis laughed. "And then there's Dale Shearer, he'll say, 'Ah, I think we're at Parramatta Stadium' and a little glint comes into his eye."

Yet as important as were his field duties, the Sherriff's part in settling the Kangaroos in their new environment was priceless. He did this with comedy, forever taking the mickey out of himself — he referred to his near bald pate as having a nine-inch wide part in his hair. That signalled he was fair game from the players too. "I give them heaps and they forget about each other's idiosyncracies and concentrate on trying to catch me," he said. Watching training one rainy morning, mud spattering the Roos' legs and faces as they splashed through the boggy grass, Hollis suddenly sauntered away and motioned for me to follow. "I just heard one of them say 'Gees, Sherriff's the only one that's clean'. I've just drifted away because they're thinking right now of rolling me in that mud." The Roos caught the Sherriff often enough, usually in the hotel lift where several would wrestle him to the floor and suddenly step out of the lift, leaving him gazing up at amazed guests about to get in.

Hollis had the spare bed taken out of his room to set up his massage table and paramedical ultra-sound and laser equipment to provide 24-hour treatment to players' injuries. The management all had rooms to themselves as did Meninga as captain and Elias as vice-captain. With a good sprinkling of friends in the squad it was no trouble for the management to room old Brisbane buddies Belcher and Lindner together, boyhood Ipswich mates Langer and Kerrod Walters, beachboys Ettingshausen and McGaw from Cronulla, Raiders Daley and Stuart, and Lyons and Hasler from Manly. The strangest alliance was that of arch 1989 grand final opponents, Roach and Lazarus, who became good friends on tour. Lazarus was married the day before he flew out of Australia and Roach joked on the second day on tour he had already spent more nights with Lazarus than had Lazza's wife.

The Kangaroos' big men were well pleased with their Ramada quarters. The hotel had been converted from commercial offices and has abnormally large rooms, each containing two queen-size beds. The Rolling Stones rented four floors during a concert tour earlier in the year and, one day while I waited for the evening audience with Fulton, country and western singer Johnny Cash strolled across the foyer in a floor-length leather gunfighter's coat. The Ramada was light years ahead of the Ilkley Moor Hotel, 25 kms from Leeds, where Kangaroo teams stayed years ago. The ARL based the team in the lee of the famous Ilkley moors apparently to reduce costs and to keep the Kangaroos out of trouble in the city. The result was the opposite, as exemplified by the famous "man in the bowler hat" incident in which a Kangaroo was alleged to have strolled through Ikley wearing only a bowler hat and carrying a brief case. The Ilkley Moor Hotel burned down in 1968 and later tours moved to the Dragonara, now the Hilton International, in Leeds.

Most mornings Sherriff Hollis and several players jogged to the YMCA Castlefield Hotel's gym before breakfast, past the Granada Television studios with the liver-brick terrace cottages of Coronation Street visible from the road, and down towards the old docks on the River Irwell beside which the hotel-gym is built. The team trained mornings and afternoons, Fulton overseeing the field work but in the gymnasium Johnny Lewis, trainer of world boxing champion Jeff Fenech, held sway. One particular morning Lewis decreed it cardio-vascular refurbishing time at the ''Y'' for the Test team. They gathered in an exercise room, pulled on lightweight boxing gloves and catching mittens and paired off — Roach punching Meninga's mitts, Bella against trainer Shaun McRae, Langer with Belcher, Hancock with Ettingshausen and so on. Right cross, left cross, they punched diagonally across the front of their bodies, eyes fixed straight ahead. The rhythmic smack of leather upon leather filled the room. Three minutes, a few seconds break, and then three minutes uppercutting.

Roach and Bella pounded away at a slow heavy beat thumpathumpathumpathumpa, Langer punched twice as fast, like a humming bird, bimbambimbambimbam, chatting and laughing with Belcher whose mitts barely budged with the blows. A rest and then three minutes of left and right hooks and the lightweight gloves were no longer light. Bella and Roach bore on, sweat running off their faces and dripping from the tips of their noses. McRae was catching Bella's shots, bouncing the mitts off Marty's fists and swaying his body with the blows. Even Meninga was now a picture of concentration, his huge biceps and forearms flexing to cushion Blocker's blows. Johnny Lewis gave the call, ''Two minutes to go . . . one to go.'' Bella picked up the pace and Roach matched him. The agony creased their faces, Bella's was wine red, Roach gripped his tongue between his teeth. On they pounded, faster, whumpawhumpawhumpa expelling hisses in unison like steam pistons, ''15 seconds . . . 10,'' and with a final flurry the pair raced to the finish. ''Time!'' and Roach gave a roar of relief, raised both hands above his head and marched around the exercise room like Rocky Balboa. ''The winner, by KO,'' he shouted to himself in the wall-length exercise mirror. Meninga was holding his aching forearms, McRae was wincing, rubbing his shoulder muscles. ''Bloody..hard..work..that, mate,'' puffed Roach slowly, but he enjoyed it and, even now, perhaps there is a heavyweight talent lurking beneath that Tigers t-shirt. After that exertion the players warmed down with a game of basketball. They'd be no threat to the Cannons or the Bullets, as Keith Barnes quipped to Allan Langer, ''Having trouble with the slam-dunks Alfie?''

The Roos scarcely needed such bruising preparation for their fourth tour match — Wednesday, October 17 — against Cumbria in Workington. On the west coast facing the Irish Sea, Cumbria comprises four second division clubs, Barrow (founded 1900), Workington (1945), Whitehaven (1948) and recent arrival Carlisle (1981). They form rugby league's most northerly outpost in England for beyond lies Scotland and soccer. Between them the four clubs boast a smattering of names from posterity, the best known by far Whitehaven's Dick Huddart, England's great running second-row forward who came to Sydney to help St George defeat Balmain in the 1966 grand final. Cumbria was always the outsider, and occasionally, the giant killer of the northern counties, defeating fancied Yorks and Lancs in the county championship in two successive years, 1981-82. But in 1985 the championship was replaced with the War of the Roses challenge between Lancashire and Yorkshire and Cumbria was forgotten. In fairness, by then Cumbria was declining, its youth unemployment rate of between 25-30 per cent pushing players with talent south. But Cumbrian fans of middling vintage remembered how in 1967 they knocked over Reg Gasnier's Kangaroos, 17-15.

Cumbria was a foregone conclusion, tantamount to Australia being matched against, say, Riverina or north Queensland. Being a composite squad they had only trained three times together and their coach, Phil Kitchin, conceded his aim was to restrict the tourists to 40 points thereby bettering the 1982 and 1986 losses of 41-2 and 48-12. This was Australia's only "missionary" match of the tour, scheduled to reward the Cumbrians for retaining the rugby league faith under sliding economic and demographic fortunes.

Autumn, season of mists and mellow fruitfulness, and haze did hang sleepily over the motorway and the countryside as I set out on the 240 km journey north from Manchester. I drove via the Lake District which had so inspired England's romantic poets. In midsummer the towns of Windermere, Ambleside and Grasmere, where William Wordsworth lived, are among Britain's busiest tourist districts. Because it was late in the day no tourists queued with me to enter Dove Cottage, Wordsworth's home from 1799 to 1808. Here he wrote possibly his finest romantic poetry, "Resolution and Independence", and "Intimations of Immortality". The cottage housed Wordsworth, his wife Mary, and his devoted sister Dorothy for eight years, but it did not contain Wordsworth's poetry. He composed that outdoors, walking up and down, speaking the lines aloud to be recorded by Dorothy. Here he wrote "The Daffodils", beginning with four of the most memorized lines in the English language:

> I wandered lonely as a cloud
> That floats on high o'er vales and hills.
> When all at once I saw a crowd,
> A host, of golden daffodils.

Thanks to Dorothy's journals we know that he was not alone, but accompanied by her on a walk to a nearby lake where they saw the shoreline covered with flowers. Beyond the cottage today the visitor finds the lakes still filled with reflections and the shopwindows filled with sturdy hiking boots. The solitudes Wordsworth loved are now crowded with tourists churning the best known mountain trails into eroded mud tracks. On every hillside caterpillars of tiny figures in brilliant multi-coloured anoraks and rucksacks crawled towards the skyline or down towards the lakes' edge. Wordsworth and sister Dorothy were stout walkers, often visiting their poet friend, Robert Southey, at Keswick, 13 miles across the high foothills. They would return the same day and Dorothy could walk it in four and a half hours. But not I, who drove by car past Lake Thirlmere's high serenity and was rewarded by a gallery of landscapes around every corner.

The roadside was bordered by autumn trees turning every shade from pale lemon through pink to amber, golden browns to russets and reds. The season's first street sweepers were at work with brooms and spades. Huge North American sycamores, their fronds curling like fingers, and giant horse chestnuts were the culprits. They formed a backdrop for small mountain ash, bright with flame-red berries and spikey hawthornes with berry clusters in shades of claret. Offstage, but making occasional, unmistakable entrances, stood magnificent copper beeches. Down by streams, lime trees, alders and willows drooped, further up hillsides larches dropped needles noiselessly. And most beautiful of all were the silver birches, their pale, fragile leaves exploding from dark, mossy limbs like disembodied stars, shimmering in a timeless memory of autumn.

I returned from Ambleside through the tarns of Coniston towards the coast. As the road climbed through the passes of the Cumbrian mountains the forests gave way to hillsides of rust bracken and then descended to the flat foreshores and beaches of Cumbria. There, just 30 kms from Wordsworth's Elysian lakes and hills, stood the bleak, forbidding tower, dome and blind buildings of the Sellafield nuclear power station. I had advanced 200 years in 30 kms, from Wordsworth's vision of the sublime heart of nature to this unnatural heart of half-life decay.

Sellafield's owners, British Nuclear Fuels, run full page advertisements and television commercials inviting the public to visit Sellafield. In 1989 over 160,000 accepted, making Sellafield the fastest growing tourist attraction in Britain. I approached with trepidation because the nuclear plant's past is a national scandal. Childhood leukaemia around Sellafield is 10 times the national average; the most recent independent inquiry, in 1990, found that workers at Sellafield who received the highest radiation doses ran the greatest risk of having children who eventually developed leukaemia. Now eye tumours have been discovered in workers' grandchildren.

I knew Sellafield as Windscale but, in 1971, after a series of radioactive leaks, Windscale became such a dirty word, BNFL decided on a new name and now spends a fortune each year promoting a new image. The key to this is the Sellafield visitors centre, an ultra-modern tourist-education exhibition designed to reassure visitors about nuclear safety. I glanced through the tourist shop where they sell games for children like Nuclear Tiddleywinks, The Mighty Atom and Fission (knock out your neighbour's neutrons!). Shelves were laden with Sellafield Visitors Centre playing cards, telephone diaries and keyrings. On special was a tapestry kit — Sellafield Sunset — a golden orange glow behind the Sellafield complex skyline.

BNFL sponsors BARLA, British Amateur Rugby League — the fastest growing sporting association in Britain — the fast breeder of juniors for Britain's professional clubs. As I drove towards Workington, 30 km further up the coast, I passed the Sailor's Distress Hotel and the Sailors Rest Hotel. Pubs often give a clue to the local industry so I suppose one day tourists will pull in for an ale at a rustic Nuclear Arms Hotel.

The drizzle had set in at Workington as the Kangaroos jogged out half an hour before kick-off to run through their stretching and ball drills. These always surprise and please English crowds because after the usual hooting and hollering dies down they can inspect the enemy lines before battle is joined. On this night the size of Carroll and Geyer, tall enough to be basketballers, set up a buzz before everyone became mesmerised by the drills that trainer Shaun McRae put the Roos through. McRae, strength and conditioning assistant to Tim Sheens at Canberra in their back-to-back grand final victories, is the third member of Fulton's four-man support crew. The fourth is Dr Nathan Gibbs. It sounds excessive until

McRae, trained in sports medicine, delivers his devastating analogy of modern rugby league — "If you put a car in the middle of the field and took to it for an hour and a half with hammers, you have the equivalent of what league does to the human skeletal system. That's why you need to manage their injuries."

Fulton, anticipating improved opposition from English clubs, created a new position to include McRae on tour. He'd never met McRae but was impressed by Canberra's obvious good hands, fitness and freshness. If the Sherriff hadn't opted to play the jester, McRae, stout, extroverted and quick-witted, could have. Instead his serio-comic nature was soon leaning towards the earnest as it became apparent that with two teams to train, Fulton required him as a clear second-in-command coach as well as chief conditioner. McRae's flair is in devising game-specific drills which simulate match skills. But above this is his gift in attacking those drills from a dozen different directions so that training never becomes boring.

At Workington, what looked like everyone darting randomly hither and thither, was McRae's favourite drill, the four-star. Players run at each other like spokes across a wagon wheel, two footballs in constant motion, passing and receiving. "When the team's under pressure the players tend not to talk," explained McRae. "With this they've got to use peripheral vision, concentrate on where the ball's coming from, who's calling them and who they're calling to." They are practising, it would seem, grace under pressure.

The Cumbrians of Workington and Whitehaven arrived in such numbers, about 7000, that the match kickoff was delayed 10 minutes to allow them in. They were in good spirits too, bursting into "Tie Me Kangaroo Down Sport" when the Australian national anthem was announced. As Benny Elias led the dirt-trackers back out on to the field, in the stand the Aussie A team gamely sang the words of "Advance Australia Fair". They were a dedicated lot these 1990 Roos.

Instead of sitting in the stand I joined the local lads jammed on the terraces where you could hear the thud of flesh on flesh and sickening knock of bone on bone. The fans winced and "Ooohed" with every tackle. The first try came inside two minutes, Mark Carroll running onto a slick short pass from Mark Geyer. Encouraged, those two giants then essayed a little field theatre, in which they were the hammers and Cumbria the car. Cumbrian halfback, Dean Marwood, resorted to a sensible kicking game — the first used against Australia in four matches — to successfully turn the Aussie pack around. After 30 minutes Benny's boys led only 10-4 and though they pushed this to 16-4 at half-time the Cumbrians deserved the crowd's ovation. The Roos handling errors, 9-2, and the penalties against them, 9-3, told the story. Fulton's explanation later — no condescension intended to Cumbria — was that the Roos were not used to making breaks on the first and second tackle and, seeing so much space, were pushing their passes.

At half-time he had a word with Carroll and Geyer about their shoulder charges which occasionally, in the open, resembled bulls missing the toreador's cape. "You're trying to come up with big hits, when all we want is for you to be effective," Fulton told them. The big hits would come for them, he said, because both could hit like all hell. "But to get a shoulder charge sometimes you have to sprint out of the line and that leaves us vulnerable," he said.

After the break I moved to the end of the field defended by Cumbria to look through the goalposts for a better perspective of how the Roos outflank opponents. Mark Geyer spoiled that theory by beginning this half as Carroll had the first, dashing straight down the blind side to slither over. 20-4. "Eh, must be bluidy chumpions to keep them pair out of Test," said a Cumbrian. Just so. Then the procession began. Tries by Elias and Shearer took it to 32-4 and then came what I'd hoped to see. From a scrum inside his own quarter, Alexander doubled around to make the extra man and the Cumbrian defence opened as if it had been keycarded. Down the field the Roos came, exploiting the numbers — four green and golds versus three black and white hoops — leaving Shearer to stride in for his second try of the night. The Roos rarely fumble such over-

laps and to watch the flawless execution made the wait in the
wet worthwhile.

At 42-4, having spoiled the Cumbrian coach's night, the
Roos became careless and showed the crowd how not the least
of their skills was how to knock on and fumble expertly. On
Fulton's count, on the last seven rucks they spilt the ball by the
first tackle. Who could blame them? The rain was tumbling
down, the ball "slippy", as the Poms term it, and what joy in
humiliating a brave county side? In amateur boxing a fight can
be stopped if one party is outclassed. Yet if such a rule had applied this evening we would have missed Cumbria's finest moment for, almost on the bell, halfback Marwood chipped low
across Australia's line for Whitehaven winger Willie Richardson to slide in to score. At 42-10 the Roos had bettered the 1982
score and had won by a wider margin than in 1986. In the
Cumbria change room I spoke to young Dean Marwood, the
best of his team. "They tuckle really 'ard," he grinned, flushed
with pleasure at such noble punishment. "Their defensive larn
cooms oop real quick so thar wasn't really a lot of gups. Real
quick they are." He towelled himself, a trifle embarrassed at
this media interest. "Thut's why I tried to brek play oop with a
few kicks in be'ind their larn, seemed to wuk though, eh?"
Sure did, I said. A wonder Wigan or Saints hadn't thought to
do it too.

All the same, motoring back to Manchester, I wondered
why the RFL no longer matched the Kangaroos against some
real opposition. From after the war to 1967 Australia's tour
schedule always included Yorkshire and Lancashire, the English equivalent of the Lions playing Queensland and NSW. In
those years Australia's record was none too smart, losing nine
and winning four. Indeed it is said that putting a Yorkshire
team together produces a strength in spirit second to none as
shown by the annual War of the Roses match between Yorkshire and Lancashire introduced by the RFL in 1985. In those
five years, although the Lancashire clubs of Wigan and Widnes
have dominated English rugby league, Yorkshire have won
five out of five, including the last by 56-12. Why weren't the

Kangaroos subjected to a little White Rose steel? One deathless victory by Yorkshire over the Kangaroos would do more for English club coffers in one night than this club by club round of death-by-walkovers.

6 LEEDS — THE STYLISH LOSERS

"You are now standing in the old dressing-rooms, where Bradman would change before entering the field, down that ramp, through the crowd to the wicket," said Joe Warham, former Leeds rugby league coach, chief executive and now club director. "You know Bradman's record here? I keep it because people ask me about it so often." He opened a small diary - 1930, 3rd Test 334; 1934 4th Test 304; 1938 4th Test 103 and 16; 1948 4th Test 33 and 173 no. "Aggregate 963, average 192.6," quoted Warham.

We were standing in the L-shaped Headingley Taverner's Club, Leeds, where I had a view of both the rugby league and the cricket fields. The club building divides the grounds and cleverly incorporates a grandstand to face each oval. Headingley is special in the history of Anglo-Australia Tests in both sports. Until rugby league moved Tests to soccer grounds in 1986 to cater for the larger crowds, Headingley always hosted a Test with crowds of 40,000. Safety regulations imposed on all British grounds after the 1985 Bradford grandstand fire in which 56 people died and the 1989 Hillsborough grandstand crush in which 95 people lost their lives, reduced Headingley's capacity to 25,000.

Before the turn of the century the city of Leeds scarcely reached Headingley, and horse drawn wagonettes brought gentlemen and ladies out for games — crown green lawn bowls, athletics, cricket, cycling, tennis and rugby. "There was a sense of being a little bit special and that's carried on throughout the club's history," said Warham. "The tradition was that we played open football but we don't always fulfill it." The club's full name is the Leeds Cricket, Football and Athletic Club but only the cricket and football remain. The club's car park used to be the crown green bowls lawn. "Don't you play the game in Australia?" inquired Warham. "We think flat level greens is a sissy's game." Crown green bowls is played on a lawn with a slight rise in the centre — a crown — from which the green slopes away on all sides. "If you set your bias with the crown your bowl will boomerang off the lawn," explained Warham. "Alternatively if you set the bias against the crown the bowl will go reasonably straight." A more difficult game than orthodox bowls, crown green bowls was once very popular but is now played only in pockets of the north, has little money and less publicity. It is what rugby league might have become had the RFL not reclaimed its heritage.

Leeds, a city of 700,000, is the capital of English rugby league. The RFL has its headquarters there, its administrators live nearby and Headingley is England's finest rugby league stadium. Immediately post-war, before Leeds United became world class, Leeds rugby league outdrew soccer. Today Leeds United averages crowds of 27,000 a match to rugby league's 12,000. Even so the *Yorkshire Post*, in its Monday morning sports lift-out, devotes six pages to soccer and four to rugby league, more than any other English morning newspaper. The Kangaroos were unknowns to the locals in Manchester because that city's football heart belongs to Manchester United and Manchester City, but in Leeds the Roos couldn't have walked the streets without being hailed. ARL president Ken Arthurson eventually conceded future tours would probably return to Leeds.

Leeds, with splendid headquarters, income from two grounds spread over 14 acres and with an entire city as its support base, is accepted as the game's wealthiest club. Only the cup-winning ways of Wigan and Widnes allow them to keep pace. If Leeds enjoyed either of those Lancashire teams' cup successes, the club would need a Wembley instead of Headingley. For being money bags, Leeds earns the envy of all the clubs on its southern outskirts — Wakefield, Featherstone,

Castleford, Dewsbury and Batley — none more than 15 kms drive away. Ex-Wakefield secretary Allan Pearman remembers once hearing the biggest cheer of the day at Belle Vue when it was announced at the ground that Oldham had beaten Leeds. ''A lot of it is jealousy at their splendid facilities,'' said Pearman. ''Leeds don't like to make a mess of their field. You get more A team (reserve grade) matches postponed from Headingley than anywhere. They don't admit it, but they mother hen it a little.''

Yorkshire County Cricket Club moved out of the main pavilion into their own quarters at the ground in 1968, but Headingley is still their home as it was to the feats of Fred Trueman and Geoff Boycott. It is the Leeds C.F. and A. which hosts cricket Tests and, having retained these formal cricket links, Headingley, and therefore Leeds rugby league club, has never really acquired rugby league's working class patina. Leeds have a tradition of playing rugby league in a manner that links the game back nearly a century to when it was rugby union. It is not enough for Leeds to go to Wembley and grind out a 7-6 victory. No, Leeds must play the game with esprit and elan and if that wins the Cup, then so much the better. Intangible though such an expectation may seem, it is nevertheless real. Said Leeds secretary, Bill Carter, ''Our twin aims are to play entertaining and enterprising rugby. Our fans demand it and though it's a burden, we live with that.'' Malcolm Reilly told me of several reasons he had for quitting as Leeds coach in mid-season 1989, but he added, ''I'm supposed to be big and strong but the pressure got to me. You not only had to win, you had to win with style.'' Having begun as a dignified gentleman's club and evolved to accommodate rugby league, Headingley reminded me of some well-heeled Australian rugby union clubs, where the committee keep one eye on the decorum of its members and guests, the other on the points competition table.

Leeds has produced a video, the Headingley Story, which dates the formation of the cricket club as 1863, 17 years before the rugby club. Headingley therefore has an unbroken connection with the Establishment and community of English cricket.

Since in the south of England cricket in summer and rugby union in winter are watched by much the same crowd, Headingley exists with a dual face. Blending these twin stratas of class is an inherited knack and Leeds C.F. and A. are equally proud of their rugby league and their cricket heritage.

The Headingley video intertwines its cricket and rugby league history naturally, moving easily from film of fiery Freddie Trueman taking 4-0 against India, to the 1950s Welsh wizard, Lewis Jones, demonstrating his famous hitch-kick, which, I noted, is identical to Wallaby David Campese's modern goose-step. The BBC's idiosyncratic commentator, the late Eddie Waring, is heard muttering drolly, ''As the umbrellas go oop, the rain cooms darn and I get wet, this kick is tairken . . . the first two are certain, the third is . . . a goal!'' Waring commentaries, delivered in a rich brogue and overlain with a dry Yorkshire humour, drew good national ratings for rugby league but his critics alleged he reduced rugby league to the level of mud-wrestling. On this video is film of the most dramatic, and possibly painful, incident in club rugby league history. In the Wembley Challenge Cup final in 1968, after a see-sawing match before 87,100 people, Leeds led Wakefield 11-7 with minutes to go. From a Wakefield kickoff the Leeds winger attempted to trap the ball with his foot, the ball skidded through on the drenched pitch and Wakefield toed it through to score almost under the posts. Leeds still led 11-10 but Wakefield's Don Fox now lined up the simplest of conversions. Said Eddie Waring, ''And all on this shot. It's not a hard shot, but it's always a hard shot when the match depends upon it.'' Some Leeds players stood with their backs to Fox, already lamenting having the game snatched from them by their own carelessness. Five steps back and . . . Fox sliced the ball wide of the posts. Fox turned to run back to his team but faltered and fell to his hands and knees and pressed his forehead to the turf. By the time he recovered, Leeds, after a disbelieving leap of joy, saw that the individual tragedy exceeded their team triumph and they surrounded Fox sympathetically. When he reached his own team Fox put his hands on his knees and wept. "What a moment to live with, what a hard luck story," quoth Waring sadly. "Ee, poor lud."

While Yorkshire is the most parochial of county cricket clubs — choosing only players brought up in Yorkshire — their brothers in the grand old pavilion have a long history of importing internationals from Australia. Most famous of all, pre-war, was winger Eric Harris, known as the "Toowoomba Ghost" for his gliding running, who scored 392 tries for Leeds, still a club record. Harris was brought to Leeds by another Australian, centre Jeff Moores, an Australian rugby union international who had returned to Australia for a holiday with instructions from Leeds to bring back a winger. Moores himself was the Gasnier of his day. When Moores died, club director Joe Warham, who as a boy had admired him, attended his funeral. "I was the only person there from rugby league football," said Warham. "Yet if he had died at the height of his fame you'd have had to bring in the police to control the traffic. He arrived as a young lad from Queensland and was buried in a quiet English graveyard."

The Australian connection continued through Arthur Clues, one of the finest second-row forwards of all time, who joined Leeds in 1947. He too never left and though today crippled by arthritis in his knees, I noted his presence at all the 1990 Kangaroos' important occasions. Another Australian, Keith McLellan, led Leeds to a Wembley Cup victory in 1957 and four years later Ken Thornett, of the famous Sydney footballing family, helped Leeds to their first league championship. In 1960 Dick Thornett, a rugby union international who later played 11 Tests for Australia in rugby league, returned from the Rome Olympics where he had represented Australia at water polo, and sat on the bench at Leeds watching brother Ken play.

When the 1982 Invincibles trounced Leeds 31-4 they left a deep impression on club secretary Bill Carter. "They were like a football machine that side, we couldn't even score a try," he said. With the lifting of the international transfer ban the following year, Jack Gibson, then at Parramatta, sent two little-known players to Warham with introductions which read, "Joe, take a look at these two boys, they'll do you a lot of good and they won't take a step backwards. If you want them send me back their air fares." The great migration began. Joe Warham, then Leeds chief executive, and fellow director, Harry Jepson, now RFL president, flew out to recruit Australians. Said secretary Carter, "Many came over for a holiday so we didn't have to talk telephone numbers — Eric Grothe was on the best contract, but nothing extraordinary. At one time it must have seemed like you couldn't get in the team unless you spoke Australian. It was like walking into Parramatta's dressingroom."

Or Cronulla's, because none are remembered more fondly at Leeds than Andrew Ettingshausen and Mark McGaw who, aged 21 and 22 respectively, were in the Leeds team crushed 40-0 by Wally Lewis's Kangaroos of 1986. Apart from their obvious talent, Sparkles and ET were cast in the Leeds mould — young, handsome, polite and well spoken. Leeds welcomed Ettingshausen back again in 1987-88 but were criticised for their excessive overseas spending, especially when many Australians would sign only short-term contracts because of their Australian commitments. By the time the RFL cracked down to stem the flood, English standards had risen to the point where, said Bill Carter, of the 10 Australians on their 1985-86 books — ignoring the age factor — only Eric Grothe's talent would make him certain of inclusion in today's Leeds side.

Yet Leeds are still recruiting and none more famous than former All Black rugby union fullback, John Gallagher, signed in 1990 for a reported $1 million over five years. To meet Gallagher is to understand why he couldn't have joined any other English club. He's in the nice guy vein of McGaw and Ettingshausen and, because he excels in sweeping with uncanny timing into backline movements, fulfills Bill Carter's requirements of playing the game in an "entertaining and enterprising" manner. Before the Kangaroos arrived I drove to Leeds to see how Gallagher was settling in. He was icing a torn thigh muscle with a packet of frozen peas and reading literature about a physiotherapy course he intended to study at a Leeds polytechnic. When I arrived the media-plagued Gallagher smiled and joked to a friend, ''He's Australian, but he's OK.''

Gallagher was contemplating buying a small cottage in Bramhope, a picturesque village in the Yorkshire Dales, about 11 kms north of Leeds. It is only a few minutes by fast car to Headingley where the All Black fullback of 18 Tests spent the early season counting tackles, maintaining positional depth, taking bombs and ignoring amateur instincts to release the ball when tackled. Some rugby union memories he has found easy to forget. ''At international level we kept the ball in play a lot,'' he said. ''But at schoolboy and club level the ball rarely got out past the first five-eighth. It was very frustrating.'' Before turning professional Gallagher had noted, via Australian Winfield Cup replays in New Zealand, how much quicker rugby league had become. ''Ten years ago the game looked very static,'' he said. ''In Britain heavyweight forwards were taking the ball up and dying with it. Now you watch a game and the ball's being thrown all over the place. I'm used to playing a fast open game with quick hands so it suits me.''

Gallagher took an accountant friend with him to negotiate with Leeds. ''Our trump was that they weren't just signing a rugby union player,'' he said. ''They were getting a high profile All Black.'' Rugby union's International Player of the Year for 1989 no less. Part of the motivation he said was that, aged 26, he suddenly imagined breaking down and asked himself what long-term security rugby union had given him. A league contract seemed good insurance. At first the jokes flew around the Leeds dressingroom about ''Mr Millions'', but that's not unusual at Headingley. Just three years earlier Garry Schofield had become the world's costliest player when he transferred from Hull for $375,000.

Gallagher, Schofield and the Kangaroos drew 16,000 to Headingley on October 21, a fine Sunday afternoon in which, locals said, there was the first hint of autumn, which to Australians meant winter. But before the game, Leeds showed how to present a tour match by inviting 160 dignitaries to lunch in a huge yellow and white striped marquee with a red carpet underfoot. It was erected on the cricket oval near the boundary where Bradman used to score so prolifically. Leeds do not stint themselves and wines were Australian in honour of the guests. Entrees were smoked salmon and shrimp, followed by rare roast beef and the county pudding and to wind up a desert of chocolate cake and hot custard, coffee and port. Each place was set with the match program — 50 glossy pages — and an inscribed Parker pen as a memento of the occasion. The meal ended with a toast to the Queen and the advice, ''Ladies and gentlemen, you may now smoke.''

The Australian assistant manager, Les Stokes, more used to addressing the Ipswich rugby league as delegate from the Booval Swifts, found himself with the unenviable task of proposing a vote of thanks at this elite gathering. Stokes accomplished it admirably. ''On these occasions I've usually been able to give the flick pass to Keith Barnes,'' he began, with a chortle. ''But . . . we've got 28 talented players and I know some are — I wouldn't say they're depressed — but unlucky not to be on the field today. It's very competitive for places and I'm sure we all wish for a good match and that the players enjoy the game, with no serious injuries.'' I suspect Les was thinking of Australia's Test players but the august audience received it as the gentleman's pledge, to participate without harm, and warmly applauded the sentiments.

As the teams ran out at 3 pm a soft sun shone from a clear blue sky but the floodlights were already on to produce the necessary light for television. The field looked perfect, a curtain raiser having been called off to avoid unnecessary damage to the pitch. I felt a tinge of pity for Leeds. The Kangaroos, with 146 points for and 38 against in four club matches, had a better attacking record than the 1982 side and a better defensive record than in 1986. Those previous two tours aggregated 71 points to four against hapless Leeds and here we were about to repay their splendid hospitality with another drubbing. Mal led the Roos' usual Sunday punch team out — minus injured Cartwright — and ET and McGaw zipped a quick interchange of passing to acknowledge the fans' generous reception. Australia, in their traditional green jerseys with gold vee, looked old-fashioned beside Leeds' blue sweaters with thin blue stripes, amber borders and blue shorts. Old-fashioned but deadlier. At least it would be a good Test trial and Fulton had already decided that all four substitutes, Gillespie, Alexander, Lazarus and Elias would be given a run to press their claims, especially the latter pair.

Meninga kicked off into a significant wind, Leeds took three rucks, got a penalty for Australia offside, took three more rucks and Gallagher ran sweetly onto a delayed pass from Schofield down the blind side. He ran into space and though the cover nailed him that was the first time I'd seen the Australian backline lanced so early in a match. Several aspects became clear in the opening stanza — that wherever Australia's kickers placed the ball, Gallagher was there to take it, that Mackay, unobtrusively, was Australia's quickest man to the tackle and that Lindner was the only Australian forward certain of making 15 metres whenever he ran. Kerrod Walters usually made ground too but, as at Wigan, he threw an early pass to Langer which went to ground, chiefly because Kerrod's eyes were on the opposition, not Alfie. Gauging the wind like a helmsman, Schofield kept play in Australia's quarter until, in the eighth minute, McGaw hurt his knee in a tackle, lost the ball and became a patient for Sherriff Hollis. Within seconds Schofield drifted wide to the blind again — where McGaw might have been — and in a carbon of their first move, Gallagher sailed gloriously through the gap. According to Leeds coach David Ward, Gallagher is the fastest in his squad over 100 metres, but he looked pretty nippy over 30 metres too as he arched for the corner and scored untouched. It was his sixth game of rugby league and his third try, one to remember for a lifetime.

In the Leeds dressingroom, coach David Ward had written on a blackboard a list of sports-psyche advice of which one was, "Visualise yourself in a variety of situations where you have to position yourself to effectively make the tackle, break the line or support the ball carrier. Rehearse it in your mind two or three times correctly." Gallagher eventually made four clean line breaks in this game so he exceeded Ward's instructions. But he got his chance to carry out the tackle theory later too.

Gallagher's try pumped the crowd no end but we didn't need them to tell us that class will out and Schofield and Gallagher were all that. Down 4-0 the Australians remained calm, they had trailed Wigan too. But, Gallagher eh? The next time the ginger-headed fullback from the Land of the Long White Cloud caught a huge bomb, Daley and McGaw were on the spot to manhandle and maul him to the ground. Nothing illegal, or even unworthy, but ex-rugby union centre Simon Irving took umbrage and threw McGaw aside. Leeds hooker Richard Gunn must have thought Brad Mackay's peacemaking gesture with his palm was a potential karate chop because he bounced a nasty punch off Mackay's head. So it was on and when the fighting was over Daley was bending over, tenderly holding his right hand. Several rucks later the Sherriff was still bandaging it.

Tempers were now frayed and when McGaw ran in to smite Leeds centre Vince Fawcett, he missed and collected a penalty instead. McGaw said later, "I knew the guy was going to get the ball and I had him lined up here," indicating his chest. "And he just ducked. That's why I got cautioned." Referee Ray Tennant sensibly called Meninga and Schofield over for a general warning and Mal ran back tapping his temple and shouting at his players, "Use your heads!"

After 20 minutes Schofield, Leeds' architect of opportunities, put up a bomb which Lions prop-forward Roy Powell got a Maradona hand to, knocking it on before Belcher could grasp it in his arms. As with Maradona in the soccer World Cup the referee missed this airborne action and awarded a fair try to Lions second-rower Paul Dixon. Leeds led 10-0 but the Kangaroos looked more disgusted with themselves than rattled. They did not resemble a team about to relinquish the Kangaroos' record of 36 consecutive wins in England. Paul Sironen manifested their frustration by charging over from 10 metres out, all sheer animal strength, with a gallant Gallagher clinging to his ankles. Australia trailed 10-6 and then lost McGaw for 10 minutes, sin-binned for dangerous kicking. In fact he was merely trying to step out of a tackler who would not let go, but McGaw's record in this match told against him. At half-time the Kangaroos moved to their dressingroom like a team puzzled by this new experience of an English club deservedly leading them. As five workmen with gardening forks strolled about the field repairing divots a statistician informed us that the last team to lead Australia at half-time was Hull who led 7-0 in 1982 — and they finished up losing 30-10.

There was no such danger of collapse by Leeds even though, soon after oranges, Sironen did it again, from the same distance out, taking a neat inside pass from Bella. Again game Gallagher clung to his ankles. Sironen, once he gathers momentum, moves with the unswerving inevitability of a cantering Percheron — perhaps that is where he gets his nickname "Buttocks". Australia now led 12-10 yet it was another 15 minutes before Lindner strode over for Australia's third try and, even then, a more determined Roy Powell might have stopped him. In the remaining minutes Daley was seen to grab at jerseys one-handed and Meninga scored a simple try to stop the clock at 22-10. Schofield and Benny Elias were joined by Steve Roach as they walked off, all old Tiger team-mates, chatting about the quality of a match in which the penalty count, 6-2 to Leeds, showed referee Tennant's good sense and both teams' discipline.

The crowded dressingrooms posed so many questions it was hard to know who to talk to first. Gallagher thought the Aussies were big and fast, backed up with great support play. "It becomes second nature to a team that's used to winning," he said. A comparison with his alma mater? "I suppose if they win another 13 games and get to 50 unbeaten then I'd put them on a pedestal with the All Blacks."

Garry Schofield hoped Malcolm Reilly would take a leaf out of the way Leeds had bustled and pressured the Kangaroos into mistakes. He thought these Roos were more workmanlike than the 1986 side. "Back then they had Sterlo, Wally and

Kenny getting the ball away to the outside backs quickly," said Schoey. "This side makes sure they don't make mistakes and they capitalise on yours. The 1986 side had a bit more flair but if you make mistakes against these boys they'll score points."

Mal Meninga saw it as a game of contrasting halves, with and against the breeze. In the first half Leeds kicked well and put pressure on the Roos. "So when we had it we were a bit tired and we couldn't create the opportunities we had in previous games," he said. "We've been winning by big scores but our ball security has been a problem in all our games so far. I'm worried about it and I know Bozo is too. This is a bit of a kick in the pants for us and we'll make it work for us."

Post-match, back under the Big Top, we partook of tea and fruit cake while Paul Sironen received a silver mug as man-of-the-match. Leeds chairman, Norman Shuttleworth, whom I had met on previous visits to Leeds, remarked sotto voce, "Does McGaw always play like that in Sydney? We had him here for a season and he wasn't like that." Like what? I replied. I was learning from Fulton, answer leading questions with a question. "Oh, this," and the venerable chairman gave his arm an imperceptible jerk. I assured him Mark would have been provoked. "They're easy to provoke, Australians," said Shuttleworth, smiling. "Always have been, just refer to their parentage."

In that tent full of dignitaries Meninga, less than an hour off the pitch, was called upon to reply on behalf of the team. He stepped forward, his impressive figure forever threatening the integrity of some bespoke tailor's stitching, and with a candour that he has learned to trust in himself, spoke briefly and to the point. He thanked Leeds club for the reception and congratulated the Leeds team for their spirited play. "Obviously it must give heart to Britain for next Saturday at Wembley and makes us realise we must improve if we are to come out victors," said Mal. "Thank you once again, hopefully in four years time many of us will return to appreciate Leeds' wonderful hospitality." Modest, but not ingenuous, and exactly what Leeds wanted to hear.

Leeds had suddenly, and radically, altered the tempo of the Roos' previously unflustered build-up to Wembley. More than that, Leeds, as Raymond Fletcher wrote in the *Yorkshire Post*, "had reduced the Australians to mere mortals and given Great Britain renewed hope." Bob Fulton had copped criticism for not altering the Sunday and Wednesday teams sufficiently to try all combinations, but until Leeds such discussions were purely hypothetical. None of Fulton's critics was seriously suggesting he change a winning game.

Yes, it was a tough match, said Fulton, but exactly what the doctor ordered. "If we'd won the toss and run with the wind in the first half, we would have put them to bed a lot earlier," he said. Australia had three or four tries pulled up because of forward passes when there were inches in it. "Then you start talking about a scoreline of forty," he said. He was right about the tries — ET had two disallowed and Lindner one. "We were a little impetuous," he conceded. "We made any number of breaks but instead of taking the tackle and looking to score on the next play we tended to push the final pass. We have won by big scores and there's a tendency to play touch football when you get in the clear."

And what about Schofield? "His kicking in the second half against the wind was marginal," said Bozo. "He's a fine player, but a bloke with a wooden leg could have kicked well with that wind." With that qualified, ungenerous appraisal of Schofield, Fulton revealed a new underlying concern about the first Test. Only a year earlier Wigan's Shaun Edwards seemed to have made the British stand-off position his for the forseeable future. But Schofield, in New Zealand and now here, by sheer weight of performance, had almost certainly displaced Edwards. If he could put an All Black through Australian gaps he could put Lions through at Wembley in six days time. That Fulton was edgy was demonstrated in an exchange with an Australian journalist:

Q: Bob, Martin Bella seems to believe his Test spot's under some kind of pressure.
Fulton: Why? Who said that?

Q: No, he seems to think so.

Fulton: Why? he spoken to you about it has he?

Q: Oh well, he just . . .

Fulton: In what way?

Q: Well if there was someone to go out of the Test side he thinks he may be the one.

Fulton: Well that's not a fair reflection of the way he's performed and that comment wasn't really required. I'm not having a shot at you but the bloke's played very well.

Fulton was then reminded that three days earlier he had said he was clear in his mind what the Test side would be. Was there any reason to change that view?

Fulton: I don't think so, do you?

Q: No, but you're the coach.

Fulton: Mate, you saw what I saw.

But of course we knew not what Fulton saw, nor what he thought. The assertiveness, bordering on abruptness, with which he now spoke contrasted with the relaxed, easy going relationship he had established with the travelling Australian sportwriters. The reason was Leeds. The clockwork football of the previous four matches seemed to desert the Kangaroos, not the least because Leeds had taken the game to the Roos instead of waiting tamely to be dismantled. Schofield had edged Daley of the sore paw; Carl Gibson had blocked Meninga manfully, and Paul Dixon must have played himself into the British Test team. On the other side of the ledger Gallagher had distinguished himself above Belcher, ostensibly the world's best full-back; Langer seemed unable to rediscover his erstwhile zest and Kerrod Walters persisted with uncharacteristic errors. Yet none of the Australians could really be said to have played themselves out of their established Test spots. Fulton, short of dropping players on suspicion — and he is a logician who only nods at intuition — would have to entrust Wembley to the Test incumbents.

After the match, when the stands emptied, a scattering of journalists remained in their seats, dictating match reports on portable telephones or composing on laptop computers. Over the stand loudspeakers came the strains of the banal aria from Verdi's *Rigoletto, La donna e mobile* — women so changeable. And so are the fortunes of football. Verdi's opera ends badly for Rigoletto the clown but, six days away from the first Test, I had no such prescience for Bozo, the clown, the Kangaroo coach.

7 FIRST TEST — THE STING

At 10.30 pm a knock on my hotel door. An attractive young woman stood in the doorway. "Hello," she said, smiling. "Is this room 2420? Yes, I've got it right, that's the number your friends gave me, may I come in?" It was so professionally done she was past in a trice. "Sarah," she said, holding out her hand. "Your friends said you'd be surprised." She was about 30, with ash blonde hair, and wore a black dress suit, black stockings and carried a black purse. Behind her winning smile lay an $80 business transaction so graciously proposed it seemed almost ungentlemanly to decline. But I did, politely, at which she shrugged, apologised for her intrusion and left. It was all so civilised until I remembered the muggings, theft, pimps and drugs which accompany the trade. Welcome to London.

It was Monday, October 22, and the Kangaroos had arrived that evening at the Forum Hotel in South Kensington, London, for the six-day countdown to the first Test at Wembley. The five-star Forum was wonderfully situated for West End theatres but disastrous for a rugby league team preparing for a Test. One side faced Cromwell Road, where the traffic noise is incessant, and the other a giant construction site where pneumatic drills hammered away in the early morning. After one night I swapped rooms, opting for the drills. Worse than the noise was the hotel's distance from any suitable training ground. To reach Crystal Palace, home of Fulham, the sole professional rugby league team in London, the Roos' bus took 50 minutes through non-stop banked-up traffic. If they trained there twice a day they would spend nearly four hours in traffic jams. Manager Keith Barnes got terse when traffic set back training schedules but really the answer lay in the British team's choice of hotels, down a quiet country lane in Essex, north of London. ARL general manager Bob Abbott struck a winner with the Ramada, but the Forum was a blunder.

Fulham's coach Ross Strudwick, former coach of the Brothers club in Brisbane, welcomed the Roos and gave them the run of Fulham's superb facilities. Trainer Shaun McRae loaded 20 kg weights on power sleds to which the players harnessed themselves like snow huskies. When the lighter players, like Shearer and Alexander, started running they pulled the sleds in a series of jerks, whereas when Meninga and Lindner took the strain, the rope stayed taut as they powered forward. Power sleds looked stressful but it was during a simple stretching exercise that a torn cartilage agonisingly locked Mark Carroll's knee.

Strudwick, Barnes and Dr Nathan Gibbs conferred. Carroll's knee and Laurie Daley's hand, swollen after Leeds, needed x-raying. No vehicle was available, would I drive them? Strudwick navigated us to the Sloane Hospital in Beckenham, Kent, 20 minutes away. My concern was for Carroll in the front seat beside me, in agony, unable to straighten his knee. Then I heard Strudwick joke to Daley, "He won't rule you out, will he?" nodding mischievously at Gibbs, for it was Gibbs who ruled Wally Lewis out of the tour. Said Struddie, "If he rules you out for Saturday you can play with my mob on Sunday." Gibbs replied that Daley would be OK, even though the hand was broken. "Is it?" I said, surprised, for that was news. "Yeah," said Gibbs. "The x-ray is to see how badly it's broken."

In the clinic Gibbs unwound a copious bandage from Daley's right hand and removed a steel splint, shaped like a spoon, which was pressed into his palm. The hand was swollen black, pink and purple. It looked impossible for him to play a Test against Garry Schofield in five days time. "Does it hurt?" asked Strudwick. "No," said Daley, flexing his fist — gingerly. "You'll only be able to use your left if there's a fight on Saturday," said Struddy. "Throw your left and then hit the deck." Laurie pretended a left hook. "Mate I'm useless with my left," he said. Gibbs chided him, "Some might say that about your right!"

Daley was first into the x-ray room. "Gees, that Schofield had a good game yesterday didn't he?" said Carroll, putting words to his concern about the Test. Gibbs returned within minutes, studying the x-rays. On one I could clearly see a thin white crack across the metacarpus of the fourth finger on his hand. On the second film, a cross-section, there was a splinter of bone lifting out of alignment. It wasn't serious, said Gibbs. But first they had to get the swelling down so that Daley could have a pain-killing injection before Saturday's Test.

While Carroll was being x-rayed Strudwick lightened the mood in the waiting room. "You're going to play three Tests with a broken hand," he told Laurie. "What a story that will make in your memoirs. When young blokes go off with a muscle tear you can say, 'What's wrong with you modern blokes! I carried a broken hand through three Tests.' You'll be in the Satts' class." (John Sattler played through a Sydney grand final for Souths with a broken jaw.) Strudwick thought aloud as we returned to my car. "If the Poms hear about this, they'll soon test out that hand," he said. Gibbs replied, "Until I speak to Bozo, if I'm asked, I'll say that Mark's knee requires an arthroscopy and that Laurie's finger was dislocated." This was my cue, for I sensed my passengers awaiting some sign of compliance. I nodded, but I doubted they could keep it secret all week.

Training had finished so we headed back into the heart of traffic-jam city a melancholy crew. Carroll's was the first serious injury of the tour and Daley's could cost Australia dearly. I dropped the wounded at the hotel and drove to Wembley for the Roos' farcical publicity session with Jason Donovan. The team walked onto the hallowed turf and gazed in awe at the grandstands towering above us. It should have been a moment to savour. Instead, with nearly 50 English popular newspaper photographers and television crews snapping and whirring away, Mal Meninga, plainly displeased, was called upon to lift the television soap star above his shoulders. To his credit the actor admitted he was from Melbourne where Aussie Rules ruled. Then why was he publicising rugby league. He shrugged. "Look, these guys are Australians, what more need I say?" he said.

The Roos were to call in at the Houses of Parliament on the way back to their hotel but their schedule was too much for me and I headed for a quiet drink with Ross Strudwick. We chatted about Daley's injury and he said, unsolicited, "To me that hand looked very bloody sore today. As a coach I wouldn't be playing him. I think they might be underestimating the British a bit." Strudwick coached Wally Lewis for many years at Valleys in Brisbane. As we talked the same thought struck us both. What irony, to leave the best five-eighth in the world at home with a mended broken arm and play his replacement with a broken hand. "That would stink a little, eh?" laughed Struddy.

At 6.30 the next morning, Mal Meninga, rubbing his eyes sleepily, walked through the empty foyer of the Forum in white open-neck shirt, green tour sweater and dark grey slacks. He was off to the ITV studios in Camden Town to appear on "Good Morning Britain" which has an audience of two million. If you want to promote rugby league you can't knock back national exposure. The joys of captaincy. It was still dark, the air cold, as we wended our way across London. "Hard for a bloke to get sleep on this tour," said Mal. "Lucky I had an early night last night — 11 o'clock!"

We were ushered into the inner sanctum of the breakfast show and handed a cup of tea. Mal flicked through the popular Fleet Street morning newspapers for signs of the Donovan photographs the day before. Plenty of bare breasts but no Donovan. The studio set was done out like a cheerful cottage lounge and we could hear the host, Mike Morris, asking producers when Great Britain had last defeated Australia in a Test series. Mal looked at me, we both knew, but at this ungodly hour, neither of us could remember. "Long time ago," quipped Mal, rehearsing his reply if they asked him the question.

As they went to a commercial break the host announced, "And next, man mountain Aussie, Mal Meninga." Mal grimaced. He was a man mountain with a sore throat, a cold, and handed me his Strepsils so they didn't bulge in his breast pocket. On camera Morris introduced him as the Kangaroos "coach" and threw to the Tina Turner promotion film, "Simply the Best". Mal softly corrected Morris, "Captain, not coach", but who cared because Tina was shaking her tail feathers. "The best ad in Australia," said Mal. "People turned their heads every time they saw it."

Morris warmed to his subject. Were there things happening on the pitch between players which even the bench weren't aware of — sledging, questioning parentage? Mal grinned. "Oh yes, definitely, a few words exchanged," he said. "Fortunately we're not miked on the field so the spectators don't get to hear about it." Mal handled the interview deftly. In his promotions job with the Canberra Raiders he's learned all about media techniques and camera work. As he walked off the stage set I handed him back his Strepsils. "What now, coach," I said. He smiled, "Hope Bozo wasn't watching."

We were chauffeured back to the Forum. It was 8.30 am, the sky lightening, the traffic heavier. We passed scampering squirrels and dogs on tight leashes in Regents Park and cut and thrust our way around peak-hour Hyde Park corner. Only weaving bicyclists wearing gauze dust masks could make good headway. In the back Mal was sleepily silent, taking in the top-hatted flunkies of the Hyde Park Hotel, the hooded display windows of Harrods and the bizarre baroque stone architecture of the Natural History Museum. At breakfast we were joined by Gary Belcher and Bob Lindner, both in t-shirts, tracksuit pants and joggers. They puzzled at Mal's television outfit. "New training gear?" asked Badge. Mal grimaced and recounted his early start. "True story," he said to their doubting looks. Keith Barnes' call of "Well done," confirmed Mal's devotion. "Captain my captain," said Lindner.

Later that morning the management decided Crystal Palace was too far and opted for nearby Hyde Park. There, amid vast, green expanses, the trainers set out the markers for drills. McRae warned, ''Watch your footing, you know it's not an even surface.'' This was the most inappropriate training venue I'd seen yet, 100 metres from the roar of Park Lane's eight lanes of traffic, no privacy and a chill wind blowing unchecked across the park. Barnes and Dr Gibbs broke the news that Laurie Daley's hand was broken and would not be risked in the Test after all. Daley's disappointment clouded his normally cheerful visage. While the team trained he took off, head down, for a long jog around the Serpentine, not noticing the nude nymph and satyr sculptures cavorting in a fountain by the path.

Bob Fulton announced Daley's replacement on the bus as the team prepared to leave for afternoon training. It was an open secret who it was, but there was some excitement as Ricky Stuart stepped off the bus. ''Great thrill,'' he said. ''But I'm upset it had to happen the way it did, Laurie's my good friend and my roomy.''

I could see Fulton's reasoning. On his grand final form Stuart added lustre to an already polished outfit. The alternatives of Cliff Lyons or Des Hasler represented a new strategy altogether, not one that Fulton wished to wrestle with five days before a Test. Stuart's selection therefore was a contradiction. It expressed exceptional confidence in one tour member to assume an unfamiliar role and a lack of confidence in others to perform in their chosen positions. I felt that choosing Stuart out of position in his first Test broke accepted rules of prudent team selection. However, like others, I dreamt mostly of Ricky's Utopian kicking transcending rugby schisms at Wembley and showing all adherents of the handling game his true class.

From Wednesday the Roos at last got their training venue right, courtesy of the exclusive Bank of England sporting club, Roehampton, in the heart of conservative south-west London. To get there they crossed Putney Bridge, where the Oxford-Cambridge boat race starts, past Rosslyn Park, Martin Offiah's old rugby union club, and the bus pulled into the green swards of Roehampton tennis courts where pre-qualifying rounds for Wimbledon are held on grass. The Roos began a game of touch and a game of rugby union began on a field next to them. Minutes later a game of soccer got underway on a field the other side. On the three adjacent fields I enjoyed the sight of the full evolution of the folk game called football.

That evening the Forum filled with ''G'day mates'' from rugby league supporters' tours. All the cracks had gathered at the hotel — Ray Price, Royce Simmons, Jack Gibson, Tim Sheens, Graham Lowe. We commandeered a corner of the ground floor lounge for Fulton's 6 pm press conference and every Aussie within cooee pricked up his ears. There were no dramas, said Bob. The team reviewed a video of the Leeds game and the players were starting to generate their own build-up. He'd chatted to Ricky Stuart and was comfortable with him at five-eighth. ''He's just a class act, Ricky,'' he said. He hadn't spoken to the French referee, Alain Sablayrolles, but he hoped to.

On Thursday the training tapered and Friday afternoon, match eve, Fulton and Barnes joined a dozen other players for a two-hour guided coach tour of London. Of the Test team only Meninga, Sironen and reserve Hasler hopped on board. Another group went shopping for leather jackets in Carnaby Street, West End. ''Famous street, Carnaby Street,'' mused trainer Shaun McRae. Famous for what? said a couple of players. Shaun shook his head in disbelief. Was it so long ago, the Swinging Sixties?

No Test players were sighted in the usual hotel haunts that evening but at 11 pm Benny Elias and Laurie Daley rocked in, having just seen the *Buddy Holly Story*. To escape the relentless Test talk, *Rugby League Week* Queensland editor Tony Durkin and I had been to see it the previous night. Benny was wearing a souvenir Buddy Holly cap. Did they dance in the aisles? I asked. ''Mate, WE danced in the aisles!'' said Benny, giving a passable imitation of Ritchie Valens singing La Bamba while Laurie mimed the Big Bopper's ''Hel-loooo Baby!''. They'd rather be playing Tests but there was a certain release in not being responsbile for whatever happened at Wembley on the morrow.

Match day, October 27, the Channel 10 crew departed at 11 am. They expected an Anzac audience of three million viewers — a million in Sydney alone. At 11.40 am a police motorcyclist arrived to escort the team bus. PC motorcyclist Maurice O'Donnell drew documents from his breast pocket. Official orders, no doubt. Wrong, six Wembley programs and would Gibbons the bus driver get the team to autograph them for a charity? A crowd of 100 excited Aussies had gathered outside the hotel, their clothes in varying stages of Roomania. Caps, scarves, sweaters, badges, rosettes, everything in green and gold. A sketch on a bedsheet-sized cloth of a charging rugby league kangaroo — "Roo Beaut" — was held against the Kangaroo's coach for the mandatory posed snaps.

The bus eased in behind the police motorcyclist and, true to my training as a young reporter to stay close to my subject, I nipped in behind the bus in my white Ford Sierra. Approaching Wembley the police escort received a radio message that the Great Britain side was also nearing the ground — delay the Kangaroos. The escort signalled Gibbons and we started turning corners away from the ground. After 20 minutes of this the order finally came to make an approach but by now there was an endless, unmoving queue of traffic pointed towards Wembley. PC O'Donnell switched on his motorcycle's flashing blue light, directed traffic coming in the opposite direction to pull over and rode over to the wrong side of the road. The coach followed. There was nothing else for it. I tucked in behind and we rolled grandly down the right-hand side — the wrong side — of the road towards Wembley. Uniformed bobbies waved us through at traffic lights, road wardens held up pedestrians; we ran two red lights, dived around the wrong side of traffic islands, ignored No Right Turn signs and directed lawful motorists out of our way. We raced towards Wembley in close convoy — the motorcycle cop, the Kangaroos bus and the strange white Sierra. I sneaked an occasional look in the rear vision mirror and saw the startled looks on some police faces as the third member of the convoy zipped past. As we neared Wembley the number of police on duty increased but it was too late to let go of the tiger. We flashed down a VIP road, past crowds cheering and jeering the Roos' bus, and at the last moment, before the coach pulled up to the main gates, I peeled off into a VIP car park alongside Rollers, stretch limos and chauffeurs, and parked. My hands were shaking and my heart racing at my own nerve-wracking road to Wembley.

Nearing 2.30 pm I gazed over the huge crowd, 52,274, a record for Tests in England, a fantastic sight, filling Wembley except behind the eastern end goal posts which looked straight into the afternoon sun. British crowds sing, Aussies hold signs, like "Where's Our King Wally?" from the Sunshine Coast and "The Graham Eadie Stand", from Bilambil on the Gold Coast. As the two teams walked out the 80-strong Philharmonia Chorus, fresh from a tour of Italy, burst into "Land of Hope and Glory", one of the most moving moments at any football match I've ever attended. The crowd all but drowned out the choir and the combined bands of the Queen's Lancashire Regiment and the First Battalion of the Royal Irish Rangers. Over came those strains, "God who made thee mighty, make thee mightier yet." They sing it at Conservative Party conferences and play it on the last night of the Proms at Albert Hall too. Stirring stuff. Mouthguards back in and, lift off!

Monsieur Sablayrolles kept a good five metres and let scrums go to the feed but after 15 minutes he was caning Australia 6-2 in penalties and from the Australian supporters — a sea of wattle amid green leaves — the first chant "Buuullshiiit" went up. The English fans looked across trying to fathom this brand new tune. Schofield's first chip kick was so finely placed that Belcher could neither field it on the full nor dive upon it safely. Schofield regathered and only ET's desperate lunge knocked down Schoey's pass to an open tryline. The straight-line Aussie defence suddenly looked like the Maginot line — dug in, heavily fortified but being outflanked. It was 2-2 at half-time but as novelist and football fan Tom Keneally said, rolling his eyes, "It could be 10-2 to Great Britain if they'd taken their chances. They're not letting Belcher link up with the backs.'' I know! I know! I said. I'd seen NSW close him out in State of Origins in the Blues' successful years.

Referee Sablayrolles' whistle-blowing in the Lions favour had stopped both teams developing rhythm. But looking at my notes, what was killing Australia were the offside penalties, four against Australia, none against Britain. Bob Lindner said later, ''I couldn't work him out except to stay two to three yards behind him. A lot of occasions guys were making the attempt to get back and he was still grabbing them.''

Before the Roos arrived in England, Raymond Fletcher of the *Yorkshire Post* told me how difficult it would be for Great Britain to break Australia's straight-line defence. ''They move up and back like guardsmen on parade,'' he had said worriedly. ''They even look at each other as if they're measuring off correctly.'' The only way, he had said, was over the top. He meant with chip kicks, not as at the Somme, but the British were about to emulate both.

The half-time truce was broken four minutes into the second half. A metre inside the Australian half Hanley accepted the deadest of dead balls from Schofield. Nothing on, yet among Hanley's unique skills is his ability to crab sideways at such speed it becomes a fluttered sidestep. Thus did he evade Sironen's lunge and then lean on McGaw's ankle-high tackle to skip around him. Having negotiated that minor maze, he was suddenly free. The tumblers rolled and the locked Australian defence fell open to reveal Hanley sprinting towards the safe arms of Gary Belcher. But no! Hanley delicately chipped over the advancing Belcher's head, leapt into the air like Nureyev to take it on the full and was brought to earth by Hancock almost over the Australian line. That was Hanley's speed and agility. Now he showed his strength, shrugging off the Roos who were lying all over him to leap up and play the ball. Daryl Powell fed Paul Eastwood who put his head down, raised a protective arm and, like a blind mole, burrowed for the line. As he modestly said later, ''I might not go 100 yards for tries and I'll never be another Martin Offiah, but from close range I can take some stopping." Great Britain led 6-2. " Here We Go, Here We Go, Here We Go!" Such pandemonium!

Eight minutes later Bob Lindner led the Australian counter attack, beginning just 10 metres from his own line. He ran through Denis Betts, put a hand on Carl Gibson's chest and propelled him backwards, sideways and away — this Gibson who had stalked Meninga all day — beat Kevin Ward's covering tackle and charged 40 metres, looking just like he was towing his power sled. It was Lindner's breakout, including ridding the defence of pest Gibson, that enabled Meninga to set a diagonal course for a try in the corner. Happiness shook the wattle tree terraces, "Aussie, Aussie!", 6-6.

Five minutes later Hanley, again with no options apparent, hoisted a bomb towards the Australian posts, Belcher spilled it, Offiah scooped it up and scooted over. That's how it looked, that's how the referee saw it, that was a try. But Belcher — spill a bomb? Only when I stopped the action frame-by-frame on a video replay did I see the sneak genius of Ellery Hanley. He follows his own kick through, eyes on the ball, to contest the catch and harass Belcher. As Belcher rises in his leap — as the ball is a screen blur about to fall into his arms — Belcher's body develops a big banana bend backwards as Hanley hits him waist high, a nano-second ahead of the ball. Hanley's timing was too good for the naked eye, no fault of Sablayrolles, but I can safely acquit Badge of what looked, prima facie, a costly error.

Great Britain ahead again, 12-6, and then 13-6 after an astute dropped goal by Schofield. As the ball sailed between the posts Steve Roach greeted the British cheers with an "up yours" middle finger. But the British were singing "You're Not Singing Any More" at the Australian section, and nor were they.

I awaited an Aussie revival but they never seemed to have the ball and statistics later confirmed that in the second half Australia had possession for only 34 rucks compared with Great Britain's 67. Sablayrolles maintained his penalty flow against the Roos, 6-1 in this half, so it was against the run of play that Mark McGaw performed another of the Roos' great feats of individual power running. He took a ruck ball five metres inside the Great Britain half, evaded Offiah's tackle from dummy half, struck through a sliding cover from Andy Gregory, ran to the quarterline and was hit by Gibson and Hampson simultaneously. Extraordinarily they collided with each other in the tackle, fell off McGaw, who rose from the knockdown and had the presence of mind to run on through to the tryline 25 metres on. McGaw's Cronulla partner ET grabbed McGaw's shoulders and shook the big centre with glee.

Mal's timely conversion meant the Lions now led only 13-12 and I thought Britain would collapse. McGaw's try seemed superhuman, a signal that against all odds Australia were destined never to lose. But while McGaw had shown the way through the foothills, the carriers could not scale the British mountain. So it was Schofield who finally claimed the Test, chip kicking with inch-perfect precision, regathering and using plain overlap numbers to link with Daryl Powell who sent Eastwood in for his second try. Eastwood leapt up and threw the biggest air uppercut imaginable, a symbol of the damage he had just inflicted on the Aussie psyche. The Kangaroo camp later decried the British tries for all having come from kicks. But to clever players like Schofield, the odds of cleanly regathering chip kicks are at worst 50-50, pretty good odds in a Test. Eastwood added an improbable conversion from the sideline for a final score of 19-12. Malcolm Reilly, sitting on his ringside bench, momentarily forgot his perennial frown.

I sat high above the action, gazing down, the final score assuming an air of unreality, as though this was some dream sequence of an imaginative British film producer. Even the singing "You'll Never Walk Alone", the soccer fans' hymn of loyalty, boomed over like a soundtrack. The song, appropriately, is from Rogers and Hammerstein's *Carousel* and it signified that Australia's merry-go-round — unbeaten in a Test in England for 12 years, unbeaten for 37 matches in England — was over. Furthermore, Britain had taken a giant step towards recovering the Ashes they last held in 1970.

On BSB satellite television, ex-Lions hooker Mike Stephenson said it all to co-commentator Eddie Hemmings, "Isn't it great Eddie, to be a Pommie!'' Steve Hampson had begun doing handstands on the field as the British team chaired their giant stuffed lion on a circuit of the stadium. The Australians walked steadfastly off, as bitterly disappointed with their own performance as with the loss, Wembley's jibe ringing in their ears, ''Eeea-syyy, eeea-syyy.''

In the Australian dressingroom it was the afternoon of the long faces — Barnes, Fulton, ARL president Ken Arthurson, all looking at the floor where perhaps the answers lay in the mess of rags, towels and bandages. Sironen just sat there, shirt, underwear and socks on, but no pants or shoes, as if he could go no further. Alfie was fully dressed but didn't look like moving, ever. Belcher had his head down running his finger around the rim of a beer can, around and around. His liquor neither frisked nor leapt.

Mal sounded flat, but was captain stoical. The final whistle had embarrassed him, he said. ''I've been involved in the last two tours over here and it's not a very nice feeling to lose a Test match on foreign soil. We've got to show a bit of character, pick our heads up. We can come back and see it right in the second and third Tests.''

Fulton braved the media and immediately granted that the better team had won on the day. ''But when you have to put up with a piggy-back ride in relation to penalties it was difficult,'' he said, referring to the Lions' 17-7 final penalty advantage. ''We'd get them up in their 22, tackle our guts out and they'd get a penalty on the fifth tackle,'' he said. ''They'd be then out to halfway after we'd been tackling like Trojans.'' What about Sablayrolles' penalties? ''Arrr, what do you do? Grin and bear it. Pointless complaining.''

It was pointless, considering that an hour before the Test kickoff English Controller of Referees, Fred Lindop, who speaks passable French, visited both dressingrooms with Sablayrolles to explain the Frenchman's interpretation of offside. ''In Australia referees tend to be lenient about the centres coming up quickly on the basis that they are not interfering with play,'' Lindop told Sablayrolles. ''In England we rule that by encroaching the centres are forcing the ball back towards the middle and therefore they are interfering with play.'' Sablayrolles agreed with the English interpretation and Lindop had explained this to both teams. Lindop agreed with Sablayrolles that Australia were offside. ''Obviously Fulton didn't digest what had been said,'' he told me.

But whatever his complaints Fulton didn't stint on praise. ''We're not playing mugs here, that should be stated,'' he said. ''We're playing Great Britain and there's some tremendous players out there. Look at Hanley,'' and Fulton shook his head. ''A super performance.'' It was indeed. On the British stats sheet Hanley had made seven clean busts, compared with five for the entire Australian forward pack. *RLW*'s Tony Durkin put the acid question. ''If you can't make a protest against the referee why wouldn't it be the same in the second Test?'' To which Fulton replied, ''Well it might be and if that's the case, we'll lose the game. I'm not trying to detract from their win. Great Britain have had a really big day today. They took advantage of what was on offer and won.''

Fulton looked at the assembled media and smiled philosophically, as though still coming to terms with the enormity of the result. ''Unfortunately, we've lost a Test match,'' he said. ''I suppose it had to come sooner or later and the sad part about it is, it's this day. But quite frankly, I'm super confident about the second Test and given a fair shake of the dice, we'll beat them.'' Since Meninga and Fulton hadn't colluded in their comments, I accepted their testimony on the second Test as more than chin-up, cheer-up propaganda. Another writer was more cynical. ''If we lose the second Test, for them it's . . .'' he said and he drew his finger across his throat. ''It's a business now, not just a sport.''

Australia's officialdom, whatever their private disappointment, remained steadfastly magnanimous. Pushed for an answer, ARL president Ken Arthurson agreed Sablayrolles wasn't the best referee he'd seen by a long shot, but he was not blaming the referee. ''I won't deny Great Britain a win today, they've been trying to beat us for a long while, they played well and good luck to them.'' he said. But after the dressingroom emptied of television lights, cameras and cassette recorders, nothing was left for the Roos except to collect their gear, and their spirits, and depart.

Malcolm Reilly's pleasure manifested itself not in praise for his own team but for Australia, the better to show what a famous victory it was. ''We were underdogs, they're a machine,'' he said. ''They take a lot of stopping, lot of ability there, and that's not bullshit. We've got a real series on our hands. I know what Bobby's like, he'll fire the bastards up for this next one, it will be war. I'm going to put crash helmets on our boys.''

More relevant was his comment that Ricky Stuart hadn't shown enough individual flair at five-eighth. ''His passing game was all right but moving the ball to the wide open space put a lot of responsibility on Meninga,'' he said. A five-eighth had to take the game to the opposition not just be a supply merchant. ''I think Ricky may have frozen,'' he said. ''I rate Ricky highly, I'm not blaming him because he . . .'' Reilly stopped and smiled, ''I better not say too much.''

What happened? I asked Phil Larder in a quiet corner of the packed Lions changeroom. ''Didn't do their homework on us,'' he said. ''They thought they could just play good football and beat us. Used to, not any more.''

Back at the Forum hotel that evening, small groups of blank-faced Australian supporters sat desultorily sipping drinks in the lounge. Players in civvy gear — not a tracksuit among them — drifted in and out of the bar. Mark Carroll, recovering from his knee arthroscopy, sat down in the piano bar, bent his huge frame to the keyboard and, with a few hitches, tenderly rendered Scott Joplin's melancholy theme from the film, *The Sting*. Sitting by the grand piano were Allan Langer, Kerrod Walters and Michael Hancock. Standing beyond the bar were Steve Roach, Paul Sironen, John Cartwright and Martin Bella. All ceased conversation and listened, their faces glowing with intimations of imminent mortality. When I remembered how negative Reilly and Hanley had been when the Roos arrived, I suddenly realised that the tune Spud Carroll was playing was an ironic parable to the biggest sting in modern rugby league history.

8 THE GRITTY NORTH

"You are playing a game of football this afternoon, but more than that you are playing for England and more even than that, you are playing for Right versus Wrong. You will win because you have to win. Don't forget the message from home, England expects every one of you to do his duty.

So spoke manager, Mr J. Clifford, addressing the British Lions in their hotel room before the third and deciding Test against Australia in 1914. On that tour the Lions had won the first Test but lost the second Test two days later. They were then due to tour New Zealand and play the third Test upon their return. Instead the Australian authorities cancelled a NSW-Lions match scheduled for the following weekend and replaced it with the third Test. Three Tests in eight days! Clifford angrily outlined the whole story of the revision of the Test schedule to the players and then issued his ringing call to arms.

The result was a classic victory for British spirit when Harold Wagstaff's Lions, though reduced by injury to 10 men, won the Test and wrested the Ashes from Australia. It became known as Rorke's Drift, the name of a Zulu Wars battle in the 19th century in which British forces overcame superior numbers of tribesmen. We should have known therefore that the 1990 British bulldog was no tame terrier, that the Lion would not lie down for the Kangaroo no matter how superior Australia's record for the past decade. Not one jot of history suggests that Great Britain willingly forfeits its rugby league birthright to the colonies.

Nor do we need to return to 1914 to find evidence that speaks eloquently of British sporting courage against the odds.

At the Exhibition Ground in Brisbane in 1958 British captain Alan Prescott broke his right arm in the first few minutes. He stayed on and at half-time Britain led 10-2. British manager Tom Mitchell wrote in his confidential report later:

> Very few of the players, if any, knew of Prescott's injury but it could not be kept from them. The captain had a broken arm, they looked stunned . . . The doctor forbade Prescott to resume and told me so. It was obvious the day could only be saved if Prescott returned to the field if only to hold the side together. The matter was put to him in the sense that this decision was left to him entirely. Without hesitation he said he would go out again. The crowd went silent as the position became clear to them . . . As I write many hours later I feel drained by the drama and tragedy of the game. [Great Britain won 25-18.]

When I read those reports in the Rugby League Hall of Fame I understood a little better the manner in which Ellery Hanley and Garry Schofield had lifted the 1990 Lions to such exceptional heights at Wembley. I tried also to imagine what culture could have produced such persistent resilience, courage and comradeship down through the years. What community would support a sport that broke away from its parent, sustain it for nearly a century and supply it with teams to joust with the best that Australia could produce? The answer is the North and its long, cruel, industry-weary history.

Before the Industrial Revolution the bulk of England's population lived in the southern half of the country, around London and the Thames Valley. From the later part of the 18th century, for 100 years, as new uses were found for coal, iron and textiles, and as railways threaded the countryside, a vast migration saw the population become most dense in Yorkshire and Lancashire. What followed was a century of the worst exploitation of labour outside the American slave trade, leaving northerners with a deep suspicion of lawmakers, privilege and capital — in short, the South.

In my six months on the rugby league trail I was living in a 200-year-old weaver's cottage in the small village of Delph, nestled among the Lancashire Pennines. The house had stone walls two feet thick and a top floor with windows all around that would have provided maximum light for the weaver at his loom. This contented cottage industry ended when the shuttle fell from the hands of the weaver into iron fingers that could ply it faster. The mechanisation of wool weaving, now mass-produced in steam-driven factories, turned old towns like Halifax and Leeds, and small hamlets like Huddersfield into crowded, unsanitary urban slums, dominated by William Blake's "dark, Satanic mills". The North entered its own peculiar dark age. Journalist Angus Reach wrote in 1849:

> Conceive acre on acre of closely built and thickly peopled ground, without a paving stone upon the surface or an inch of sewer beneath, a deep trodden-churned slough of mud forming the only thoroughfares. Conceive . . . the idea of a town built in a slimy bog . . . and you have, I am sorry to say, a fair idea of Leeds."

At its zenith in 1890, the woollen industry employed 275,000 workers but by then wool had been well and truly eclipsed as Britain's leading export by the giant cotton manufacturing industry. Cotton turned small entrepreneurs — Karl Marx called them "new-fangled men" — into wealthy capitalists. Oldham, 8 km west of where I was living, boasted more cotton spindles than all of the U.S. or France. When factory land in Oldham became scarce, investors flocked over the hills to nearby Shaw which eventually became known as "the richest town in England" — all from cotton goods.

The reverse side of the wealth was the mill factory in which staff were expected to labour on the shop floor the same hours as the owner in his office. Workers' lives became tied to the machine, the mill bell summoned new shifts, the steam engine never tired. Even children worked 12-14 hours a day. Talk to any Pennine oldtimer today and he will tell you how his parents grew up working from 6 am to midday in the mills and then spending the afternoon at school.

Wherever I drove in the north, in every village and town the relics of the mill era survive, massive flat-topped brick or stone factories, six or seven storeys high, covering hectares of ground. The soot of a century has stained them dirty grey, their

thousand window panes are smashed, and towering overhead, as obsolete as the steam engines they served, stand 50-
metre high chimneys, the mastheads of rampant profiteering.
Pollution from these chimneys was so bad that in 1906 one resident of Delph complained that, ''on going into his bedroom he
believed it to be on fire, the place being so filled with sulphur-
ous fumes.''

But even cotton was dwarfed by coal. In 1900 Britain had a
million miners. They outnumbered textile workers by two to
one and were producing a quarter of the world's coal. From the
shelves of libraries, history books condemn British society for
its treatment of coalminers. Mining deaths were the road fatal-
ities of the day — 1000 a year from 1850 to 1913 — and for those
who survived there was pneumoconiosis (miner's asthma) and
nystagmus (miner's blindness). Coalmining employed children underground as trappers — opening and shutting ventila-
tion doors to control the flow of air through the mine as coal
was removed. Just across the Pennines from my village, in the
tiny community of Silkstone, is a graveyard monument to 26
mineworkers — 15 of them boys and 11 girls — trapped underground by a flash-flood in 1838 and drowned. The average age
of the boys was 10, of the girls, 11. When I eventually found the
mine site, in a small sycamore wood near Silkstone common, it
was marked by sculptures of two children emerging from a
shaft. Four years after that tragedy the Commission on the Employment of Children recommended the end of child labour.

Coal, cotton and wool were the three heartbreaking industries which formed the backbone of the North. Miners walked
home blackened with coal dust to homes blackened by the
smoke and smog from coal-powered factories. Family life suffered, health suffered, hopes vanished. If an omnipotent
power had set out to divide a nation economically, socially and
culturally, it could have done no better than the Industrial Revolution in England. Generations of workers in Yorkshire and
Lancashire passed on to their children both a resentment of in-
equality and a pride in their capacity to survive.

When the Ten Hours Act of 1847 introduced time for recreation the impact caught workers by surprise. A Lancashire spinner noted in his diary, ''For a while we did not know how to pass our time away. Before it had been all bed and work; now, in place of 70 hours a week, we had 55 1/2. It became a practice, mostly on Saturdays, to play football and cricket.''

The football was soccer and rugby union. Blackburn Olympic's team which defeated the Old Etonians in the final of the soccer FA Cup in 1883, contained several spinners and weavers from the Lancashire cotton trade. But rugby, with its greater emphasis on physical strength, belonged to the miners. Coalminers worked, ate and showered together, they worked in teams, depended on each other, developed wordless communication and daily were bonded by the dangers of the pit, an experience akin to a peacetime battlefront. They became close mates yet if one was taken out they welcomed his replacement and got on with the job. Nothing so closely resembled the milieu of the coalface as the rugby field.

The Hall of Fame descriptions of Rorke's Drift in 1914 and Prescott's epic in 1958, spoke to me in tones of comradeship, loyalty and heroism which I recognised from reading of mining life in the North. From British Coal, who sponsored the Tests, I sought out Parkside mine near St Helens for an unexpurgated look at life underground. Before I descended the manager inquired whether I liked sweets. Why? I asked. He simply gave me a handful. Why? I insisted. ''The dust, they help you to swallow,'' he said. I was dressed in boilersuit, steel-capped boots, safety helmet, battery lamp and self-rescuer — a mask which, in case of fire, converts fatal carbon monoxide to carbon dioxide.

After descending 650 metres by lift it took us an hour to travel four kilometres through tunnels to the coalface. We walked and rode man-riders — like fairground rail carriages — dropping ever deeper until we were 1000 metres below the surface. It was so black that all I could see was the cone of light from my helmet lamp. Scrambling through the tunnels, if I looked down I hit my helmet on objects above, if I looked up I stumbled on floor junk below. The tunnel roof was held up by steel arches twice as thick as railway lines, yet I could see where "mother earth", as it was fondly called by my guide, Ron Silver, had buckled even these. Sometimes the tunnel ceiling seemed to be lower. "No," said Ron Silver. "If the arches don't buckle, Mother Earth lifts the tunnel floor instead."

Modern mining uses the equivalent of a giant chain saw which bites into the coalface and spits coal onto a conveyor belt. I heard the blades of this shearer-loader from some distance off, a terrible banshee shriek and the nearer we drew the more deafening, dirtier, dustier and hotter it became. Once at the coalface the safest place was under the outstretched steel arms of the line of hydraulic roof supports. To traverse the 200-metre wide coalface we crawled through the machine lair of the jacks, surrounded by coils of cables, hanging hoses, gauges, pressure taps, and telescopic legs. I suspended fear because there were too many dangers to attend to, all overlaid by the scream of the shearer-loading monster. As the coal is removed the hydraulic supports are moved forward and the unsupported mine ceiling behind is allowed to cave in. Ron Silver had forgotten to tell me this. As we crawled between the hydraulic jack legs the first I knew was a terrifying cracking, rumbling, collapsing roar about a metre behind the wall of jacks. Blinding black coal-dust spewed out, noise enveloped us, all senses were overwhelmed except my sixth sense which said flee. When the air cleared Ron was smiling at me. "Motherf . . . earth," I spat out.

Emerging eventually from this ordeal we came upon a group of miners eating white bread sandwiches, their hands and faces so filthy they looked like black and white minstrels, especially as their pink lips were wiped clean by the bread. With the noise and their broad accents I couldn't comprehend much, so I laughed and nodded, getting by until Ron Silver approached. "How's tha gettin' on wi' th'stralian roogby lud," he asked the miners. "Dorn't knaw," said a miner. "Ah been talkin' t'm for 20 minutes un 'e 'usn't spairk a bluidy word!"

After three hours underground I stepped from the lift at the shaft top, black-faced, bent and exhausted, filled with unend-

British coach Malcolm Reilly, a hard man as a player, still superbly fit, drove the Lions to within 20 seconds of squaring the Test series and almost pulled off a shock Ashes victory. (Unless otherwise stated, all photos are by Andrew Varley.)

Bobby Fulton, brilliant as a player, shrewd and aggressive as Australia's coach, lifted the Kangaroos' spirit and hauled them back from the brink of defeat.

The 1990 Kangaroos. *Back row*, from left: S. Roach, A. Ettingshausen, M. McGaw, J. Cartwright, M. Geyer, M. Carroll, P. Sironen, M. Bella, G. Alexander, D. Hasler, M. Hancock. *Middle row*, from left: J. Lewis (trainer), B. Hollis (trainer), C. Lyons, D. Gillespie, L. Daley, Kevin Walters, R. Stuart, D. Shearer, B. Mackay, M. Sargent, G. Lazarus, Dr N. Gibbs (medical officer), S. McRae (trainer). *Front row*, from left: Kerrod Walters, A. Langer, C. Johns, L. Stokes (co-manager), B. Elias (vice-captain), R. Fulton (coach), M. Meninga (captain), K. Barnes (manager), G. Belcher, R. Lindner, B. Fittler.

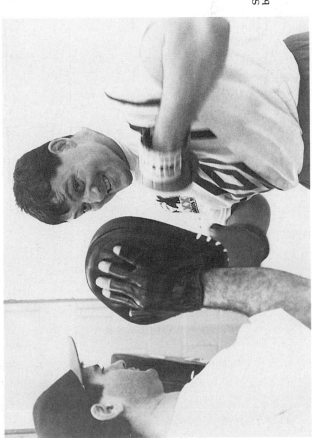

Steve Roach doing a ''Rocky'' during cardio-vascular boxing exercises, with Benny Elias holding the mitt.

In power sled harness or out of it, "Man Mountain" Mal Meninga accelerated with the same awesome torque. (Photo — Steve Moorhouse/Qld Newspapers)

Second day on tour. Glenn Lazarus with the British coal miner. Lazarus vowed he was there to play Tests and did, displacing Martin Bella.

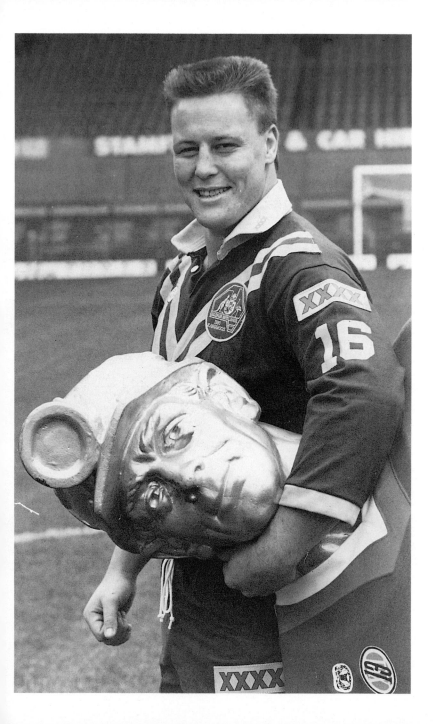

St Helens. Bob Lindner crashes through prop Bernard Dwyer with Kerrod Walters in support. Lindner exuded power like a heavy-duty battery, producing great form in match after match. He was favourite player with the thousands of Kangaroo supporters.

St Helens. Allan Langer escapes prop John Harrison watched by Kiwi Shane Cooper.
Langer lost his Test place but became alternative captain in matches when Meninga and
Elias did not play.

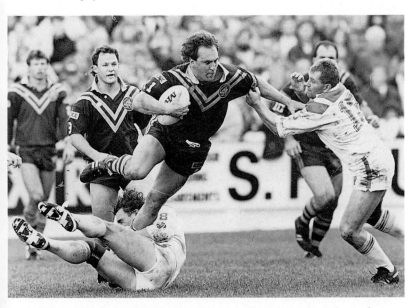

St Helens. John Cartwright takes the ball up as hooker John Neil goes low and prop
Dwyer goes high. Cartwright was man-of-the-match here but later lost his Test place.

Wigan. Gary Belcher swerves to evade Ellery Hanley with Ettingshausen in support. After his superb form here ''Badge'' was closely marked in future matches.

Wigan. Andrew Ettingshausen on the way to one of his hat-trick of tries, showing the perfect balance and timing of his sidestep. Denis Betts in defence has no hope.

Wigan. Michael Hancock shows his amazing strength for a winger, despite Andy Gregory, Shaun Edwards and a third Wiganer around his legs. Hancock's tour was later ruined by injury.

Wigan. The shape of things to come. The "Black Prince" Ellery Hanley turns on his remarkable sideways speed to easily round Paul Sironen for one of his trademark breaks. "Sirro" finally nailed him in the third Test. (Photo — Bruce Greer/*Yorkshire Post*)

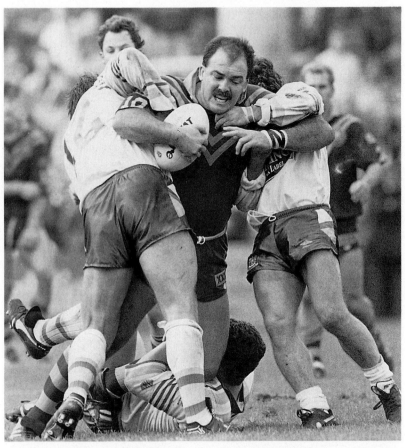

Leeds. Martin Bella in typical attacking mode — still moving forward despite the efforts of three Leeds defenders. Bella was later among the players who paid the price for Australia's first Test loss.

Leeds. Referee Ray Tennant appeals to the captains, Garry Schofield and Mal Meninga, to calm their players after a Mark McGaw swinging arm sparked a brawl. Tennant refereed well, awarding only eight penalties.

Leeds. Paul Sironen is congratulated by Kerrod Walters after thundering over for one of his two tries which saved the Roos. On the ground is ex-All Black fullback John Gallagher who was run over by Sironen each time.

First Test. The Hanley break-out that led to Britain's first try. Offiah screams in support and referee Alain Sablayrolles is superbly positioned. In Hanley's trail are Cartwright, on the ground, Sironen diving, Walters and Lindner, well back, and Belcher.

First Test. Distressed Kangaroos after Britain's first try.

First Test. Ellery Hanley's brilliantly timed tackle on Gary Belcher produces this fumbled ball. Mal Meninga is off the ground acting as a blocker. Martin Offiah hovers — seconds later he pounced on the loose ball.

First Test. Offiah slides over while Belcher looks up to protest to the referee and Daryl Powell acclaims the try. Meninga is aghast, Allan Langer and Andrew Ettingshausen arrive too late.

First Test. Offiah and Hanley celebrate their try with a high handshake.

First Test. British hooker Lee Jackson, 80 kgs, gets run over attempting to tackle Mal Meninga, 107 kgs.

First Test. Mark McGaw's super solo try which momentarily dragged Australia back into the Test. McGaw has risen after centre Carl Gibson (on the ground) and fullback Steve Hampson collided tackling him. In the background are prop Karl Harrison and Kerrod Walters. (Qld Newspapers)

First Test. Ecstatic Ellery Hanley and Karl Harrison after their victory. This photo was in a series which won *Yorkshire Morning Post* photographer Graham Lindley the British Regional Press Photographer of the Year award.

Mark "Spud" Carroll at the piano where he displayed unexpected talents after the first Test to play the theme from the film *The Sting,* an appropriate choice after Great Britain's shock win.

Castleford. Cliff Lyons draws fullback St John Ellis before in-passing to Gary Belcher. An identical move with Mal Meninga produced Australia's matchwinning try in the third Test.

Greg Alexander shows his beautifully balanced, grass-cutting style of running. Alexander was chosen for every match on the English tour, seven as substitute, but did not leave the bench in the second Test.

◄ Castleford. Paul Sironen falls to a tackle by Graham Steadman. The hand on his face, close to his eyes, shows the dangers of defenders going high, as Sironen later discovered against Widnes.

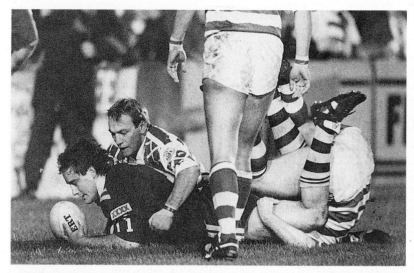

Halifax. Mark Geyer plunges over for Australia's first try after Halifax spilled a Greg Alexander bomb on their tryline. Geyer was unlucky to compete with Sironen and Lindner for a Test place.

Halifax. Mark Sargent is sinbinned. The Roos were often punished for trying to free their feet when English players, like Alan Platt on the ground, clung on in tackles to slow play down.

Second Test. Mal Meninga attempts to calm Steve Roach after he is penalised for roughing up Denis Betts.

Second Test. Benny Elias evades Andy Platt while Steve Roach looks on. Elias's elusive running from dummy half confounded the British forwards and won Elias man-of-the-match.

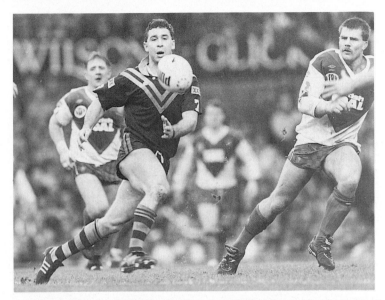

Second Test. With Australia leading 10-6 Ricky Stuart (photo above) risks a huge cut-out pass. Tall replacement centre Paul Loughlin — "a giraffe" Bob Fulton called him — stretches out a long arm (just visible in photo above) to intercept (photo below) and race 50 metres for a try to tie the score 10-all.

Because of his broken hand, Laurie Daley uses only a couple of fingers to collar opposing centre Daryl Powell during the second Test. Despite his injury Daley set up an important try in the third Test. (Qld Newspapers)

Sequence of photos over page.

Second Test. The try that turned the Ashes. Ricky Stuart ➤ first sidesteps hooker Lee Jackson (No 9) near the Australian line and takes off downfield looking for support. Mal Meninga controversially bumps aside centre Carl Gibson with Loughlin and Gregory in pursuit while fullback Hampson (No 1) closes in. Stuart, in classical passing pose, picks up Meninga who has rebounded off Gibson to cut back inside. Meninga receives as Hampson and Gibson sandwich Stuart. The final photo in this dramatic sequence captures Meninga touching down with his outstretched hand, leaving Eastwood and Schofield sprawling in his wake. (Series of photos by Peter O'Halloran, from Channel 10 video)

Stuart gives a congratulatory pat to Meninga, both exhausted from their match-winning 90-metre dash. (Peter O'Halloran/Channel 10)

Minutes after their sensational series-saving try, Ricky Stuart and Mal Meninga — elated and relieved.

Widnes. Welsh speedster Jonathan Davies falls after an unorthodox body block by Allan Langer. Second tackler Dale Shearer had not gained a yard in chasing him.

Widnes. Two Kiwis, props Joe Grima and captain Kurt Sorensen fail to stop Steve Roach getting his pass away. Roach was later sinbinned after a blow-up with Sorensen in a scrum.

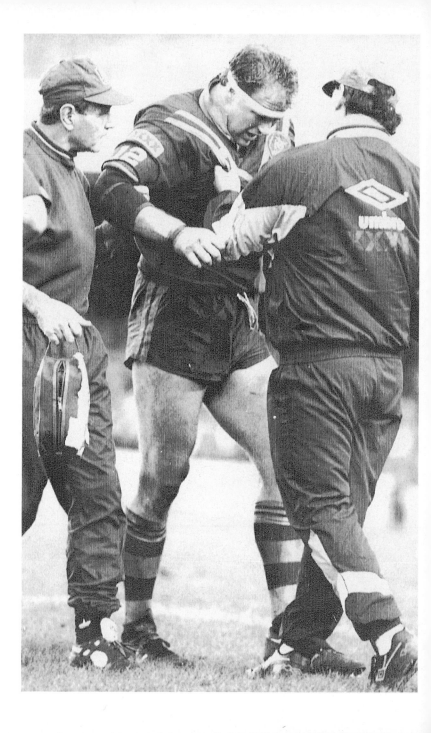

Third Test. Bob Lindner's face shows the determination which made him the player-of-the-tour. Gamecock Andy Gregory takes him on with Andy Platt following up.

◄ Widnes. The incident which sparked the eye gouging controversy. Paul Sironen is helped from the field by trainers Brian Hollis (left) and Shaun McRae after being poked in the eye with a finger in a Kurt Sorensen tackle.

Third Test. The reason Garry Schofield's tactical kicking game was blotted out of the Test. Benny Elias's speed from dummy half gave him no peace. (Steve Moorhouse/Qld Newspapers)

Third Test. Glenn Lazarus making a typical charge. Lazarus showed great courage to play two Tests with 17 stitches in his forehead.

Third Test. The moment of truth for Garry Schofield (No 6), watching as Meninga slides over for the try that sealed the series. Schofield's attempt at an intercept left a huge gap instantly exploited by Cliff Lyons and Meninga.

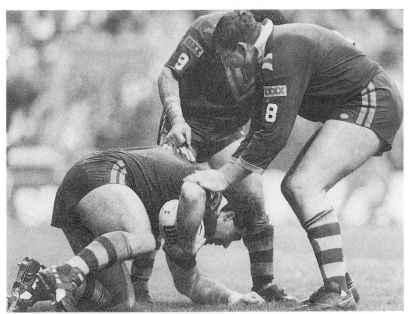

Third Test. Delight shows on the face of Steve Roach as he and Benny Elias (obscured) help Mal Meninga to his feet after that crucial second-half try.

Third Test and Victory. Captain Mal Meninga summons his players over to show their appreciation for the support of the thousands of Australians in the crowd.

Third Test. The winning team breaks into a victory song. From left: Mackay, Meninga (obscured), Alexander, Hasler, Elias, Sargent, Shearer, Belcher, Daley, Sironen (obscured), Lindner, Stuart, Roach and Lyons.

ing admiration for the miners of the past whose ranks filled the first division teams of English rugby league. As far back as 1841 a physician, examining coalminers, wrote that although the average 20-year-old miner was already showing signs of chest and breathing problems, "his body was hard, spare, and had extraordinarily well-developed muscles and sinews." In the early 1960s Wigan's pack boasted three Test forwards — all miners — Brian McTigue, John Barton and Frank Collier. Parkside miners still speak with awe about Collier who, when playing for Wigan, thought nothing of working the midnight-to-dawn shift, nipping home for a quick kip, and playing at Central Park, Wigan the same afternoon. In 1964 he is said to have shovelled coal until late on Friday, caught the Saturday morning train to London, played for Widnes in the Challenge Cup final that afternoon at Wembley and won the Lance Todd Trophy for man-of-the-match. Collier was a tunnel ripper, using pick and spade, the hardest physical work. But perhaps Collier was exceptional. He transferred from Wigan to Widnes in 1963 and is reputed to have asked which change room peg Vince Karalius used. When the "Wild Bull" entered Collier deliberately walked over and, amid awe-filled silence, hung his coat on Vince's peg. "This thy peg, Vince?" he asked genially. "Thars's plenty more in room for thy tackle."

Former Wakefield secretary, Alan Pearman, ran through an early-1970s Trinity team for me, listing from fullback: a carpenter, miner, accountant, miner, policeman, plumber (the present coach David Topliss), miner, policeman, miner, miner, miner, club employee and unemployed — half were from the pit. Pearman estimated Featherstone Rovers' teams would have been 75 per cent miners in the same period, and Castleford's 60 per cent.

The days when, as the saying went, you could walk over to the pithead and shout down the shaft for a few forwards are long gone. Today it is difficult to find a miner in a first division team in England. Lancashire which had 25 pits with 26,500 miners in 1963, by 1990 had just three pits employing 2000. Yet the miner's affection for rugby league remains undiminished.

In the lamp room at Parkside I had noticed that on the blinking red electronic screen above the entrance, the normal safety advice had been replaced by the message, ''10 free tickets, Australia versus Wigan, contact . . .'' Three hours later the message was gone, swamped by so many miners that there had to be a ballot.

If national character is tempered by traumas, then the North is fired by coal. Though the miners are disappearing their legacy is not, and occasionally it is expressed upon the sporting field. What Great Britain displayed at Wembley in 1990 was a modern manifestation of Rorke's Drift and Prescott's Brisbane, a defiance of all odds, born from a century of social suffering and the toil of inhuman industry.

But perhaps even more remarkable than those sagas of individual and team courage was the course the North itself followed to create the game of rugby league. Because to split a sporting code as well founded as was rugby union in 1895 was tantamount to splitting a modern political party, or perhaps indeed a small nation. The Great Split of 1895 was a social protest as much as a sporting upheaval. It had it all, North versus South, amateur against professional, Oxbridge versus the workers, all conducted with thundering debate and ending in sporting civil war.

The rebellion by the northern clubs against the English Rugby Union must be viewed in the context of the times. It is unlikely the North would have attempted, or succeeded, in challenging the English Rugby Union in the downtrodden social, political and economic climate of the preceding century. But the last decade before the turn of the century was an extraordinary period of change in Britain. The Miners Federation, founded in 1888, flexed its industrial muscle when 300,000 miners went on strike for five months in 1893. The same year the Independent Labour Party, forerunner of the modern Labour Party, was formed after a six-week-long strike by workers in a silk and velvet mill in Bradford. The industrial workers of the North had combined to fight the worst excesses of capitalism with a loose federation of trade unions, accident insurance societies, permanent relief funds, trading co-operatives and working men's clubs. John Wesley's Methodism, with its self-governing and democratic traditions, had stolen a march on the hierarchical Anglican church. A sense of equality, the beginnings of a massive labour backlash, was abroad. An era of commercial and industrial oppression had bound the working classes of the North in a spirit of comradeship and self-containment that is evident today.

The 1890s was also a decade of twilights and dawns and witnessed the overthrow of the intellectual and artistic strictures of Victorianism. "The Red Flag", the workers' hymn of revolution, was composed after a dock strike in 1889, the same year that Gustave Eiffel, master of iron engineering, built his Paris tower, a symbol of revolutionary technology. In 1891 Thomas Hardy published his harrowing, anti-aristocracy novel, *Tess of the D'Urbervilles*. The following year Conan Doyle silently lampooned bureaucracy with Sherlock Holmes and George Bernard Shaw's first play heralded his long career of scepticism and criticism. In 1893 Aubrey Beardsley's drawings shocked accepted sexual mores while in 1895 H.G. Wells challenged imagination with *The Time Machine* and Oscar Wilde took London theatre by storm with his satire and hedonism. It is not easy to point to another decade in which English literature produced such works of revolutionary distinction. Everything was new — New Humour, New Drama, New Unionism, New Politics and soon, New Football.

Oscar Wilde certainly had "nowt" to do with rugby league but the arts both lead and reflect national moods and movements. In the North workers were amazed to find that reduced hours gave them time to make furniture, join libraries, attend lectures, learn instruments, sing Haydn, hold concerts and play sport. Once unleashed the North caught a whiff of the nation's new liberalism. Though the North's delegates to the English Rugby Union were middle-class, self-made men of industry and commerce, they rubbed shoulders with club members who were artisans and workers. The industrialists who supported rugby union clubs, the clerks who ran them, and the labourers who played for them, were not immune to the new gusts of cultural enthusiasm.

That a North-South social divide existed in rugby union is evidenced by a northern report of an 1893 match between York-shire and Middlesex. The journalist wrote that when Yorkshire got on top towards the end:

> For 10 minutes before time they were leaving the stand in long streams and the study of some of their faces would have been a good thing for an artist to portray despondency. The followers of the game in the South are evidently swells and the writer has never seen as many top hats at a score of matches in the North as he saw at Richmond that day.

The North, driven by blue-collar endurance and an un-forgiving temperament, began to dominate rugby in England. It has been suggested that in it's own macabre, Darwinian fash-ion, the Industrial Revolution culled the weak from the people of the North. Others argued that a grudge was as good as a goal. Whatever the reason, by the 1880s it was considered that any England scrum needed a good injection of Yorkshiremen to oppose the strength of the brawny Scots. From the inaugura-tion of the English Rugby Union's county championship in 1888, through to 1895, Yorkshire won the title six times out of seven, and that loss was to Lancashire.

Rugby provided a welcome haven from the drudgery of the industrial workshops, but under the Factory Act, Saturday work didn't finish until 1 pm. Yorkshire and Lancashire work-ers playing away-games couldn't make the kickoff on time un-less they left work early and lost wages for their half-day shift. In southern England rugby was played by gentlemen of the professions, old boys of public schools and ambitious lads from the commercial world — the upper and middle classes. In the North however rugby competed with soccer to become the people's game and labourers could ill afford to lose half a day's pay. Northern club officials began lobbying the English Rugby Union to permit clubs to give players a small "broken time" payment for away-games. The conservative attitude of the ERU may be summed up by its president, Mr A. Budd, who wrote in 1892:

> The answer to those who urge that the working man ought to be compensated for the loss of time incurred by his recreation is that if he cannot afford the leisure to play the game, he must do without it.

The prevailing amateur ethos — that sport was a leisure, character building and spiritually uplifting — ignored the truth that for the monied classes rugby was a relief, a neutral zone where they could compete, elbow and knee, without risking status, capital or their family's good name. To the working classes of the North, rugby increasingly became attractive as a source of income, a reward for athletic ability and a way to scale the economic and social ladder. In short, a profession. From as early as 1889 the northern clubs were pressing for leagues — organised competitions — as against the informal, friendly invitations by which matches were traditionally arranged. They wanted to take competition seriously. But the ERU had seen the formation of the Football Association's soccer league in 1888 as the bastard son of professionalism and would have none of it.

When soccer professionalism could no longer be ignored, the FA council patiently and diplomatically managed the issue without splitting the code, their common aim being to regulate a universal game. The ERU, by contrast, was again characterised by Budd who wrote:

> The amateur must refuse to submit himself to the slow extinction which has been going on in the sister game (soccer), and say at once that henceforth he will play and compete with his own class alone, and let professionals for the future look among themselves for opponents.

Although the ostensible difference between the North and the South was the issue of broken time payments, conservative ERU forces were meting out widespread suspensions upon Northern players said to have received match payments — nothing to do with broken time compensation. Fear of creeping professionalism verged on a witch-hunt. In 1892 Yorkshire and

Lancashire clubs twisted the ERU's tail by forming county competitions — the dreaded leagues. Yorkshire then moved to provoke a decision by calling a meeting of the ERU for 20 September 1893 with the announced intention of proposing that the rules of professionalism be modified so that "players be allowed compensation for bona fide loss of time."

Posterity has it that Yorkshire was naive to so telegraph their move, for the South immediately set about lobbying and by the time the ERU met at Westminster Hotel, London, the vote was sewn up. A counter motion defeated the North, on a show of hands, by 282 votes to 136. One delegate sealed Southern victory by producing 120 proxy votes, most of which Northern delegates alleged were irregular, coming as they did from individual colleges at Oxford and Cambridge universities which should have been allowed only one vote each. The result was greeted with loud cheering, and waving of hats and walking canes in the air, but the South were dancing upon the hopes of rugby ever becoming a force against soccer in Britain, in Europe, or of a single rugby code developing in Australia.

After that emotional meeting in London nothing changed immediately. Not a single northern club resigned. However, not content with victory, the South set about drafting such rigid rules of amateurism that a split was virtually ensured. And this was achieved on August 29, 1895, when 21 clubs — from the Yorkshire Senior Competition and the Lancashire Combination — met at the George Hotel in Huddersfield and 20 resigned from the ERU to form the Northern Rugby Football Union. Only Dewsbury was odd club out and they joined three seasons later. Of the nine clubs the 1990 Kangaroos played on tour only Castleford was not among those original rebels. The ERU moved swiftly to shut out the northern rebels. On 19 September, 1895, three weeks after the George Hotel meeting, the ERU voted that under rugby union rules the Northern Union clubs were professionals. The split was complete.

The courage of the North may be seen by the ERU's edict that after a period of grace all Northern Union players who did not return to the fold would be banned for life from rugby union. If the Northern Union had failed hundreds of players would never have played rugby seriously again. The North responded by joining the Northern Union in droves. By 1907-8 Yorkshire membership of the English Rugby Union had sunk from 150 clubs to a mere 14 and rugby union has never recovered its strength in the North since. The Northern Union prospered, growing from the original rebels to 59 clubs in 1896 and 98 by 1898. Ironically by then Northern Union officials realised broken time payment rules were unworkable and by 1905 professionalism was a fait accompli.

Leeds director Joe Warham remarked to me one day, "I ask myself, had we never changed the rules of rugby, what would have happened? Because if you take the parallel with every other sport — boxing, cricket and tennis — the professional game is miles ahead of the amateur game. Rugby might now be one powerful association. But once we changed the rules we became distinct entities." RFL chief executive David Oxley asked himself a different question. What if the clubs which broke away had been based around London? Because by the time rugby league had established supremacy in the North, soccer had swept the south, and indeed the nation. Rugby league has never spread beyond Yorkshire and Lancashire for a variety of reasons — because of the sheer weight of soccer's numbers and because of fierce opposition from rugby union.

That a mutual North-South antagonism still exists was evident at a London Sports Writers Association lunch held for the touring Australian journalists at the Strand Palace Hotel during Wembley week. Several times hostilities rippled the surface with soccer writers heatedly defending soccer's poor record of crowd control. Rugby union writers took umbrage when Keith Barnes jokingly suggested the Kangaroos could give the All Blacks a 30-point start and a beating. British manager Maurice Lindsay, with true northern tenacity, didn't let it rest. "We'd like to issue a challenge, at Wembley, 40 minutes our rules, 40 minutes theirs, proceeds to charity," he said. RFL chief David Oxley added fuel with the damning statistics that only one in five rugby union internationals who turn professional become rugby league internationals. "There are a lot of expensive failures," he said.

Curiously the RFL has never seriously challenged the south with rugby league, never put its heart as well as its cash into a southward thrust. And this exposes the hidden element in the equation of rugby league regionalism. It stems from the North's very strengths — its pride, obduracy and parochialism. The Northern Union's withdrawal from, and ostracism by, the ERU cultivated a defensiveness in rugby league rather than any desire to evangelise and convert. This became wedded to the North's peculiar inverted snobbery that northerners are altogether a finer, friendlier, tougher type than southerners. Rugby league is quite happy to take their showpiece, the Challenge Cup final, to Wembley, just as they were happy to play Australia there. But rugby league belongs in the North.

In that same North in 1990, students left school at an earlier age than in the south yet a lower percentage of them found employment. The North has higher rates of births outside marriage but lower co-habitation rates, therefore more single mothers. Car thefts in greater Manchester average 15.5 per 1000 cars compared with two thefts per 1000 in Surrey. All but six of Britain's 70 most prosperous towns are south of Sheffield, rugby league's most southern outpost. Southern homes, on average, are worth twice as much as in the North; southerners earn 27 per cent more, own twice as many stocks and shares, have four times the amount of private medical insurance and live longer. Week after week market research reveals a new demarcation, more proof that the North is disadvantaged. The social antagonisms underpinning the North-South divide in England make the Queensland v NSW State of Origin in sport seem a friendly.

The whirlwind of inspired red, white and blue jerseys which swept aside Australia in the first Test at Wembley defied all previous form, individual reputation and rational explanation. Despite the Lions' reputed weakness in defence, lack of upper body strength, lack of intensity in their overcrowded match calendar and the backwardness of some of their club coaches, I suspect that what the Kangaroos encountered was the physical embodiment of a century of fierce northern tradition. Wembley became a match in which the descendants of those people cast off by an industrial revolution, and of those sportsmen cast out from the old rugby diaspora, showed that although they may only be the North, in rugby league they are unequivocally Great Britain.

9 BOBBY BACK AT WARRINGTON

Little can be read from Bobby Fulton's face, still less from his clothes. At his first press conference back in Manchester after the first Test, he appeared in the hotel's lower bar in a cheerful yellow t-shirt, black Hard Rock Cafe shorts and Nike thongs. He was definitely not in mourning and nothing about his demeanour suggested he was at risk of becoming the most famous losing coach in Australian rugby league history.

Already the British media were relishing such a prospect. "Kangaroos Beaten to the Punch", said the *Observer* headline, "Hanley's Heroes Back Australia into a Corner" wrote the *Guardian* and "Oz Super Flops" crowed the *Daily Mirror*. The 1990 Kangaroos had been labouring under the burden of the undefeated records of their illustrious predecessors, but if the Test loss lifted that monkey from their backs it did not leave them unburdened. They were now saddled with the fear they could be the first Kangaroos for 30 years to lose a Test series in England. Whatever the portents, a new urgency informed the Kangaroos' camp. Even the staff of the Ramada, most of them soccer fans, shared their guests' disappointment. Trainer Shaun McRae told me quietly one day, "I know how the players feel because, personally, I got beaten as well at Wembley. Just like they did." But the man who felt it most, and who now had the job of lifting everyone's game, was Bob Fulton.

When objecting to what he considers unfair criticism, Fulton is legendary as a counter-puncher. But what Fulton really objects to is defeat. The taint of it, the taste, the hangover. When he was still coaching Manly he said, "You can learn from defeat but once you can handle defeat you should get out of the game." His record as a player and a coach bespeak an archly competitive perfectionist, pushing people, issues and the laws to the brink and sometimes over.

He was immensely irritating as a player because he fretted to play the ball quickly and, like Wally Lewis, was strong enough to shed tacklers seeking to delay him. He was notorious also for sledging in tackles to goad opponents to give away a penalty, the "Chappelli" of the football field, the supreme opportunist who never gave mugs an even break. Apart from his legendary play he is remembered in England for a dive he took in a 1973 Test resulting in referee Billy Thompson sending off Britain's Brian Lockwood for a high tackle. When Australia's trainer arrived with sponge Fulton is reputed to have opened one eye and said, "Don't go throwing that water all over me." When I met Thompson, now retired, he told me Lockwood had confessed to him years later, "If ah'd uv' caught Fulton raht thut day, his 'ead would have coom darn in Wigan! Ah joost missed 'im." Thompson felt justified in marching Lockwood for intent.

In his playing days Fulton was compared with Reg Gasnier; once retired he was the benchmark from which to judge Wally Lewis. He won premierships with Manly in 1972, 1973 and 1976, and played 20 Tests, including captaining the 1978 Kangaroos on the tour which broke the ground for the 1982 Invincibles. His record as a player was so impressive that it actually became an albatross to him when he became a coach and lost grand finals, first with Eastern Suburbs and then Manly. His fanatical rejection of defeat culminated in 1987 with his being reported for saying he would like to run over referee Bill Harrigan with a truck. In those days what cut Fulton deeply was the pub lore, and boardroom bandy, that great players don't always make great coaches — "Look at Fulton".

Roos trainer Brian Hollis attests to the hours of research Fulton put in at Manly. "Every time I've been to his place, and that's often, he was watching a game, the back play the forward play, fast forward and rewind on the video. Now that didn't make him unique but he could read a game so quickly too. I'd be sitting on the sideline for Manly and over the radio he'd say, 'Get out there and tell them to watch for the short kick', so out I'd go and sure enough, short kick. Happened too regularly to be coincidence.''

Fulton finally quietened his critics with Manly's 1987 grand final victory, consolidated his reputation when he became Australia's coach in 1988, and hadn't looked back until . . . Suddenly he could hear all the familiar caterwauling back home, ''How could Fulton lose with the team he took over there!''

How indeed? In the *Sunday Times*, the week before Wembley, columnist Stephen Jones had presaged:

> I have a suspicion that some of these Kangaroos — like the All Blacks — manage to hide individual weaknesses under the proud collective umbrella, but to reveal them you have to hammer away at all points.

Hammer the British did, and hairline cracks around the Australian scrumbase suddenly split open. If Fulton was correct — that penalties had cost Australia the first Test — then he had no need to change the Test side. Having painted himself into that corner he leapt nimbly clear by announcing that Laurie Daley was a certainty for the second Test — he did not even have to play another match to be included. Beyond that, Fulton would not go. Since he had not uttered a public word of criticism of any player since the tour began, we were left to piece together clues.

The Kangaroos desperately needed a five-eighth, preferably with two good hands. Daley, his hand still swollen and healing slowly, was not included in the Kangaroo selection to play Warrington, Fulton's former club, in the seventh match of the tour, but other omissions and inclusions showed how Australia's fixed Test side was being prised open.

The biggest surprise of the team to play Warrington was 18-year-old Brad Fittler at five-eighth. ''I've got a lot of time for him,'' said Fulton. ''He's one of the coolest kids I know. Boys of his age, they're not men and they're not boys and sometimes they try to prove they're an adult. But he's just taking life as it comes, taking everything in his stride. He's a fantastic young man.'' It was inconceivable however that Fulton would throw such a tyro against Garry Schofield, indeed ''Freddie's'' selection for the Wednesday game shifted the Test spotlight to Cliff Lyons who was named as a reserve against Warrington.

Almost certainly Lyons would play the following Saturday's match against Castleford and it had become axiomatic that whoever played the weekend match was favoured for second Test selection. Benny Elias and Glenn Lazarus were in the mid-week team against Warrington so they still had the job ahead of them. Des Hasler at halfback wasn't good news for Allan Langer because it left Ricky Stuart available for the weekend team and it went without saying that Stuart's career as a Test five-eighth was over. Langer was fulfilling Alex Murphy's requirement that he ''clear the traffic jam'' around the rucks but he was presenting opposing teams with little threat from the scrumbase. For those of us with vivid memories of the slim, blond-haired Ipswich halfback magically jinking his way downfield at Lang Park, Brisbane, Alfie's form was a mystery.

Warrington, on the River Mersey, halfway between Manchester and Liverpool, is boxed on three sides by the M6, M56 and M62 motorways — the ideal industrial estate, except it's a town. Part of the M62, as straight as a rule, was once the main runway of an airstrip used by the Americans for the Berlin airlift. The strip is now Burtonwood where you can walk for a kilometre through row upon row of American jeeps, gun and personnel carriers. Burtonwood gave Warrington its GI brides and today Coca Cola, Boeing, Du Pont and Goodyear continue the Yankee connection. The other face of Warrington's industry are eerily silent, tree-lined science parks with tenants of the scale of British Nuclear Fuels and Mercury Communications, or with names like Advanced Micro Devices and Spectra Tech Europe. Mothballed wartime munitions and high tech science parks are the different ages of Warrington, officially designated as a New Town and now the flourishing, white-collar Boom Town of the north-west, with an unemployment rate well below the national average. I thought to find a softer, friendlier core in the heart of Warrington, but the very town centre is dominated by the industrial towers of Lever Bros, makers of Persil. Warrington rugby league are known as the "Wires" because larger even than soapmaking was the local wire weaving and cable industries where many of Warrington's football families worked. When British Steel and British Aluminium closed operations 10 years ago, so did many of their subsidiaries, but the nickname lives on.

"Ale, the King" said the poster on the side of a Warrington bus, which would have been a nice welcome had Wally toured. Unfortunately Greenalls, the Wires' major sponsor, had recently ended 207 years brewing ale in Warrington, undone by the marketing drive of Australian lagers like the Kangaroos' Fourex. To add to the Australian takeover, Warrington's coach was ex-St George fullback, Brian Johnson; a local hero was the infamous Les Boyd of Cootamundra; and most-favoured son since 1984 was former Penrith forward Bob Jackson. Brian Johnson played the same three years at Warrington as Boyd and remembered with amusement Boyd's amazing popularity. "They just loved his style," he said. "They loved him bashing people, not that he did, they just loved the anticipation of it. He was a good player but, mate, to them he was God!" Johnson was no slouch himself in the wide open spaces of English football. He recalled, "You'd be in your own quarter and make a break and the ball would go through five different pairs of hands 70 metres upfield and we'd drop the ball and they'd come back 45 metres and kick into the corner on the second tackle. There was no defensive style but there was always something happening."

Those Australians are successors to a Warrington tradition begun back in 1945 when the club signed a young RAN seaman who became the greatest try-scorer of them all. Of the 10 players in the Rugby League Hall of Fame, Brian Bevan looks least like a rugby league champion. The bandaged-legged, knobbly-kneed, baldy-headed winger scored a phenomenal 796 tries, a record unlikely ever to be surpassed. Warrington secretary Ron Close remembers the skinny-framed Bevan possessing an uncanny ability to beat an opponent. "So often I saw him come to the touchline where there was no room and somehow he'd get through and then use his speed to go all the way," he said. "Yet he looked anything but a rugby league player." Bevan never returned home and so never played for Australia and nor did St George's Harry Bath. He arrived at Warrington three years after Bevan and still holds the club record for most points scored in a season.

During the Bad Boy Boyd years the Wires developed a poor disciplinary reputation but under former school teacher Johnson, Warrington became the reformed good guys. Oddly enough Johnson found upon becoming coach that epithets which would wash off Australians at training, were so taken to heart at Warrington he had to rein in light-hearted abuse. "Unless you live here you can't appreciate the subtle differences between Australian and English societies," said Johnson. The difference which most impeded his efforts at Warrington initially was the low priority players gave rugby league. "They had their jobs, their families, having a good time and somewhere down the list they fitted in rugby league," he said. "In Australia if you want to be successful you fit your life around the game and everything else comes a distant last. It amazed me. I had players turn up late for training and say the boss wanted them to work, not 'Hey, it's 4 pm, I've got to go.' "

Nor did the attitude of employers help. "I'll give you an example," said Johnson. "I've got a centre, Tony Thorniley, worthy of a Lions tour spot except for injury. He was told to make a choice between football and his job because a downturn in trade meant his employer wasn't willing to risk him taking time off with injury in the future. It just couldn't happen in Australia, in fact the opposite would apply, the boss would exploit the kudos of having a champion player on his staff."

Johnson had struck what I would call the peasant/lord-of-the-manor syndrome, a hangover from a past industrial age, which still pervades many companies in the North. No Australian coach begrudges an employer's right to value-for-wage from his footballer-workers, but it need not always be totted up by hours on the shop floor. Over at Castleford, coach Darryl Van de Velde, a financial consultant when in Brisbane, encountered a similar outmoded attitude from employers. "Everyone loves to meet sportsmen," he said. "If employers had any brains they'd use their high profile players to attract business, because most English towns simply buzz rugby league." Van de Velde began ringing firms and offering to pay the player's wages for time off to prepare for a match. That worked until one said, "Hang on, we've got a lot of work on here," so Van de Velde paid the firm so they could employ a replacement. Van de Velde's complaint matched Johnson's. "The players work all day and leave no time for match preparation," he said. "I get them at 6 pm for a Yorkshire Cup semi-final, it's a knockout match and I say, 'Listen fellahs, in a little while it's win or bust, a once off, lose this and it's all over, so I want you to go out there and do this, do that and bash these blokes!' and they're still thinking about work."

Brian Johnson took over Warrington in mid-season, 1988, and made his first task survival in first division. "That's one great pressure Sydney coaches don't have," he said. "The bottom three teams go down to second division and three come up. You struggle to keep your head above water and you worry about experimenting in case it rebounds on you." Johnson and the Wires avoided relegation by two points then got a flying start to 1989-90 going nine matches unbeaten, winning the Lancashire Cup and making the Challenge Cup final at Wembley. Oddly, considering Johnson's attacking skill as a player, Warrington's 1990 form leading up to the Kangaroos was marked by two consecutive losses without their line being crossed — or them crossing the opposition's line.

Apart from Great Britain, Warrington were the only team on the Roos schedule who could say that they won the last time they met. Warrington and Widnes defeated the Kangaroos in 1978 but Widnes lost in 1982 and 1986 when Warrington didn't fulfil the criteria to be placed on either tour schedule. So October 11, 1978 was given five-page prominence in the match program, including pictures of the 15 players that historic night, and excerpts of their heroic memories. Forward Mike Nicholas recalled taking the second tackle of the night.

> Five Aussies came into me like a salvo of bullets. I stood up to one, two, three, four but the fifth was enough. I kneeled over with my head full of floodlights. Dragging myself up from the ground I thought, 'OK Nicko, it's them or you.'

Heady stuff! Another forward, Roy Lester, remembered going to work the next morning "to find the entire shop floor standing up and applauding." So, despite a persistent drizzle, a capacity 10,200 packed Wilderspool for the return bout with the 1990 Kangaroos. Wilderspool is set amid the most unprepossessing surroundings in rugby league. On one side it is separated by a narrow lane from the backyards of nearby homes, on another side stands an old blackened fibro factory building, windows covered with wire netting and yard littered with industrial rubbish bins, and at the back of the ground runs a raised railway line with coal hoppers seemingly permanently parked. Inside Wilderspool, along one touchline, where a grandstand and terraces once held 10,000 spectators, is a decrepid leisure centre and snooker club which I can describe no better than Wires secretary, Ron Close, who dismissed it as, "that monstrosity". The approach to the Wilderspool main gates is through the back of another grandstand clad with cliplock galvanised iron, painted powder blue. The lot reminded me of the depths to which English rugby league must have fallen 20 years ago.

Yet here were the Wires' fans, cheerful, singing, passing around money buckets for player testimonials, streaming towards the ground as though they were heading for seats at Her Majesty's. As an ordinary football goer in Australia it used to irritate me to hear the endless praise heaped upon English fans, their loyalty, their singing, et cetera, et cetera, but having experienced the conditions under which the majority watch matches I will concede their grit. Everyone seemed to be eating the Lancashire special — a pie on a plate drowned in mashed green pea gravy — including Broncos manager John Ribot, Martin Bella, Bob Lindner and Channel 10's Billy J. Smith.

Rumours flashed around supporter groups — Langer versus Stuart, Elias versus Walters, why not Alexander instead of Belcher? It was October 31, exactly halfway through the tour and, contrary to all expectations, the Kangaroos' mood seemed volatile.

Benny Elias was particularly wound up, pounding his chest guard like some primate, and within minutes he instigated Australia's first try, harassing Warrington fullback David Lyon as he steadied to punt clear. Lyon hurriedly on-passed to rugby union convert, stand-off Kevin Ellis but Brad Mackay charged down his clearing kick and then fell on the ball to score. It was a typical 1990 Kangaroos score, nothing gorgeous to behold, just pressure, patience and pounce.

The Warrington defence, swarming as seaweed, solid as the shore, lived up to their reputation, led by former Lions captain Mike Gregory and Aussie Bob Jackson. When Australia spread the ball wide to Meninga there was Gregory, all compact muscles and headband, waiting to nail him. Overnight it seemed the English had cracked the Kangaroos' code — who was dangerous, who not. Once their machine was blunted the Roos were dependent upon individual brilliance to score and that was not their strong suit.

After 27 minutes Warrington scored from a loose ball snapped up by Mike Gregory, quick pass to Tony Thorniley who strode through Meninga's tackle — ''A badly missed tackle'' one commentator called it — to level the scores at 4-4. Meninga still protects his arm-guarded arm, far preferring a full body hit to a jarring swinging arm tackle. Mark Sargent replied for the Roos in a manner other teams rarely can emulate. Using his speed and size he barged down the blindside, scattering tacklers, carrying several with him for the last five metres to score in the corner. Mark Geyer followed suit, leaping to mark a Benny Elias bomb to take the score to 14-6 at half-time. Australia's scores had come from their big men, but the team seemed to have lost the rhythm they brought with them from Australia.

It took the Roos until three minutes from full-time to improve on that half-time score and then only because ingenue Kevin Ellis floated a speculative pass near his line which Fittler accepted for a strollover try. Another try on the bell by Hancock provided a thoroughly unjustified final scoreline of 26-6. Nobody was fooled, least of all the players. Brad Fittler said with some suprise as he came off, ''The best defence we've played, a great team, they'd measure up against any Sydney side I've seen. With 10 minutes to go I remember thinking, 'This is like a premiership game at home.' ''

Fulton agreed. ''They're the best side we've played, throw in Great Britain too,'' he said. His audience's faces must have reflected disbelief, so he expanded. ''They were spirited, committed, never flinched and it took us until the last five minutes to subdue them. If they'd been given the same refereeing latitude as Great Britain, they'd have beaten us, and by more points,'' said Fulton. ''Take out Wigan and that's our best display.''

You'd have thought Warrington had lost the cup final by their mood. They thought they could have beaten Australia, it seemed. This was the club scene Australia would face for the rest of the tour, rejuvenated, confident, no longer overawed by the myth of Australian supremacy. That was the legacy of Wembley. ''A lot of Australia's success has been that we're always beaten before we go out,'' said Mike Gregory. He had turned in a Test candidate's performance but he wasn't expecting a call from Malcolm Reilly. ''The way the boys played on Saturday, they played out of their skins,'' he said. ''Far be it from me to take one of their jerseys off them.''

Brian Johnson was dismayed by the penalty count. Huh? But it was 10-8 to Warrington? ''I know, we probably struck the fairest referee in all bloody England, you expect a bit more leniency our way!'' he said, laughing. How come Warrington were able to so stifle the Roos' attack? ''In Australia it's back five yards, quick ruck and spread it while the defence is still organising itself,'' he explained. ''Over here the refs let you lie on the player more in tackles so when you move the ball wide the defensive line is set ready.''

Later in the week I tested this theory on Mark Sargent, one of the few who did break the Warrington line. Yeah, he agreed. What often appeared to be dead-end, one-off running was in fact an attempt to open up set defences by punching up the middle, he said. I spoke with Mark in the player's recreation room after training one day. Des Hasler was playing a solo game of pool, and a country and western singer was sorrowing away on the juke-box. Sargent, originally an outsider for a tour place, was slowly working his way into Test calculations, though Glenn Lazarus was probably a stride ahead of him. Sargent, intelligent, modest, the only tourist from the Newcastle Knights, had quickly earned himself the respect of everyone on tour. He hails from Newcastle but in 1985, aged 20, went to Sydney and spent four years with Canterbury when that club overflowed with such forward talent as Peter Tunks, Peter Kelly, Geoff Robinson, Darryl Brohman, Steve Folkes, David Gillespie, Paul Langmack, Phil Gould . . . "A galaxy of stars," as Sargent put it. No wonder they won back-to-back grand finals in 1984-85. He'd always been a Canterbury supporter from afar and remembers to this day the moment his hero Steve Mortimer walked into the dressingroom and said to him, "How're you goin' mate?"

Not so well as it turned out. In 1986 Sargent was out for 10 weeks with torn knee ligaments from trying a defensive dance to match the mobile, twisting stepping of Noel Cleal. Next season, 1987, he was not named in the first grade squad and one night, training in the rain, concentrating on his internalised anger instead of the suspect turf, slipped and broke his leg. In 1988 he experienced his worst pain of all when the bones of his pubic arch dislocated in a tackle. "Mate, I walked off the field like this," said Mark, rising and heel-toeing his way across the carpet. "Felt like someone had a knife up my backside, Ohhhhh!" By mid-1988 he was negotiating with Newcastle and though he was a substitute in Canterbury's 1988 grand final victory, he was the only player not to make it off the bench. So he's played in a premiership winning team, but not in a grand final. ''I did the lap of honour but it's not quite the same,'' he said.

Touring England, with it's parochial football fans, reminded him of his 1989 return to Newcastle. ''Newcastle is working class and the people pay their money to see an hour and a half of Newcastle versus the world,'' he said. Narrowminded Sydney had an image of Newcastle as coalmining, steelworks and rough heads, he said. ''They never acknowledge the beauty of Newcastle's beaches, bush or people, so they never see the prettier side of our football either. Just think we're boring. Sheer prejudice.''

Newcastle's mass following has become a two-edged blade for Knights players. ''You can't walk down the street without 'Hey Sarge, Hey Sarge, Hey Sarge', when all you want is privacy,'' said Mark. ''But then, before matches we go for a warmup on an oval across the road and we look back and the ground is forever packed — 32,000 for our last game against Balmain — just a sea of red and blue, and no matter how you're feeling, you just go, 'Yeahhhh!' '' In Newcastle, Sargent is a shining advertisement for what rugby league can bring a young man. Aged 26, unmarried, he has bought a house at Redhead, 20 minutes drive south of Newcastle and two minutes walk from the beach, has passed his mature age university entrance exams to study Arts communications, and reckons on another four years in rugby league. But he appreciated he was no Brad Fittler, aged 18, with time to make the tour a learning experience. So he was giving every match his best shot and hoping. ''Mate, I'd give anything to play in a Test,'' he said, with sigh.

Until then he was enjoying the total experience of the tour, including sharing a car with room-mate Martin Bella. They bought a 1979 Austin Allegro for about $700, and later Ricky Stuart and Mark Carroll bought into the consortium. The tiny Allegro's bonnet was always ajar, the back seat was half out, the carpets torn and lifting and it was severely dented — a nice little goer. ''Marty couldn't get it started one day but we reckoned it probably had run out of petrol,'' said Mark. ''He was going to drive to Halifax but the hotel guy said 'You're not going to drive that heap on the M62 are you? The coppers will eat you.' So he drove by the backroads.'' As poorly as the Austin went, it was a limousine compared to the 1970 Citroen stationwagon that Brandy Alexander and his Penrith teammates, Cartwright, Geyer and Fittler bought for $625. ''It's been crashed into walls, bounced off buildings and it's a mess,'' said Brandy, laughing. ''We won't try to sell it. It's basically a mass of dents.'' Benny Elias, Block, Sirro and Lazza bought a clapped-out Capri which I occasionally saw parked haphazardly in front of the ritzy Ramada. Sometimes it had one wheel on the footpath, other times it rested diagonally across the tour bus's parking possie, much to driver Gibbons' amused disgust. Said Mark Sargent, ''Whenever we walk by someone just goes Bang!, another dent. People look and say, 'Hey, they're kicking someone's car.' ''

The players were finding the cost of living in England so high that their 262 pounds a week allowance was not covering meals and living expenses. Perhaps it was coincidental that, four days after the shock of Wembley, the ARL president Ken Arthurson chose to announce an increase in the allowance to 300 pounds, a $100 a week rise. It would be subtracted from the players' bonuses at the end of the tour but at least it was some joy. The tour management also gave the whole squad two days off training after Warrington to refresh them for the arduous haul ahead.

Whatever the Roos' physical condition it was a neat piece of sports psychology because their natural reaction was to work themselves into a lather of guilt at training to expunge memories of defeat. Instead about 20 players adjourned to a local wine bar one evening to relax with drinking and word association games, the penalty being to skoal a half pint. With such games the more you lose, the more you lose and while those with mental blocks were being caught out amid much hilarity, a condom was secretly passed around the group and gently laid across some unsuspecting player's shoulder, there to sit as a source of much mirth until the player twigged. If Martin Bella was caught once he was caught 10 times — more penalty half pints. It was all harmless fun and knitted the players together in their unspoken adversity. Football tours concertina and exaggerate the normal proportions of life.

The raison d'etre for these players, once they arrived in England, was to come away with the Ashes. Before they left Australia, and after they returned home, they could distance themselves from the series and examine the results dispassionately, but for the moment the mood of the camp was dominated by the peril of the Ashes. Present in that circle of joviality and touching everyone on the shoulder, was the ghostly spectre of Madam Loss who, at her whim, could send them home without honour and unsung, but with a crushing new title, the 1990 Nonentities. Not until the second Test on November 10 could they begin to pick up the pieces of their tour and that was another two club matches and 10 frustrating days away.

10 CASTLEMAINE NOT CASTLEFORD

I was in two minds whether to attend the English Rugby League Writers' Association annual dinner, held at the grand Kilhey Court Hotel outside Wigan. For an Australian to venture among 150 English journalists, players, coaches, club executives and sponsors just five days after the first Test invited endless ribbing. "You're a brave lad," said the *Yorkshire Post*'s Raymond Fletcher, smiling, as I pushed through the throng at the pre-dinner bar. Yet the English sportswriters were not euphoric and certainly not patronising towards two other Australians, Keith Barnes and Bob Abbott, who were also guests at the dinner.

The chairman of the RFL, Bob Ashby, in his opening address, couldn't resist a gentle dig. "Keith Barnes has taken the defeat very well," he said, gesturing towards Barnes who had fixed a wan smile to his face. "He's here," said Ashby, "but the rest of the Aussies haven't surfaced yet, still got their heads under their pillows I think." Kangaroos hiding? Barnes' grin grew thin. "Last Saturday we gave you journalists enough to write about for the next 12 months. We should toast the lads of Wembley, because I've been praying for that win for years." He raised his glass but the assembly responded half heartedly and the explanation of their reluctance came from the BBC's Neil Harmon, sitting next to me: "Nobody wants to count their chickens," he whispered. Perhaps there was some embarrassment also at toasting victory with the vanquished as guests, because the last toast of the evening was to the Australians, "who made rugby league really competitive by putting themselves up there to be knocked off!"

If the Wembley loss was producing friction within the Australian camp it was not evident to the travelling media corps for we had to learn from Sydney that two players had allegedly been involved in a scuffle in the hotel. Keith Barnes formally denied it and said the players concerned had laughed when the newspaper reports were read. "I hadn't heard," said Barnes. "Nor had Les Stokes, Bob Fulton, Brian Hollis or Mal Meninga and they're all pretty close to the players." Nor had we though one story was that some Broncos were skylarking, imitating the Three Stooges. Even if there was some discord between players it had nothing to do with the loss to Great Britain. The whole camp was unified and focused upon the second Test at Old Trafford, Manchester, and new incentive had been created by Fulton's team selection for the Sunday match against Castleford. Five changes had been made from Wembley — Stuart in for Langer, Elias for Kerrod Walters, Shearer for Hancock and Lazarus for Bella. As expected Lyons was given the five-eighth spot vacated by Stuart, and Brad Mackay had moved in as lock when Bob Lindner replaced John Cartwright in the second row.

Fulton wasn't available for the usual media conference so Keith Barnes stood in and gave us our first non-combative analysis of team selection on tour. Australia's tactics in the first Test had been primarily based on a sound kicking game, a powerful pack of forwards and a top defensive effort, said Barnes. "Our forwards invariably get on top of the opposition and pave the way for the flair in the backs," he said. "But after some early mistakes in the Test the team became overly conscious of ball security. Bella put the first ball down . . . it wasn't a good pass from Kerrod."

Barnes then revealed for the first time that Fulton had been disappointed with the forwards' one-out running. "The ball carrier had very little option, the support wasn't there," said Barnes. "That's not the way Bozo trains and that's not the way he coaches. Yet invariably when Great Britain ran they had support players." The amazement evident in Barnes' voice spoke for all those mystified by the reversal of roles at Wembley. The British had also varied their kicking game intelligently, he said. Schofield had used a short kicking game for Leeds and he and Hanley continued with it in the Test. ''I know the message was sent down to our boys to vary their kicking against Warrington,'' said Barnes. ''Bozo has already looked at a sweeper to collect the short kicks at Old Trafford.''

Old Trafford was never far from everyone's mind but before then the Kangaroos had two club matches, the first against Castleford. The north of England was being criss-crossed by scores of buses carrying Kangaroo tour supporters. The Australian High Commission in London estimated there were 1500 supporters on organised tours and at least the same number travelling privately. The Sydney-based *Rugby League Week* magazine alone had organised 13 coaches carrying 500 supporters. Each passenger paid an average of $6000 for 35 days overseas, including air fares, first-class hotel accommodation and match tickets — half what it would cost them had they followed the tour privately. Some arrived via Ireland, some via Europe but all were converging on the North for the most crucial Test in modern rugby league history.

I had arranged to travel for a day with one such coach load of Roo supporters led by Steve Ricketts, rugby league writer on the Brisbane *Courier-Mail* whose previous Kangaroo tour experience gave him inside knowledge of the English football scene. Steve had turned tour guide for the 1990 visit and his flock were bedding down in York before driving on to Castleford on November 4 for the Kangaroos' eighth match. Wally Lewis told me that on past tours, when the Australians were quartered in Leeds, many players visited nearby York which impressed even the most cultureless of Kangaroos. So I drove to York, the medieval city whose name marches through English history to the shout of trumpets and beating of drums and whose antiquity rivals that of Rome and Venice.

York is the original capital of the North of England and, until 1400, even had pretensions to usurp London as the nation's capital. Its history spans the Roman Emperor Constantine, who was crowned there in AD 306, as well as the Vikings who named the town Jorvik, and the Normans who began building York Minster in 1220 and completed it 252 years later. Christianity's "Big Four" in England are St Paul's Cathedral, Canterbury Cathedral, Westminster Abbey and York Minster. The rivalry between York and Canterbury to be the centre of the church in England did not abate until 1354 when Pope Innocent VI cleverly declared the Archbishop of York Primate of England, but the Archbishop of Canterbury Primate of 'All' England.

Early one morning, with a bitterly cold, knifing wind blowing, I set off walking from my hotel towards the Minster. York all but subsides under the impact of three million tourists annually but this late in the season visitors were mercifully sparse. I made my way down streets whose names, merely by repeating them, give the town's flavour — Shambles, Ogleforth, Coppergate and Swinegate, Gillygate and Fossgate, Friargate and Nunnery Lane. The streets abruptly awoke to the pealing of the Minster bells, 10 descending chimes, summoning congregations to prayer as it has for 750 years. Whenever I entered a small lane the chimes echoed in confusion off other buildings but the Minster, a masterpiece of high medieval civilisation, is visible from everywhere, riding like a great ocean liner above the fields of rural Yorskhire. I emerged into Petergate opposite the Minster entrance and let the peals break over me, sound waves of physical clarity.

For a better view I climbed the medieval garrison wall which girdles the Minster from Bootham Bar — an entrance to the old city — to Monk Bar, a 700-metre walk. The Minster was silhouetted against the rising sun, its serrated spires speared the pale blue sky like swordfish snouts, stone adornments were weathered to gaunt bones, the sculpted faces to featureless skulls. Green moss and black mildew grew like beards upon the faces of gargoyle cornices. The wall's high earth ramparts are Roman-built, the turreted wall itself medieval. For centuries York, into whose backyards I now peered, has lived out its generations in the presence of this inspired monument to a dwindling devotion.

The Minster's bell towers were clad with scaffolding, weather erosion threatening what successive fires could not. In 1829, Jonathan Martin, a regular church-goer afflicted by a religious mania known as ''ranting'', began pinning notes to the Choir denouncing the clergy for its opulence. He wrote ominously, ''Your Gret Charchis and Minstairs will cum rattling down upon your Gilty Heads.'' One evening he hid behind a tomb and, when the church was locked, made a bonfire from hymn books. Yet Martin's fire was not as severe as another in 1840 which brought the Minster's ten great bells crashing and bellowing one by one down from the towers. Nor as damaging as that begun by lightning strike in 1984 which burnt out the entire south transept, including its 500-year-old oak roof vaults. Marian Nicolson, who owns the Memories of York gift shop 50 metres from the Minster, remembers the fire still smouldering when she arrived at her shop. A large sorrowing crowd had already gathered from all over Yorkshire. ''They were desolate,'' said Marian. ''It's the heart of the city and of Yorkshire. It's the mother church.''

I returned to the Minster for Evensong and sat in a timber pew in the Choir where all the daily services are held. There came 20 cherub-faced choir boys and 10 senior choristers, two abreast, all wearing white surplices over startling scarlet cassocks, an angelic line against the multi-hued, pagan parkas and windjackets of the congregation of tourists. The choir sang an anthem, ''How beauteous are the feet who stand on Zion's hill'', soaring and falling in sweet harmony in praise of Jerusalem. The early 19th century poet, William Blake, in his poem commonly known as Jerusalem — from whose lines came the title for the film Chariots of Fire — questioned whether Jesus had visited England and built a Jerusalem, ''among these dark satanic mills?'' If He did it was certainly York.

Two weeks later the Minster echoed to the hymn of Blake's poem at the funeral of Len Hutton, a true son of Yorkshire who, as a 22-year-old, once upstaged Don Bradman himself. In a Test against Bradman's Australians at the Oval in 1938, Hutton scored 364 runs to break the Don's world record Test score. Sir Leonard Hutton was the greatest English batsman of his generation and the first professional, as opposed to gentleman, to captain England. One eulogy was delivered by his erstwhile opening partner, the Rt Rev David Sheppard, now the Bishop of Liverpool, and the faces in the crowd further filled in the score sheet — Compton, Bailey, Trueman, Statham and Eric Bedser. Remembering their deeds, England could use their like today.

Back at my hotel I teamed up with Steve Ricketts' tour mob who mostly hailed from Brisbane Souths, where Mal Meninga, Gary Belcher and Bob Lindner played their pre-Sydney football. At Headingley, before the Leeds match, Belcher had given them all a wave during his warm-up. They were halfway through their 37-day tour and had followed the progress of the Roos closely.

Doug Cory is patron of Brisbane Souths rugby league club, Richard Welch president of Souths-Sunnybank Junior rugby league club, and Col Egan a long-time Souths supporter. They had watched the Leeds match and the Wembley Test and weren't happy with what they saw.

Col Egan: "After Leeds we said the Test would be no cakewalk because Leeds held us for so long. Our weakness is the scrum halves."

Doug Cory: "Yeah, the weak link was the Broncos — Walters, Langer and Hancock, and we're all Broncos supporters. Kerrod never ran from dummy half and Langer hasn't been the same since he broke his leg."

Dick Welch: "Langer just played a passing game. I saw the Sydney grand final and on form Ricky Stuart should be the number one halfback. At the moment Australia haven't got a general out there."

Doug: "The whole team looked jaded, they've had a hard season. I don't think they can be too happy. Mind, they got a rough deal from the referee."

Col: "Yeah, both teams were offside but Great Britain weren't penalised."

Dick: "I don't go along with that. I've been watching the

Poms since 1962 and they've learned how to defend. They're not tackling high, they're not slipping off tackles and they're not going in with swinging arms. No, they definitely outplayed us."

Col: "I'd agree the difference from 1986 is the condition of the English forwards. They used to be sloppy, fat and over-weight. They look pretty fit now.'

I interrupted. Weren't we told this was the strongest squad Australia had ever sent away?

Doug: "They still are so if they're not firing you have to look at the coach or the captain. It's either that, tiredness or dishar-mony."

Col: "You can't blame Fulton, he's not out there on the field. I don't want to stir but they miss Lewis. He could always read the game on the field."

Dick: "Bobby has taken over an undefeated team and is ex-pected to win. Malcolm Reilly took over with England in the doldrums. He's been building this team for three years. Reilly was an aggressive player and he might be a great coach."

As we left York heading for Castleford, about 50 kms away, tour leader Ricketts took up the bus microphone and addressed his followers — their tickets were for the popular stand, stand-ing room only but with an overhead roof. "I think you'll enjoy being next to the British supporters but it can get a bit rough and difficult to get to the toilets, so you might have to impro-vise if you get stuck!" The coach erupted into moans and laughter. They were mostly of an age with grown children and Steve's jokes broke the monotony which overtakes even the best of bus tours. "We're passing the John Smith Brewery where Malcolm Reilly works," said Steve. "So if you want to give a big raspberry as we go by . . ." On the spare seat beside Steve lay his tour bibles — the AA book of British villages, the AA book of British towns and the British Coal Good Beer Guide for 1990.

Halfway into our 40-minute trip Steve played a Channel 10 rugby league promotional tape on the bus video, which took us "From the teeth rattling cold of the nation's capital on a misty

July afternoon, to the sweet autumn sunshine of Surfers . . . camaraderie and mateship . . . victory laps and broken men with nowhere to hide . . . bigger than Artie, more electric than Bozo . . . Reggie the Rabbit, Pricey and the Crow . . . the nation bows not so much to the Queen of England, but the Emperor of Lang Park . . . rugby league truly is, simply the best.'' The Tina Turner video followed, a commercial idea that certainly grew to be better than all the rest. She put us in the mood for the next number which Steve now jammed into the audio cassette on the coach console. ''OK, here's our song, let's hear it,'' he said. The music came on and slowly, gently I heard the voices behind me pick up the verses of a typically sonorous Mike McClellan guitar number, The Heartland. When it reached the chorus all shyness melted as the 33-strong mob behind went for it.

> How do you feel, under clear southern skies,
> Does to hear Aussies sing, bring a tear to your eyes,
> How do you feel, when you call this land home,
> Does the song in your heart, ever leave you alone.

As they sang we drove under a sullen grey sky and fading light — even at 2 pm — passing fields of wintering pasture, long, bare hawthorne hedges, tiny neat villages, distant manor houses and castellated stone fortresses of country squires. As we neared Castleford the concrete cooling towers of a power station and the spinning wheel of a coal mine gantry rose above the skyline. To hear the coachload join in that chorus, ''under clear southern skies'', lifting their voices in unashamed Australianism, gladdened this Aussie's heart. At the end they all gave a loud rebel yell, partly to hide some embarrassment but mostly because they meant it. Australians used to burn gum leaves in their Earls Court flats in London to sniff the eucalypt and ease homesickness. If Channel 10 wanted a rugby league promotion tune for 1991 they should have been on that bus.

I had scarcely the heart to ask the questions I intended because loyalty must colour their replies. I picked up the bus mike: ''How many of the 33 on board picked Great Britain to win the first Test? '' Five had. How many think Great Britain will win the second Test? Only four. That meant those four supporters also thought Australia would lose the Ashes. In that emotional atmosphere even one defection was remarkable. How many would keep Walters at hooker? Only five. And Alfie? Just two. "Fickle fans," said Steve, grabbing the microphone. "And you're supposed to be Broncos supporters!" We buttoned up jackets, pulled on gloves and hats and prepared to step into Castleford's chill air.

Castleford is a small industrial town, an ex-coal, steel foundry and glass centre on the River Aire, 15 minutes drive out of Leeds. Some 12 per cent of all Britain's bottles are still made at nearby Knottingley, hence Castleford's nickname, "The Glassblowers". I had visited the town weeks earlier, in early dusk and pouring rain, and walked past heaps of rubble and empty buildings, a depressing scene of a town centre trapped in a post-industrial recession. Castleford has a main street but no core, no heart, because it was always just a dormitory for local industry. All of which was about to change in 1991 with a $50 million shopping development facelift.

Castleford is also home to Burberry waterproof gaberdine raincoats, Sirdar knitting wools and Rowntree-Mackintosh chocolates. But the major employer and principal Castleford rugby league team sponsor is Hickson Ltd., suppliers of chemicals for soap powder. Before green politics Hicksons poured waste into the River Aire near a weir which churned the liquid into great cumuli of putrid foam. Soap bubbles overflowed the banks and floated along the riverside streets, leaving indelible stains on houses, clothes and cars.

Castleford has never liked being incorporated into the borough of Wakefield thus it was with great delight that Classy Cas, as they are known, downed Wakefield Trinity in the Yorkshire Cup final earlier in the season. Castleford is on the perimeter of an arc of Yorkshire clubs which circle the southern outskirts of Leeds. The arc extends through Featherstone, Wakefield, Dewsbury, Batley, Huddersfield, Halifax, Bradford and Hunslet. None is more than 30 minutes drive from Castleford. RFL public affairs executive David Howes told me,

"Leeds has a population of 700,000, Featherstone 12,000, yet the clubs are on each others's doorstep. If we were launching rugby league today we'd look at one club per major town." But Howes' boss, David Oxley, remembers a move once to close down Doncaster football club which had entered the *Guinness Book of Records* for going 40 matches without a win. "They were the league joke but suddenly a changed regime did wonders," he said. "Now they're a good side, excellent ground, and in the top half dozen clubs for second division crowds. Yet they were the club everyone would have wound up."

Castleford are certainly not candidates for closing down. Their 1990 finances enabled them to pay a world record transfer fee of $425,000 for five-eighth Graham Steadman, and $375,000 for prop Lee Crooks. It is extraordinary that a club can spend so much on two players yet can't afford minimum seating comfort for the majority of its fans. As with most English clubs, Castleford's decrepid grandstands are strong arguments for player salary caps. Castleford's most prominent past star, Malcolm Reilly, beams down from photographs on the club's boardroom walls as both player and coach. He coached Castleford to victory in the 1986 Challenge Cup and was lock when Castleford downed Reg Gasnier's Roos in 1967, the last time a Yorkshire club defeated Australia. The word was that Castleford were disappointed Australia lost the first Test because they wanted to be the first team in England to beat the Roos. Admittedly they narrowly lost to New Zealand 24-22 the previous season, but truly, Wembley was turning people's minds.

In gathering gloom the ground lights were turned on 30 minutes before the 3.30 pm kickoff with the crowd of 9000 very nearly a sellout. After only seven minutes Elias, Stuart and Lyons, all new Sunday game boys, burst Castleford's fantasy. They combined for Ricky to loop around and slip a neat pass to Brad Mackay. Deceptively fast, Mackay accelerated into a gap, dummied and put ET through for his seventh tour try. Stuart and Lyons were Australia's sixth halfback combination on tour but that try augured well for the new partnership. At 6-0 the

Roos held steady until, in the 20th minute, disaster befell them. Steadman, dashing across field, was caught by Lazarus and McGaw who came over the top to stymie Steadman off-loading. Lazarus's head crashed flush onto the side of McGaw's right knee and the more serious injury at first seemed to be to the big Canberra prop who stayed bent double, exploring a deep gash in his forehead. But McGaw had also collapsed in agony and when Shaun McRae reached him the pain on McGaw's face suggested the worst.

After the wounded departed Belcher, when he was stopped short of the line with five tackles still in hand, uncharacteristically threw a backward flick pass which went to ground. Fulton would make oblique mention of that little foolishness later. Then, after an uncoordinated loop around, Belcher bounced a short pass off Shearer's hands. Seasoned sportswriters couldn't recall Belcher making two such simple errors in half a dozen matches for Canberra. That became the Roos' ninth handling error in 25 minutes, sheer carelessness through over-confidence and while the Roos got away with it against clubs, it encouraged bad Test habits. An exception was Benny Elias, forever inventing moves only to see his assistants bungle the finale. Finally Elias cruised sideways, the defence held off — he and Lyons are past masters at this — and he picked up Lindner charging at an angle. Lindner galloped over — I say gallop, not dash, because although Lindner's tour weight was listed at under 15 stone, he was well over 16 stone — for the Roos' second try. 12-2 to Australia.

Nearing half-time Australia scored from a bewildering series of passes and changes of direction. Peter Frilingos of the *Sydney Mirror*, suddenly elbowed me, ''Quick! . . . 9,7,6,1,16,3,2.'' I hurriedly scribbled them down and he translated. Elias (9) at dummy half had passed to Stuart (7), to Lyons (6), to Belcher (1) who doubled back and threw a speculator caught by Bella (16), who wisely fed Meninga (3), who made the break and handed off to Shearer (2) to score under the posts. In the more modern Australian stadiums football writers have video screens for instant replays, but Frilingos showed he hadn't lost the old touch. Australia led 18-2.

At half-time Laurie Daley, who had been sitting in front of us, returned from the dressingroom and announced darkly, like a harbinger from a Gothic tale, "Sparkles has done his medial ligaments and Lazza has the biggest cut in his forehead you've ever seen." Though a gloomy report it also portended fresh selection challenges for the fringe Test players now resuming the field for the second half. It was noticeable that when Steadman chipped over the top, Lyons was in position to shepherd the ball while Belcher collected. As an adept at the chip-kick himself, Lyons sees them coming early. But he almost botched the next try, fading cleverly towards the corner where, instead of delivering Meninga a parcelled up overlap, he called Mal inside. It looked like becoming a clumsy move until Mal rescued it with sheer power, running through a tackle or two to curve over and score. He had a wide smile on his face as he turned and shrugged to Lyons, as though to say, "Anyway, it's a try." Australia 24-2.

From there on most of the action was with Blocker Roach and Lee Crooks, a running battle of heavy threats but light cuffs. Yet it was Marty Bella who seemed to become most inflamed and his burst of advice to referee Gerry Kershaw would not have helped his Test chances. Meninga was kept busy racing around calming his players like a sheep dog until Cas coach Van de Velde called Crooks off before he was sent off. In the second half referee Kershaw reeled off penalties 14-4 in favour of Castleford who could scarcely fail to prosper with so much ball. Thus 35-year-old captain John Joyner, who played his first Test against Australia back in 1978, produced some vintage touches for Castleford winger David Plange to complete a Classy Cas scoring move. It was cold comfort for long-suffering local fans, feet frozen and hands too numb to applaud and at fulltime Australia had run out easy winners 28-8. The final penalties were a worrying 17-7 against Australia, six of which were for backs creeping up offside. If Australia wouldn't learn that lesson Alain Sablayrolles would whistle the Ashes from Australia's grasp at Old Trafford.

A mild air of consternation pervaded the Australian dressingroom, centred around the dejected figure of Mark McGaw, packing ice around his wretched knee. It was sad to see that Promethean figure from the first Test laid low, his tour over. Said Fulton, ''He's been among our top half dozen players. He causes any defence problems so, yes, we're going to miss him.'' And Lazarus? ''He's got 17 stitches in his forehead, looks like a haversack. But he'll be OK by next weekend.''

Fulton declined to comment on the key trio, Elias, Stuart and Lyons, but he was not reticent about other elements of an ordinary Kangaroo display. He was disappointed with the ball control, not across the board, just a few players. ''We don't get much ball so whatever we do get we've got to control,'' said Fulton. ''We all know there's holes when you change the point of attack against English sides. But we aren't getting any continuity in our attack.'' This was the most severe public criticism Fulton had levelled at his team and coming just six days before the second Test it revealed a worried man.

''Sometimes a bloke might make 15 metres of hard ground and then throw the ball back 10 or 12 metres so all that hard work he's done goes out the door,'' he said. I reckoned that was Belcher he was referring to. ''Another time we've got three or four on two defenders and instead of just drawing and passing they try and do something smart, pass behind the man,'' he said. And that, I suspected, was Lyons.

The final blast was for players losing their tempers. ''We've spoken about it, we know we're going to get served and it's something we've got to put up with,'' he said. ''No matter how hard you've been done by, you should not overreact. Tonight we've given penalities away when in possession, which is unforgivable.'' That, I thought, was a subtle dig at Bella. Yet Fulton was more understanding on this score. ''It's OK for you and me sitting in the stands, but you don't know what happens out there,'' he said. ''Players have barriers they go through and some are a little closer to boiling point than others.''

Unstated by Fulton, but a gathering consensus among camp followers, was that Elias was too good to leave out of the second Test, and that Brad Mackay — the most impressive forward on the field against Castleford — had all but sewn up the lock position. Stuart, who sparked the moves which led to Ettingshausen's two tries, seemed to have narrowly ousted Langer but McGaw's injury left the rest of the backline wide open.

It was a sombre group of Aussie supporters who waited outside the dressingrooms afterwards, chatting with Castleford fans, remarking upon the similarity of place names in England and Australia. Newcastle, Penrith and Canterbury, all English and all Sydney premiership teams. ''Castleford? You got a Castleford?'' asked one local fan. An Aussie wag joked back, ''Nah, but we got a Castlemaine!''

11 A HEX ON HALIFAX

The old stone village of Delph, where I was based during my stay in England, was typical of the Pennines, four pubs and three churches in a main street so narrow that once, as I edged past an oncoming car, our rear vision wing mirrors clashed. The year Captain Cook sailed into Botany Bay, 1770, the farmer-weavers of Delph built the local Methodist church. John Wesley preached there 10 years later and it is recorded that suspicious villagers were on their best behaviour — they did not "clod" him. Delphians were highly superstitious and in 1835 three village reverends were kept busy exorcising witches, and bogarts, creatures who took the form of a woolsack with blazing red eyes as large as dinner plates. If the cow was ailing, a witch was in the bail, if the weaving warp moved badly there was a bogart in the loom.

With just one club match, against second division Halifax, before the second Test there could have been a bogart in the Kangaroo camp judging by their form against Castleford. In the Ramada I sensed an edginess, as though no one knew how to deal with uncertainty, a new experience for Kangaroos on tour. I retreated from Manchester to spend a few quiet days away from football. But I couldn't retreat far enough. Standing in Delph village high street — old stone, low lintels, quaint shopfronts — I caught a flash of maroon, gold and white outside The Swan Hotel. I stared hard — two men wearing Broncos jerseys. It was so incongruous — like finding a computer in a Dickens counting house — I approached, shook hands and discovered they were Oldham lads who had recently returned from a holiday in the Queensland sun.

Delph was surrounded by public footpaths leading through farms and up to the moors. One day I followed a path by a stream rising into the hills and was about to turn back when I heard a peculiar sound, a methodical sigh and tramp from ahead. I rounded a bend and came across an old building, blackened with age, mildew and soot. I crept up and peered in a small window and beheld a sight to transcend time.

Under dull fluorescent lights I could make out huge rolls of grey woollen yarn being wound onto hundreds of yellow spindles by a machine on rails which advanced, unwound several yards of thread from the rolls and backed off a few metres, stretching the thread and spinning it onto the spindles in a blur of speed. The machine advanced and retreated on its rails over its entire length, some 30 metres, like a bleak, remorseless machine from H.G. Wells's own 19th century imagination. The air was misty with fine wool dust, the floor greasy black with a mixture of dark wool fibre and lanoline. A factory hand suddenly appeared and as I withdrew he beckoned me in. His name was Albert Bowker, this was a woollen spinning factory and he was a spinner — a mule spinner, because the machine with the monotonous mind was known as a mule. This small, family-owned mill was the last of those which once dotted the Delph valley — a century-old industrial relic, somehow still working profitably in 1990.

Another wintry day I took to the hilltops in search of the site of a Roman encampment. As I passed a farmhouse two dogs came bounding and barking at me. One was a huge wolfhound, the other a snarling cattledog. I stood stock still, baled up, until I noticed a small boy playing in the farmhouse front yard. Excuse me, I said, evenly, would you mind calling your dogs, please. "Aye," he said helpfully. "Thuh big 'un, 'e is called Tasha, and thuh small 'un is Polly," and resumed his game.

Modern Delph has been largely taken over by Manchester's urban gentry, living in modernised stone terraces and barns and driving expensive European cars. The first of the well-appointed pubs I tried was the tiny White Lion. As the licensee pulled a half pint I studied him with a sense of deja vu. He was West Indian, slight, wore glasses, was gentle of speech and, most noticeable, had long slender fingers. I took my drink into the lounge and there on the wall was a painting of a cricketer in sweater and floppy hat, rolling his arm over — Sonny Ramadhin, the great spinner who played in the tied Test at the Brisbane Gabba in 1961. I felt as if I had found an old acquaintance. Ramadhin, shy as he is, must have a soft spot for Australians so readily did he respond to my queries. ''I was fielding at deep fine leg, with my back to the scoreboard and I thought we had won by two runs,'' he said, smiling at the memory of the tied Test. A remarkable match, he agreed, but his best, he said, was at Lords in 1950, the West Indies' first Test win in England. He took 11 wickets in all and at home a calypso record was composed to honour the spin twins Ramadhin and Valentine.

Ramadhin settled and married in England, toured with the Windies and played as a professional in county and league cricket. A diabetic, he retired from Test cricket when his legs gave out. ''I was fine up until tea, but after that my energy seemed to drain away,'' he said. He and his wife June took over the White Lion in 1962 and he contented himself with local league cricket where, aged 47, he took 134 wickets to break the season record. I could just imagine the favourable conditions, no covers overnight, moist pitches, no sight screen, and the light none too clever. Sonny chuckled. ''My action was that quick most of them didn't pick me over here,'' he said. He misses cricket, but not its legacy, swollen and aching arthritic finger joints which, in cold weather, hinder his golf grip.

When Ram, as his regulars called him, first came to Delph as a star sportsman the pub thrived but, over a quarter of a century, that changed with competition from colour television and video and the attention of traffic police with their breathalysers. The White Lion made no fortune. In 1990, under a Monopolies Commission ruling, the White Lion's owners, Bass, were compelled to divest themselves of nearly half their 7000 hotels. They offered the White Lion to Ramadhin for $500,000, which he did not have and one day, as I walked past,

I discovered the hotel was boarded up. Sonny had been waiting for a council house, a sad conclusion to a distinguished career.

Delph was 30 minutes drive south in the Pennines from Halifax, the Kangaroos' ninth tour match. On Tuesday, November 6, I drove there, circling to arrive via Haworth, 16 kms to the north. The Bronte family once lived in Haworth and I wanted to visit their former home, the Parsonage, built in 1778, 10 years before Captain Phillip sailed into Sydney Cove. It was at the Parsonage that Charlotte Bronte wrote *Jane Eyre* and Emily wrote *Wuthering Heights*. Indeed, according to a sketch drawn in 1837 by Emily on her diary paper, she and Charlotte wrote their novels in the dining room immediately on the left of the entrance hallway. Each evening at 9 pm their father, Reverend Patrick Bronte, whose study and bible room was opposite the dining room, locked the front door and called in to tell his daughters not to stay up too late. He then wound the grandfather clock on the landing halfway up the stone stairs. But the sisters wrote until quite late at night, discussing ideas as they walked round and round the large, square, mahogany dining table. There too is the roll-sided leather sofa upon which Emily died, of consumption, aged 30, refusing to admit she was ill.

Both sisters' novels were set among the moors which, in their day, reached right to the Parsonage's front door. I walked through the garden, beside the graveyard and up a narrow laneway lined with sycamores onto the moors. Where the sisters walked is now known as the Bronte Way and a sign said, "2.5 miles — Bronte Falls, 3.5 miles — Top Withins". The latter was an Elizabethan era farmhouse, now a ruin, said to have inspired Emily's *Wuthering Heights*. I walked out on the moors and read, from Charlotte's *Jane Eyre*, her midnight flight across the moors.

> There are great moors behind and on each hand of me; there are waves of mountains beyond that deep valley at my feet . . . I struck straight into the heath; I held on to a hollow I saw deeply furrowing the brown moorside; I waded knee-deep in its dark growth.

As it was late I hurried on to Halifax to dine in the town that was voted second in a national survey on the quality of life in English towns, ahead of such beauties as York (4th), Cambridge (5th) and Wakefield (17th). Halifax must be England's most picturesque football town. It is built on a hillside, deep in the Pennines and every street seems to curve away to reveal a backdrop of green, bald hills rolling into the distance. By the time Queen Victoria was crowned in 1837, textiles had made Halifax one of England's richest towns. Sir Charles Barry, who designed the Palace of Westminster, designed Halifax's Town Hall. Victorian architects were the ancient Egyptian builders of their age, their stone cutting so finely crafted that virtually no mortar was necessary between their stone blocks. But Victorians were also the great polluters and it is said that Halifax's forest of coal-fired textile chimneys inspired Blake's vision of dark Satanic mills.

The city elders vigorously policed the Clean Air Acts of the 1960s and, with stone cleaning, modern generations were delighted to find their town a butterfly emerging from the muck and grime of a century. A further boost came in 1982 with a heritage scheme to restore the town's original genteel Victorian face from the ravages of unfettered post-war commercialism. In 1987 Halifax's efforts received royal imprimatur. Prince Charles, with 40 national company chairmen in tow, paid a visit to show his guests how shopfronts need not destroy a town's face.

Halifax's motto is, "Unless the Board keep the City, the Watchman Watcheth in Vain" and this was never more true than at Thrum Hall, home of Halifax rugby league club. In 1990 they acquired a new board of directors after the club was found to be $2.25 million in debt. Ten years ago Halifax was a typical "yo-yo" club, being alternately promoted to and relegated from first division for five consecutive seasons until in November 1984 the club rang former Canterbury stalwart Chris Anderson, then playing five-eighth for Hull KR. Said Halifax secretary, Russell Murphy, "He turned up here one night, pouring rain, muddy and there was no one to meet him, so he stood outside on the pavilion steps. When the bagman arrived he looked at Chris and said, 'Who are you?' Chris said, 'I'm your new coach.' "

Anderson, then 30, employed the good offices of his father-in-law, Peter Moore, secretary of Canterbury to recruit some of Australia's best young talent, including Martin Bella, Paul Langmack, Geoff Robinson, Joe Kilroy and Cavill Heugh. Some 13 Aussies graced the register at one stage but no signing was more fortuitous than bringing former Kangaroo fullback Graham Eadie out of semi-retirement. "He knocked on joost three tarms in two year," an old-time Fax fan assured me. "If he were to coom back tomorra' they'd pack ground and he'd be given freedom of t' city." Anderson gave Halifax three glorious years, winning the first division championship in 1985-86, Wembley in 1986-87 and losing at Wembley in 1987-88. But those successes masked a real decline which saw them fall from on top of the league table in 1985-86 to near relegation by the time of their second visit to Wembley. Sudden death Cup successes can be notoriously misleading.

Anderson retired and the reins were handed to ex-St George halfback and Brisbane coach Ross Strudwick. He arrived in a town sublimely unaware its team was sliding. "I'd walk into a pub and they'd put me on their shoulders, sing to me, and they hardly knew me," said Strudwick. "I was totally embarrassed." But it slowly turned sour and Strudwick's unorthodox coaching took the full brunt. "All I was doing was using a short line defence," he said. An orthodox back line defence stands wide, moves up in an arc and forces the attack back inside. Strudwick reversed this, bunching his defenders close to the ruck and showing the opposition his tryline. "They think there's a gap out wide, but there isn't because my blokes have numbered off and know their man," he said. "It looks ridiculous because I exaggerate but the opposing side gets sucked in. They start throwing Wally Lewis-size passes — and they always drop a few of those — to get the ball wide." Strudwick's theory is that having moved the ball the breadth of the field, the opposition wastes the next ruck or so because their forwards are still plodding over from the far side. "They're attacking and should be dictating play, but in fact you're shifting them all over the paddock," he said. Penrith now used it, he said, the Broncos and Widnes used it and Australia used it against Leeds. "But Halifax couldn't accept it," he said.

After seven months Strudwick departed, Illawarra's John Dorahy and then Castleford's Alan Hardisty succeeded him but by 1990 the club was in second division with horrendous debts. Said club secretary Russell Murphy wistfully, "When we reached the peaks we did with Chris Anderson, the pressure was on to maintain it, otherwise we were disappointing everyone — ourselves, our fans, the town. Probably our directors let their hearts rule their heads. Our signings just didn't come off." A new five-man board — including local lad Tony Gartland, one of England's wealthiest businessmen — took over in April 1990, investing $1 million to pay out Halifax's creditors. They also inserted an unusual clause in the new company's articles of association — they are not allowed to borrow money. Said new club chairman, Peter Marsland, "We were quite adamant we wouldn't go down the same path again. We can't borrow. If you'll forgive the example, it stops us going into debt to buy Australian players who want half a dozen air tickets for their family, accommodation, car, school fees, gas and electricity bills and permission to go home in February for the start of the Australian season."

Thrum Hall was an old hilltop farm — many of the local farm collectives were called halls — and thrums were the lengthways threads left on a loom when the woven cloth was cut off. Thrum Hall's name was a leftover from days when farmer-weavers ran a cottage industry on the hillsides. The Halifax Cricket, Football and Athletic Club bought the farm in 1886 and after a gesture at levelling, laid out a football field which today still slopes an extraordinary 3.6 metres away from the grandstand touchline. While the site provided superb views, Thrum Hall's high position had its drawbacks. Because it is so high it is frequently snowed in or iced over when fields lower in the town are playable. Cavill Heugh, of Brisbane and Leeds, remembered growing a beard when he played with Halifax to protect his face against nicks from ice slivers.

On an increasingly chilly evening I parked on the Gibbet Street approach to Thrum Hall. A gibbet is a guillotine and Halifax used the beheading blade until 1650, nearly half a century after it had been abandoned elsewhere in England. It was a common sentence for thieves who stole dyed woven wool stretched to dry on tenterhooks outside weavers' cottages. Since the cloth was often the weaver's sole income such a theft could condemn the weaver and his family to starvation.

As I locked my car I ran into some media colleagues including the august Jack Gibson who, all the way to the football ground, stopped amenably for photographs and autographs. Jack recounted how the owner of the hotel at which he was lodging had rambled on endlessly about the hotel's history and how it was once visited by the King. "Wally, eh?" Jack had said, amused at having finally stumped the proprietor. Thrum Hall was filling with nearly 9000 fans, with one third of the main grandstand taken by Aussies. Some wag had hung a sign over the boundary fence: "Free Russ Hinze, He Only Took What He Could Eat." Little pieces of Australiana like that threw me after so many months away. Laurie Nicholls arrived in his trademark singlet but was soon flapping his hands and wrapping his arms around his waist. I learned later he came down with a cold after this evening. The cosiest fan of all was a north Queenslander inside a tan-coloured kangaroo suit leaping about the field. Col McLean, otherwise known as Skippy, had become popular with English crowds and television audiences since he bounced out of a *Rugby League Week* tour bus onto the sidelines.

McLean, 30, hailed from Yungaburra (when I initially spelt that Youngerborough I knew I'd been too long in England) and worked as a machinery serviceman in the Kidston goldmine, 500 kms west of Cairns. He played a bit of rugby league at Tugun on the Gold Coast, watched the mascots in the Sydney competition — the Rooster, Magpie and Reggie the Rabbit — and realised he had never seen a Roo out in front of the Austra-

lian team. Having booked into a supporters tour he started
ringing around Cairns fancy dress hirers and canvas makers
before tracking down a theatre props artist who worked with
foam rubber. They visited libraries to get the kangaroo physiology right and then began countless fittings, cutting and joining. "At first every time I moved the foam would tear, so we'd
throw that away, cut it bigger and glue it again," said Col.
Three months and $300 later — including a $60 pair of top class
Maddison boxing gloves — McLean's Roo was rarin' to go.

Having grown up in the country he knew kangaroo manner-
isms but found it difficult to maintain the kangaroo crouch for
too long. "When I straighten up it kinks the legs," he said.
"When I hop there's a fair weight on me legs and they get sore
after a while. But if you find a post or something you can lean
on it, like an old 'roo leanin' on a fence." For a bit of fun he
practised the Ali shuffle, hanging his gloved hands loose and
then delivering a flurry of sharp left and right hooks. "One Friday night I gave her a trial and bounced through the
Yungaburra pub in her and brought the bloody house down,"
said Col. "They loved it, I jumped around hookin' and
shufflin' until I was done in."

Col wasn't sure how his suit would be received in England
but when his bus tour leader, *Rugby League Week* photographer,
Col Whelan, saw the outfit he grabbed McLean and said,
"Come with me," and using his media pass he hustled McL-
ean swiftly past puzzled gatekeepers. "Wembley security officials had a bit of a look," said McLean. "They frisked the
padded parts but once I got known they'd say, 'Here's the
Roo, away you go.' So I head for the nearest tunnel out of the
way and when we score I run on and do a bit of a dance."

Skippy was a welcome boost to Aussie morale but alone he
couldn't match the impact of Land of Hope and Glory at Wembley. Waiting for the Halifax kickoff I spotted Trevor O'Rourke,
owner of Travelworld, the company which had organised the
Rugby League Week tours. What was the bush telegraph like between the buses? I asked him. "Excellent," he replied.
"Why?" I put my idea to him to marshall the enthusiasm of the

thousands of travelling supporters. Malcolm Reilly had admitted that when Great Britain were met by the 80-strong Philharmonia Chorus and two military bands, it had both moved and stirred his players. The Kangaroos must have been daunted but we couldn't help them. British football crowds are supreme stadium singers, Aussies a little self conscious and besides, we were vastly outnumbered.

In Tolstoy's *War and Peace*, before the Battle of Borodino, Prince Andre Bolkonsky reflected that in war a battalion is sometimes stronger than a division and yet sometimes weaker than a single company. "Have we not seen, thanks to some resolute madman, 5000 men have held their ground against 30,000?" he said. "Success can depend on one private who shouts 'Hurrah!' " Or, perhaps, on one small section of Old Trafford singing the one song all Australians will sing, aggressively, wholeheartedly. I told Trevor, "We have to welcome the Kangaroos onto Old Trafford with the song that should have been our national anthem — Waltzing Matilda!" O'Rourke, a true patriot, lit up. "Good as gold, leave it with me," he said.

Allan Langer captained the Kangaroos in the absence of Meninga and Elias — was this a consolation for another honour soon to be lost? Anyway, these Tuesday nighters took off like a team still contesting Test places while Halifax set out to prove that they were worthy opponents for the tourists. It made for an explosive mix but it was Mark Geyer who collected a spilled bomb to score first. Halifax drew level at 6-6 when their speedy Australian centre, Greg Austin, sidestepped his way over — Austin led the English league tryscoring several times during the season. His try encouraged an ill-natured Halifax crowd no end and sitting as we were, in amongst them, they let us know. "Get on t' phone now, pal, get on t' bluidy phone now," a spectator goaded 2UE's Ray Hadley who was calling the scores to Australia by portable telephone. Oh, it was fun out there in those opening minutes with Halifax breathing fire and brimstone.

But after 15 minutes the pressure fell in Halifax's mill and the Kangaroos steamed in for five more tries before half-time. They went chronologically to Sargent, Alexander, Kevin Walters (who was struck on the head after he scored by a one pound coin thrown from the crowd), Johns and Hancock. Referee Brian Galtress was exceedingly benevolent with two rulings — Walters' try came after a blatant knock-on and Hancock touched down after the half-time hooter had sounded. Johns' try was the best, handling twice in a spectacular exchange with Dale Shearer. As livewire Johns walked back he waved to the Aussie supporters who began a song in praise of him. What were they singing, a Halifax lad behind me asked his father. "Some sort of Aboriginal chant probably," said the father knowledgeably. Listening carefully I deciphered:

> That's the way, Johnsie does the hula,
> That's the way, Johnsie does the hula,
> The hula hula hula hula hoo.

"It's just a fun bus tour song," explained a supporter afterwards. "We got fed up with the Poms singing at us all the time." The first half showed how imprudent it can be to match an outclassed second division side with Australia. The fixture raised the expectations of the home crowd which in turn increased the pressure on the home side. One way Halifax slowed play was to cling to the Kangaroos' boots in the tackle. Mark Sargent was sin-binned for lashing out with his feet, trying to free his legs. The Aussie frustration was clear to all except the Fax fans who were urging, "Send the bastard off."

The Roos led 32-6 at oranges however *Rugby League Week*'s Tony Durkin, working the sideline for Channel 10, said later that the Halifax coach, Peter Roe, had approached referee Galtress at half-time and growled, "Put your brain into gear!" Having allocated penalties 5-4 to Halifax in the first 40 minutes, Mr Galtress suddenly found 10 more against the Roos in the second stanza to finish the match tally 15-6 to Halifax. He also pulled up three tries, one of which, by Dale Shearer, sprinting through to latch onto a Langer chip, ranked with any try on tour. Finally referee Galtress gave Langer 10 minutes sinbin for an offence committed by Greg Alexander. Galtress didn't see it so accepted the word of his linesman. But Martin Bella insisted, ''That linesman was looking into the crowd when it happened. He turned around, saw the player on the ground and put his flag up. No bullshit, we were standing right there.''

Given this flood of penalty possession Halifax ran in three worthy wingers' tries in the second half to the Roos' one. The final bell, at 36-18, was a relief to all and when we finally squeezed into the visitors' dressingroom we found two depressed men. One was Michael Hancock who was slumped on a rubdown table icing his ankle. It seemed only a minor twist when he was replaced but Dr Nathan Gibbs was giving him only 50-50 of making Old Trafford. Hancock was so profoundly depressed I left him with his thoughts. The other person suffering was Bobby Fulton. His face was a mask of shock and confusion. ''That referee decided 32 points was enough, shut up shop,'' he said. Fulton ran through the litany of disallowed tries — 18 points worth which would have produced a final score of 50 points — and penalties. ''The second half was exactly the same as the Test,'' said Fulton. ''It just goes to show that any side can compete with you with the help of penalties. That mob were legless until they got 10 second-half penalties. No wonder our blokes get frustrated.'' However familiar Bozo's song may have sounded, referee Galtress did dictate the second half. Yet the newspaper match reports I read the next morning all lauded Halifax's second half revival without recording the vital penalty statistic. The reports camouflaged a substantially improved performance by Australia and even though only Shearer from this team ended up in the Test side for Old Trafford, their play augured well as a reflection of squad spirit.

That night, returning from Halifax across the Saddleworth moors to Delph, I struck heavy fog on the peaks. I slowed and in a less dense patch suddenly glimpsed the edge of the moors with the lights of Manchester glowing dully in the distance. The wind was blowing the fog up a bluff, streaming into the night sky, backlit by the city, like a blizzard blowing off the top of Annapurna. It was so stunning I pulled into a layby, dimmed the headlights and got out to watch. The air was freezing, the wind numbing, no traffic, no noise except the swish of air blowing across the lonely, empty gorse and bracken moors. Gazing at this bright white aurora something made me turn, look behind and to the side. Nothing. Just the diffused red of the tail-lights and the mist twisting and whirling. I sensed neither witches nor bogarts but I jumped back in and drove off a shade more quickly than was sensible given the visibility.

The next day I drove back up to the spot and pulled in at nearby Snoopy's Snack Bar, a tea and coffee caravan. There I learned from the proprietor, Don Clayton, that this was where the infamous moors murders were committed by Ian Brady and Myra Hindley a quarter of century ago. When police finally arrested the pair they found an audio tape destined to become the most notorious piece of evidence ever presented in a British court of law — 13 minutes of 10-year-old Lesley Ann Downey, screaming and pleading for her life. Only three bodies from five murders were originally found. With the help of Hindley and Brady the search for the two last victims was renewed in 1987 and a fourth grave uncovered. The last victim, never found, was Keith Bennett, a cheerful bespectacled 12 year-old-boy. Don Clayton served me a steaming hot cup of tea. "See that black car over there," he said, nodding. "That's Keith Bennett's uncle. He comes here every Sunday with a metal detector." Bennett was apparently wearing metal framed glasses and a snake-shaped, metal belt buckle when he disappeared. "It's too wet to search today," said Don. "It's wet like this 80 per cent of the time on top of the moors."

Later in the week I rang Trevor O'Rourke regarding our planned Matilda assault at Old Trafford. He reported word had spread — a tour leader, Scott Rigney, had photocopied the words of Waltzing Matilda and distributed them among the buses. Coachloads had been practising in hotel foyers and cruising along the motorways. "That's just our 500," said O'Rourke. "The message has spread to other tour operators and each bus has appointed a song leader." Kangaroos manager Keith Barnes looked pleased when I told him. "Great," he said. "It'll give the boys a helluva lift when they walk out." We Aussie supporters were ready with our shout of "Hurrah". When you're one down and two to go in the Ashes it has to be War not Peace.

12 SECOND TEST —
MAGNIFICENT MENINGA

A funny thing happened to me after the first Test at Wembley. I joined the throng in the joyous Great Britain dressingroom, introduced myself to Ellery Hanley who was sitting on a bench and congratulated him. Hanley stood up, muttered something inaudible and turned his back on me. Second rower Roy Powell, sitting beside him, urged, "Yeah, go on, you tell him, Ellery!" I knew of Hanley's dislike of the media but had heard only good reports on Powell. His spontaneous outburst bore Hanley's influence and Hanley's media vendetta requires explanation.

The Black Prince, the Black Pearl, "The Trymaster" as his photograph is entitled in the Rugby League Hall of Fame, is well known to Australians from his stints with Balmain and Wests. Mark Sargent one evening remarked to me, "Gees that Hanley's strong. Everyone says move up quickly and grab him, but grabbing him is only the first part, keeping hold of him is another. In the Test he brushed off blokes like Paul Sironen. No one in Sydney brushes off Sirro." Suspicions that Hanley enjoyed privileged status in England were raised before the Kangaroos arrived. He was sent off for backchatting England's leading referee, Robin Whitfield. According to Whitfield, as Hanley departed he warned Whitfield he would end up refereeing second division. Hanley's two-match suspension was halved on appeal and Whitfield was banished to second division for six weeks.

News of Hanley's anti-media stance spread quickly after Wembley, even soccer-mad Fleet Street papers carried page features describing the full Hanley history. He was born in

Leeds to West Indian migrant parents who subsequently returned home. He grew up amid some hardship but by the time he turned 17 had begun to make his mark in junior rugby league. At this stage most newspaper profiles lapsed into euphemisms leaving a gap in his football career unexplained. It was northern-based Alan Thomas of the *Daily Express* who published the exact details. Hanley was jailed for three and a half years for burglary, and three years later was given another six months for dishonest handling of goods. Thomas, vice-chairman of the Rugby League Writers' Association and a journalist of high repute, was not thanked by the RFL hierarchy for rehashing this during the Test series. But as he explained to me, once his London sports editor decided to publish, any sub-editor could have pulled Hanley's record from the computer files. Of course the remedy was also in Hanley's hands.

Yet it was not publication of this criminal record which soured Hanley. In 1988, when captain of Great Britain, Hanley was involved in a paternity suit which provoked the expected headlines, including one labelling him a "Rugby Rat". What Hanley could not forgive was discovering a *News of the World* photographer in the shrubbery outside his bedroom window in Leeds. Hanley's disgust was entirely justified but not his persistent refusal to differentiate between scandal-mongering tabloid spies and rugby league writers, most of whom had reported him in good faith for years. At full-time at Wembley, Hanley pushed past the BBC's Grandstand television camera, ignoring one of the nation's biggest rating sports programs. It compared poorly with Mal Meninga's early morning appearance on ITV in London, to promote the game of rugby league.

By ostracising all media Hanley embarrassed RFL public affairs executive, David Howes. "I agree it is probably ethically, morally and managerially wrong and Ellery knows the decision could cost him the captaincy," said Howes. "But the fact is the players regard him as the captain in Great Britain's dressing-room whether he has the title officially or not." According to the *Observer*'s Paul Wilson, moves to depose Hanley were scotched by coach Malcolm Reilly because Hanley threatened he would not play unless captain. Hanley was annoyed by one of the new spate of newspaper features and protested about it to manager Maurice Lindsay at training before the second Test. Hanley's antagonism towards the media was backfiring on his mental build-up to the most important Test of his career.

On Wednesday 7 November, the morning after Halifax, Fulton read out his second Test team. Injuries and form had produced six changes from the first Test so we were about to examine Fulton's claim that every member of the tour squad was Test standard. Cliff Lyons was five-eighth, replacing Stuart who moved to his normal position at half, displacing Langer. That night Langer, having a bad trot at cards, exclaimed, "I'm having a great tour aren't I. I've done my Test spot and now I'm doing my dough!" Even Queenslanders agreed that Benny Elias, after years of understudying Royce Simmons, Greg Conescu and then Kerrod Walters, deserved his hooker's spot. The pack lost 20 kgs but gained speed with Brad Mackay at lock, Lindner shifting into the second row to replace Cartwright. Hancock's crutches gave Dale Shearer his chance though with 13 Tests under his belt "Rowdy" was a safe choice.

Martin Bella had lost out to Glenn Lazarus who would play with special taping around his wounded forehead. And Laurie Daley, at centre, would have pain-killing injections in his hand and wear a leather protector. For the latter pair, Fulton was fortunate to have on tour Johnny Lewis, vastly experienced in protecting world champion Jeff Fenech's knuckles and repairing boxers' eyebrows. Lewis was an unusual addition to the team of trainers but there was an extra dimension to his role. "I don't know too many people like Johnny Lewis," said Bozo admiringly one day. "He's never ruffled, never rattled. The players love him. He's a fatherly type. I'm a bit young to have that type of a role, not that I'd want it anyway."

Clearly Australia's hopes rested on the performances of Lyons and Daley, both of whom coincidentally played their early football in Group Nine in the Riverina, made inauspicious debuts in State of Origin football but had won Sydney premierships. Daley, 21, Junee born and bred, was spotted as a school-boy by Canberra coach Don Furner and signed with the Raiders in 1986. Two years later he was in Country Place of Origin Firsts, thrilled to be lining out beside Peter Sterling. The next year, 1989, he hit Lang Park in the first State of Origin and, on his own admission, was overawed. "I think I was just glad to make the side," he told me. "I didn't sort of realise I had to keep going. It was so quick and intense, 26 great players."

Daley's snake eyes, spikey hair and speed made him a ready villain for Queensland crowds, but in truth he is friendly, intelligent and observant. At Fourex promotions — usually socials in local pubs — he initiated conversations with drinkers and they responded to his interest. None of which was going to help him at Old Trafford. Would he ever throw a punch on a football field again? Laurie laughed. "Definitely not, it's a bit of a lesson eh?" he said, examining his hand. "But, you know, I would have felt worse if I hadn't gone in and helped Sparkles."

Cliff Lyons, 29, had long dwelt in the shadow of Wally Lewis, but his representative career was also hampered by an unpredictability not appreciated by selectors. His Dally M player-of-the-year award in 1990 had demonstrated a new maturity and won him his tour. Born in Narrandera, outside Wagga, second eldest of six Aboriginal children, he moved to Sydney for schooling and didn't return to the Riverina until he was 18. There he played Group Nine for the Gundagai Tigers against the south-west NSW towns of Cootamundra, Junee and Harden, usually on dustbowls, learning all the tricks of elusive and economic running that were to become his trademark. His trail took him to Sydney Norths, Leeds, Manly and Sheffield Eagles and though he's classed as city for Place of Origin, "I'm country at heart mate," he said. In the deciding match of the 1987 State of Origin, Lyons made two potentially match-winning breaks, neither of which succeeded. Lyons' reputation, undeservedly, took the full impact for NSW's loss. Fulton knew all about Cliff from coaching him at Manly and he took the medicine man approach — he would not exorcise the villain from Cliff for fear of losing the genius.

Cliff enjoyed cards, often with Benny Elias, Chris Johns or Allan Langer, and listening to him explain his slanting running, I recognised the gambler in his approach to football. He's genial, not as complex as his football, and accompanies a wry humour with just the ghost of smiles. As soon he was selected he rang his mother, Melva, and organised her flight to Manchester for his first Test. His one stipulation when she arrived, ''I told her she had to leave me alone, I had a lot on me mind.''

Fulton closed the Test team's training session to television the next day — Thursday 8 November — though no spy in his right mind would be out on such a morning, so cold I could take only brief notes before my fingers seized. Every few minutes I plunged my hands into my pockets to thaw before scribbling some more lines. All the media were wrapped in a variety of ski anoraks, parkas with hoods, hats, gloves and fur-lined boots. I wrapped a scarf around my head, prompting colleagues to liken me to a Franciscan monk, while others less kindly referred to me as Mother Theresa.

The following day, match eve, I was invited to discuss the Test on the BBC's Greater Manchester Radio with their rugby league caller Malcolm Lord. I found myself suggesting that the Kangaroos would show what they were made of and win a close match, or else succumb to the pressure and be well beaten. Lord raised his eyebrows at this, expecting no doubt a more gung-ho Aussie appraisal. Look at the scrum base trios, I argued. Great Britain's Hanley, Gregory and Schofield had 76 Tests between them compared with Mackay, Stuart and Lyons with a total of just two. Even so, I said, ''I'll be shocked if we lose because it would mean that, unbeknowns to us all, Australian rugby league standards have slipped backwards and English standards taken far greater strides than we could have imagined. And I don't believe that is the case.''

I might not have been so sanguine had I known what was transpiring back at the Ramada Hotel that Friday evening. In the aftermath of Wembley, Fulton had emphasised that a priority was an interview with French referee Alain Sablayrolles. He would be telling the Frenchman there were two teams playing in the Test, that Great Britain was equally offside and he would demonstrate it with a video if necessary.

A meeting was set for Friday afternoon at 3 pm, however Sablayrolles' flight from France was delayed and he did not reach his hotel, the Periquito in Oldham, until 6 pm. The English RFL Controller of Referees, Fred Lindop, rang Fulton and invited him to the hotel for a conference. Sablayrolles knew full well Australia's unhappiness with him. Lindop told me, ''What worried Alain was that Bob wanted to go through the videotape with him and crucify him, as you can with every referee after any game.'' Accordingly Sablayrolles had received instructions from the French Rugby League that if anyone wished to interview him they had to come to him. Fulton angrily said he had had enough. He had been waiting for three hours, he said, he had a dinner engagement and it wasn't his job to drive all over Manchester chasing referees. Lindop was in Sablayrolles' room, together with a competent translator — the daughter of Sam Shephard, the Referees' Development and Recuitment officer — who knew her rugby league. Said Lindop, ''He's not the most gentlemanly of characters is Bobby. I refereed him for years and he can be very abrasive. He had the temerity to insist that the referee come to him, he assumed this God-like status and got shirty about the whole operation. That was a major blue by the Australians.'' As a compromise, Fulton requested Lindop, with the help of the interpreter, relay to Sablayrolles the Australian complaints about the play-the-ball offside penalties.

If it wasn't so serious it would have been laughable. Because I lived the other side of Oldham I drove the route to the Ramada a hundred times during the tour. Oldham was 16 kms from the Ramada and at that time of the evening it would have taken Fulton 20 minutes to reach the Periquito hotel. Fulton had made Sablayrolles almost the sole issue of the first Test loss — rarely a day went by without some reference to the Frenchman. Even in his final Thursday evening press conference Fulton had said, "We won't be changing our style, it's up to the referee to change his." Here was the Australian management declining the opportunity to air their grievances in a calm atmosphere, with an official interpreter and England's top refereeing executive in attendance. Fulton prided himself on meticulous attention to detail in match preparation. But obstinacy, as well as a strength, can be a failing and his behaviour over Sablayrolles was not consistent with his professed concern that the Kangaroos receive a fair deal from referees on tour.

When I queried Fulton after the Test he said, "Lindop could have been saying anything to him but the bottom line was that the first penalty of the game went against Britain for offside so maybe he said something that was positive from our point of view." Lindop told me he spoke with Sablayrolles that Friday evening and on Saturday morning the Frenchman accompanied him to a seminar for English coaches which Lindop holds annually at Old Trafford cricket ground. That same morning, NSW Referees Coordinator, Dennis Braybrook, on holidays and staying in the Periquito as well, took a phone call from the Australian management trying to contact Lindop. Suddenly they were anxious to know that their message had got through to Sablayrolles. Braybrook joined Lindop at the Old Trafford seminar and afterwards they had a broken English-Franglais discussion about offside with Sablayrolles. He gestured that in France, when players infringed the five metres but were returning onside, if they came back with their hands in the air he knew they were not offside. "Braybrook went in and told that to the Australians and I told Great Britain," said Lindop. "That breakthrough was lucky for the Australians. Alain couldn't be stood over. He was completely and utterly without nerves. He wasn't Latin in manner, or on the field."

At Old Trafford I pushed through ticket queues in showery rain and stepped into the Red Devils souvenir and clothing shop, as big as a commercial sports store. Jerseys, shirts, the whole United rig, plus festoons of colours, scarves and caps. For two quid you could buy a pair of women's white briefs embossed with a small, red, pointed-tailed figure and the words, "I've got the Devil in me." Don't tell me you sell many of these, I said to an attendant, incredulous. "Not in your size sir, ha, ha." Although the Test was a 46,000 sellout, the shop was not busy — there is little cross-pollination between rugby league and soccer fans.

The floodlights were already on as I took my seat behind that dynamic 2GB pair, Peter "Zorba" Peters and Greg "Hollywood" Hartley. Those two belligerents provided the pre-match entertainment because they don't call a match they shout it, at the decibels required to drown a trail-bike race. They got off to a good start with, "WAR with football boots on at Old Trafford today it'll be!" The Waltzing Matilda singing sheet for the Aussie tour followers instructed them to begin after the cheers died down when Australia took the field. "Sing it loud and proud folks," a footnote added and so they did, perhaps 5000 strong, and were rewarded by Dale Shearer and Steve Roach trotting over to acknowledge them. I felt a tinge of pride that Australia weren't overwhelmed pre-match as they had been at Wembley.

Among the media benches a ballot for the final score resulted in 21 favouring Australia and 19 Britain and the match proved just as even in the opening minutes. Laurie Daley pulled off two superb tackles, first running down fleet Offiah and then driving iron-man Hanley backwards — no mean feats either of those. Despite 20 minutes camped in Australia's half, Britain could not score, Schofield missing with two ill-advised attempts at drop-goals. Hanley found himself storming cul-de-sacs in attack and resorted to playing tight in defence where he was topping the tackle count. Australia countered this midfield defence by swinging the ball wide. Eventually Lyons, Stuart and Daley, each under pressure of tackles, strung together a line of fingertip passes to give Shearer an unmarked dash to score. Steve Roach gave the in-goal Pom crowd two huge fingers up as Rowdy skidded over. He's some patriot, Blocker. I had originally doubted the wisdom of playing Daley but, of all things, his handling dexterity made Shearer's try. Nobody expected Meninga to convert and he didn't. I awaited the judgement day when lack of a goal kicker must cost Australia a match, and hoped it wasn't today.

Great Britain made it 4-2 after Eastwood goaled from a doubtful penalty, awarded through an erroneous intercession by linesman, Mr B. Turgoose. That was the signal for Zorba to holler at 2GB listeners, ''God gave him a beautiful name didn't He? The Goose! He comes from York, beautiful place, but this bloke's as archaic as the town!''

At half-time the Lions were exhausted. Assistant coach Phil Larder ordered them to sit down. ''Don't talk, take four minutes to recover, take the air in,'' he commanded. The Lions were knocked up, resulting from often superfluous cover-defending against Australia's wide ball strategy. Hanley noted that one of the Lions' strong points, their communication, had fallen away as they tired. They should also name drop Australia's danger men, particularly Elias. ''If we name him — 'I've got Elias' — we'll force him to move the ball earlier,'' said Hanley.

Early in the second half Britain lost Offiah, replaced by tall Paul Loughlin, and Australia lost a certain try when Elias was held up over the line. The British response was for Schofield to turn the defence inside out with a dummy that conned Elias, Stuart, Roach and Sironen into looking the wrong way while Schofield put Paul Dixon though a gap. Just as at Wembley, when McGaw bounced through two tackles, so Dixon leapt up from Belcher and Meninga's tackle collision to plunge over. Britain now led 6-4 but five minutes later Australia scored the try of the decade which by rights should have sealed the Test. No fewer than 15 passes preceded the score, by Lyons. I later timed the ball to be in non-stop play for 36 seconds; Elias handled twice and Lyons three times; Elias began it and Lyons finished it. The Kangaroos refused to let the ball die, running it razzle-dazzle, probing, battering at the British defence, reforming and attacking again, all in the one movement until, in the closing moments near the tryline, Ettingshausen centre-kicked — a much maligned rugby union tactic — for Lyons to collect a perfect bounce and dive over, punching the air in triumph. It was Cliff's try — his first Test try — and he will never score one better.

The curious feature of that try was Britain's apparent willingness to let Lyons run. "We didn't decide to," Phil Larder told me afterwards. Britain's error began earlier in the week after a conversation Widnes coach Doug Laughton had with Laurie Daley about joining the club. Daley idly commented that Australia were surprised by the intensity of the British defence and might slow Britain down with chip-kicks. Laughton relayed this intelligence to Reilly who devised a counter, dropping a sweeper back — a bobby the Poms call him — and the task fell to Schofield. "I bobbied from the second or third tackle," said Schofield later. "So in the second half Cliff had a lot more freedom." Whatever decided Reilly to adopt such a rigid pre-match plan, Daley's aside to Laughton assumed the proportions of counter-intelligence disinformation as Lyons swooped and sailed through undefended space. Perhaps Reilly should have forgotten tactics and advised Schofield, "Use the Force" — rely on instinct — as Australia ran to a 10-6 lead.

Britain twice raided to the Australian quarter and twice Elias the thief, Elias the magpie, stole possession by raking in the play-the-ball, depriving Britain of at least eight attacking rucks. How the British must have detested him! Emboldened by success, and perhaps by the chants of "Aussie, Aussie, Aussie" Ricky Stuart moved into overdrive, torpedoed an arcing pass to Brad Mackay on the halfway . . . and instead found Paul Loughlin. The big British centre stretched out an arm — "a giraffe" Fulton called him — juggled the ball into the air and intercepted. Away he swept, for 50 metres to swallow-dive over. Only Laurie Daley's hopeful chase kept Loughlin from veering in under the posts. That surely was the Ashes clincher. I began composing magnanimous thoughts, that the Poms deserved to win, that it was healthy for the game, and other such nonsense. The Kangaroos gathered on their line, Lazarus's stitches seeping blood, Lindner looking hollow-eyed, while Stuart held his hands on his head in horror. First Meninga and then Belcher spoke to him. "They told me to lift my head, I had to go on with it, we were still in it, we had 12 minutes to go," said Stuart later. "But it's hard to lift your head when you've let down not just the blokes there but the whole touring party. Mate it felt like I'd had a death in the family." But death holds no fear for Heroes. When they set out on an adventure they either triumph or lose their all. Stuart's journey was not yet complete.

Paul Eastwood was one of the first to congratulate Loughlin and to ask him if he wanted to take the vital conversion. It was not difficult but was from left field and suited right-footed Loughlin more than left-footed Eastwood. Loughlin shook his head. Those who suggest it was Loughlin's kick have forgotten that in 1988, at 6-6 in the first Test in Sydney, Loughlin had a similar kick to give the Lions the lead and missed. So as Eddie Waring would have said, "The Ashes, all on this kick." Eastwood was plainly nervous, checked his boots once more, took a deep breath. And missed. 'Ee, poor lud. 10-10 with 10 minutes left. "Come on England, come on England!" the crowd chanted, forgetting the Great Britain connection momentarily.

No playwright would dare script the closing melodrama. First Stuart's field goal missed, then Schofield's. Daley was abused for grubber kicking on the fifth instead of feeding Stuart. Finally Australia set it up, Elias at dummy half, Stuart perfectly positioned, but Andy Gregory, way offside, dashed at Stuart and Benny's attempt skidded under the bar. "Andy read it and came at 100 mph," said Elias later. "I've kicked many a field goal but I felt terrible when it missed, especially when Ricky let me know it was his kick. You have to cop it, but I never said anything to him when he passed that intercept." In the heat of play Benny could not have realised that the intercept was gnawing at Stuart's guts and that, to Stuart, it appeared he had been denied the chance of redeeming himself with the field goal. The video vindicates Elias but Meninga said of these stuff-ups later, "We didn't play with too much thought and some guys took it upon themselves to perform miracles." Not much grace under pressure there.

In injury time Schofield elected for a draw or an Australian error and punted the ball into touch five metres from the Kangaroo line. The stadium applauded this sensible football, the ball now 90 safe metres from the home tryline. Perhaps a drawn match mentality overtook Britain because on the fifth tackle the British defence seemed somnolent. Lyons ran left, nothing on there, and then doubled back to the open side and passed to Stuart. He ran to the advantage line, brushed past Lee Jackson's ineffectual arm and suddenly saw not just an open field but divine absolution ahead. As Stuart crossed his own quarterline I caught the blur of a figure in the background accelerating forward far faster than all others — Mal Meninga.

Stuart ran like a hare and in pursuit came Hanley, Gibson, Gregory and Loughlin. On the edge of the pack was ET and mowing them all down from the rear, like a champion racehorse, came Meninga. Over the halfway line, 30 . . . 50 . . . 75 metres downfield, almost in slow motion. So much in rugby league is hidden or confused, yet this sequence took on the clarity of a stage performance, every step imprinted on the minds of 46,000 spectators. Hanley was first beaten — there comes a moment when even a champion athlete must align himself with his consciousness and watch his physical being fail. No one could catch Stuart but fullback Steve Hampson loomed. Stuart reined back, heard ET's call but saw ET was covered. He heard Mal's call, glanced left, glanced right, no Mal. Meninga had reached the point where only the extremely gifted continue. Blocked for a run he cannoned into Gibson and shouldered him aside. Stuart prepared to chip ahead for ET, peeped left one last time and there was Mal! ''George was absolutely flying when he got the ball off me,'' said Stuart later. ''I was rooted, but he was travelling like a truck and that was the best feeling in my life when I saw him score that try.''

We were all on our feet, the entire Australian press corps, stamping, thumping and roaring. ''What a try! What a f . . . ing try!'' I shouted, and suddenly remembered Zorba and Hollywood's open radio lines in front of me, but as usual they were shouting even louder. Mal and Ricky were bent double, hands on knees, utterly spent. The Brits were on their haunches, mortified. The green and gold terraces burst forth with Waltzing Matilda once more and seconds later, when the siren sounded, Mal held his padded arm up like a giant crab claw and called his team to pay tribute to the singing Aussies. Then came the emotional embraces, Mal and Ricky mostly. Stuart, once heir to Australian rugby union captain and half-back Nick Farr-Jones, showed what a gain he was for rugby league, while Meninga showed what a magnificent Olympian he could have been. Their try was already being written into history, snatching a miraculous 14-10 victory for Australia.

The dejected British players shook hands with the Kanga-roos — Hanley fleetingly, Schofield generously. The Australian dressingroom was locked to us for several minutes though I could hear the chorus of Aussie Boys through the door — ''We had a win today, we are the boys you know, we showed them how to play, we are the Aussie Boys.'' Steve Roach sat, still in working kit, steam rising from his body. ''How many times did I pray they wouldn't kick a field goal,'' he murmured. Cliff Lyons' eyes reflected a deep merriment. Proved a point to his critics had he? ''They can all go jump now, can't they?'' he said, grinning. Meninga was contemplating some warm inner glow. Know who you knocked out of the way? I asked him. ''Yeah, Carl Gibson, that's legal, you can do that, you can shoulder charge when you're both running for the ball,'' he said, with a wicked grin. And his magnificent run? ''ET was there too,'' he said. ''I think I breezed straight past ET didn't I? Sheer pace and acceleration!'' For modest Mal to even joke about his ability showed how elated he was. From Dr Nathan Gibbs we learnt that he had treated Mal for gastric pains and di-arrhoea all night. Said Gibbs, ''For him to run 90 metres in sup-port of Ricky in his condition in the last minute of a Test is just awesome.''

Benny Elias's mind went back to the 1989 grand final when he and Balmain lost to Canberra in extra time. ''Now I know how Canberra felt when they scored with a minute to go,'' he said. As man-of-the-match he had to go upstairs to receive his award and such was the crush he stood on a table to reply.

Thus positioned he was overcome with delusions of Marc Anthony and began a classic oration, "Out there" . . . pause . . . "this afternoon, at Old Trafford, on the 10th of November, 1990" . . . pause . . . "you've witnessed one of the greatest games of rugby league of all time." And so on. He has a sense of occasion has Benny. But no more so than ARL chief Ken Arthurson, who was moved to state eloquently, "They talk about Rorke's Drift and the Battle of Brisbane, but the commitment, tenacity and determination of the Australians not to buckle in the face of insurmountable odds today, made everyone proud of being Australian."

Quite so, and for Bobby Fulton the relief made him a happy, effervescent coach. Did his heart sink with the intercept? "Oh mate, I couldn't believe it, but Ricky and Benny touch the ball more than anyone else, it's a game of inches and there was inches in it." Would he have accepted a draw? "I'd be a fool to say otherwise, but we shouldn't have been in that position, we were a 10 point better side on the day." The referee? "I don't even know what the penalties were. 12-8? Who's way?" said Fulton, and didn't bat an eyelid.

The third Test would be a stormer, an English reporter suggested. "I don't think so," said Fulton. Stormer meant a great game, a cracker, the journalist explained. "Oh, sorry, stormer, yeah it will be, sensational." Fulton thought a moment. "Malcolm's a super coach, he'll bounce back harder," said Fulton. "Only thing is that after he's looked at a video he might have to make a few changes and that's when things start getting sticky. I'm fortunate now that whereas the pressure was on me after the first Test, now the pressure is on my old buddy Malcolm."

The manner of the loss actually made it a lot worse for his old buddy Malcolm. Reilly was still lamenting Eastwood's missed conversion after Loughlin's try. "Had Paul scored under the posts, we could have been two points up, and maybe psychologically that would have lifted the lads," he said. Reilly was so down it seemed an intrusion to question him. He couldn't think about the third Test yet, he said. "I shall tomorrow, I'm just a little too disappointed now," he said. "I can't start thinking too greatly about that."

Back at the Ramada, supporters packed the ground floor bar which they would drink dry — every drop of beer, wine and spirits and even the most exotic of liqueurs — by 4 am. Brad Mackay joined his father Lyle and Brian Smith, Brad's St George coach for 1991. "I was tired from the start, and tired at half-time," said Brad. Smith opined the first was mental, the second physical. "And I've got bruises down my back, my side and legs, even though the ground was soft," added Brad. That was definitely physical, said Smith. Nearby, the Canberra connection of Mal, Badge and Ricky were being photographed with their Raiders coach Tim Sheens. "I can't get Mal's eyebrows in," joked the fan photographer. Soon after I saw a familiar face across the crowded room, Wally Lewis. He was surveying the scene, smiled and gave me a wave. Malicious rumours reached England that Lewis had applauded Australia's first Test loss. I didn't believe it, of the man, or the patriot. At Old Trafford, Lewis was in the Channel 10 box with match-caller David Morrow who told me that when Meninga scored his last-second try Lewis leapt from his seat and punched the air in a dangerously vigorous victory salute. I believed that. Still, amid these victory celebrations, Wally was neither fish nor fowl but soon found his milieu with two other ex-Roos, and friends, Royce Simmons and Chris Mortimer.

Buying a drink at the bar was impossible so David Morrow and I fetched beer from his hotel room fridge. Morrow's voice was hoarse from having to call the two best tries of his career above the roar of Old Trafford. He slipped a video cartridge into an editing machine and we leisurely watched Lyons and Meninga's tries all over again. I timed Meninga's try from the time Stuart received the ball to when Mal hurtled over. The digital readout stopped on 13 seconds, for nearly 100 metres in full football regalia, bumping Gibson and catching the ball. I noticed also that Hanley was one of the first to drop back in the chase after Stuart. Britain's assistant coach Phil Larder had told me in the dressingrooms, "Ellery is the second or third fastest player in our squad in training and he couldn't make a yard on Stuart.'' Larder continued, ''If you put Carl Gibson and Meninga over 100 metres Carl would beat Mal by 10 metres, no joking, Carl's quick, yet Mal overtook Carl and bumped him aside.'' Larder explained, ''Why? They were knackered. They'd given everything, they'd nothing left to give.'' Thirteen seconds broke British hearts that afternoon. We rewound the tape and watched the tries again.

13 CRUSHING HULL

The day after the Test a palpable sense of relief swept the Kangaroo camp. Bob Lindner told me, "You can't believe the pressure that's been lifted. You know, there's a generation of Australians who have grown up never knowing anything but Kangaroo success in England." To lose a Test series was one thing, said Lindner. To disappoint — disillusion — hundreds of thousands of fans was another. There were occasions at Old Trafford, he said, when if he had slipped a pass, Australia might have made another 30 to 40 metres. "But you thought, 'No, not today. No mistakes today.'"

The English newspapers were full of "What if . . ." stories. What if Offiah hadn't gone off injured, wouldn't he have caught Stuart? Probably, but would he have taken Loughlin's intercept try? What if Loughlin had scored closer to the posts? He could have and risked Laurie Daley running him down. Others questioned why Britain had not reprised Wembley's successful kick and chase game. Fulton provided the answer: "Because Ricky was there waiting." Which raised more questions. If Stuart was "bobbying" for the Roos why hadn't Schofield found the same space as Lyons? And so it went.

Some writers seriously questioned the legality of Meninga's collision with Carl Gibson. NSW Referees Coordinator, Dennis Braybrook, said that from his seat at Old Trafford it looked legal. He said the referee's rule book contained a specific reference to "illegal interference", an example of which — in the context of Meninga's try — would have been Meninga grabbing Gibsons's jumper to prevent him tackling Stuart. Legal interference occurred when two players bumped each other racing for a loose ball. "Meninga, while taking up a position in support of the ball carrier, doesn't have to stop or step around an opposing player if that player is in his path," said Braybrook. "It's clear in the rule book but it can be a grey area on the field. It was up to the English touch judges to rule against Meninga, and they didn't."

Martin Kelner in the *Sunday Correspondent* ranked Mal's try as, "Among the best seen in international rugby," deliberately including rugby union in the comparison. The *Daily Mail*'s Jeff Powell — British sports feature writer of the year — wrote:

> When the scoreline comprises such a potent mixture of multi-pass movements, startling opportunism, subtle kicking and raw courage, you begin to wonder whether the Rugby Union establishment prohibit them (rugby league) from Twickenham as much from fear of comparison as from righteous amateurism.

Both the *Guardian*'s Paul Fitzpatrick and Raymond Fletcher of the *Yorkshire Post* agreed that Cliff Lyons' try was worthy of the 1982 or 1986 Kangaroos and Fulton finally felt free to compare and contrast too. "They're a good side Great Britain," he said. "Our '82 and '86 teams, they'd have trouble beating that side."

Sunday, November 11, was Remembrance Day, and for some, the anniversary of the sacking of the Whitlam Government. It will also now be remembered by 450 *Rugby League Week* tour supporters who gathered for their gala get-together lunch in a huge conference centre at Manchester University. They had been promised they would meet the Kangaroos and all were in high spirits. Brad Mackay's father, Lyle, could even laugh about his son being listed in the Test program as Greg Mackey, the Wollongong five-eighth then captaining Hull.

RL Week delayed starting lunch until 1.30 pm but eventually began with Bob Lindner the sole Kangaroo present. I joined ARL chairman Ken Arthurson and his wife Barbara at the top table, together with ARL general manager Bob Abbott and *RL Week* editor Norm Tasker, an old colleague of mine. Tasker took the microphone and apologised for the absent Kangaroos. He had hoped 20 would attend but Bob Fulton had unexpectedly required them back at the hotel. "I'd like to thank Bob Lindner for . . ." and his voice was drowned as the hall rose to give Lindner a 30-second, cheering, standing ovation. I looked across at Ken Arthurson and saw a mixture of embarrassment and anger flicker across his face. Replying, Arthurson praised *Rugby League Week*'s coverage of the game and sincerely thanked the supporters. "Although you were greatly out-numbered yesterday you made your presence felt," he said. "That the players appreciated it was shown when they ac-knowledged you at the end of the game." When he returned to the table Arthurson said in a tight voice, "I've just sent the bus driver back to the hotel to round up the first half-dozen players he sees and bring them out here. This is not good enough!"

It transpired that Fulton had called a team meeting at the Ra-mada for 11 am, which didn't get under way until 11.30 and didn't finish until 1 pm. Bob Lindner had turned up at the supporters' lunch because he had not heard of the team meet-ing. On stage, Channel 10's Billy J. Smith interviewed Lindner. "Bob, we all knew you were going to win, but could you do it a bit earlier next time," he joked. "Ken Arthurson had four heart attacks yesterday." Lindner replied, "Well, we still had plenty of time though, there were still 20 seconds left!" The au-dience, hanging on every word, included some famous names — ex-Kangaroos Bob McCarthy, Johnny Rhodes and Johnny Lang, and former Australian coach Terry Fearnley. They were all tour leaders and when I interviewed them for a Channel Nine camera crew, to a man they felt keenly the disappoint-ment on behalf of their supporters. At 2.30 pm driver Gibbons, having scoured the hotel and found Mark Carroll and Brad Mackay, returned with them as the lunch was breaking up. Too late.

Fulton's explanation was that Sunday mid-morning was the first chance the team had to get together after the Test. "We had a few beers and watched the game," he said. "I left it to the players whether they attended the lunch. Just because it's *Rugby League Week* doesn't mean God says go." He said that had the luncheon been official, the players would have attended. Fulton said the team had been harrassed by drunken supporters, resident in the Ramada, knocking on players' doors seeking autographs at all hours. "I've already spoken to Bob Abbott and recommended that no supporters stay in the team's hotel," he said. Further, he said, the players had enough official functions to go to. "The lunch would have been like here in the hotel last night," he said. "It was a dead set zoo, I had to get out of the place. Imagine them going to the lunch and being pestered by 500 people. Do you think they need that?"

Fulton was mistaken. The *RL Week* supporters were neither animals nor pests. They were a special interest group dedicated to rugby league and Bob Lindner would vouch for their responsible behaviour. *RL Week* editor Tasker tried to be fair to the absent Kangaroos. He understood the pressures on touring teams but the lunch was always intended to be relaxed affair. "This trip is the biggest thing many of these people will do in their lives," he said. "It was a chance for them to brush with fame, to meet people they admire, respect and, in a funny way, love." He was puzzled because so many players had given the impression to *RL Week* they were looking forward to the lunch. Tasker said Fulton had given *RL Week* staffers the impression he was not sympathetic to the magazine. "He said *RL Week* had niggled at him through the tour, which we had, and which is our function I suppose," said Tasker. "But touring teams do become a bit insulated, especially if you've got a very intense coach, which they've got. It would have been marvellous for the team to recognise the contribution these supporters make to rugby league."

Four days later we discovered where some of the players went. On 14 November, the *London Sun* appeared with a headline, "Aussie Yobs Riot in Bar". The paper's report ran:

> Drunken Aussie Rugby League stars terrified guests as they rampaged through an indoor cricket centre. Police were called as players smashed plates over their own heads, threw food about and scuffled in a bar. One guest at the centre in Stockport, near Manchester, said, "They were absolutely drunk and going bananas."

No one was arrested after the incident which happened on Sunday, 24 hours after the Aussies' Test match win over Great Britain.

The tour management investigated and, in the absence of any police action, Keith Barnes said the players had no case to answer. To support his decision he said the cricket centre owner had assured him the players would be welcome back. And so the whole tortuous episode became a sad postscript to a wonderful Test win. *Rugby League Week* probably erred in not obtaining official ARL sanction to advertise the Kangaroos' presence at their function. Yet Fulton knew of the lunch and his impromptu team meeting contributed to the players ignoring the invitation. Only the players know in their own consciences which would have been the better venue to celebrate their win — the indoor cricket centre or the supporters' lunch.

Perhaps more than anything the events demonstrated the extraordinary pressure the Kangaroos had been under and what a release was Old Trafford. My own feeling was that if this stress was the Invincibles' legacy then the sooner Great Britain won back the Ashes the better. But with Wembley just a bad dream the psychological advantage had now swung back to Australia. I sensed the Roos were improving and that the British had peaked. Reilly, with the deciding Test only two weeks off, had the devil's own job of lifting his players after such a heartbreak. Yet the beauty of this compelling series was that the two sides were so equal. The contest had carried far beyond rugby league's usual borders, even to the tabloids of Fleet Street whose rugby league correspondents scathingly referred to their newspaper sports sections as "soccer sections". The RFL pondered whether they could transfer the third Test from Elland Road, Leeds — a soccer stadium which held only 33,000 — to Wembley, which they would fill. But too much was already attached to Elland Road, not the least the accommodation bookings in Leeds of the thousands of tour supporters. RFL executives gazed wistfully at the large photograph in David Oxley's office of Odsal Stadium, Bradford on 5 May, 1954, when a world record rugby crowd of 102,575 overflowed the ground for the Challenge Cup replay between Warrington and Halifax.

Odsal was just over the Pennines from where I lived, a shrine for any Australian on the rugby league heritage trail. Odsal's surprise is that instead of a field surrounded by grandstands, it is a huge bowl in the earth, all below road level, surrounded by terraced sides. It was once a steep-sided, open-ended valley which was gradually closed by urban tipping in the Victorian age. Standing looking down is like gazing at a scenic view, so far below are the goal posts. Odsal, like Wembley, is also a speedway and the cycle track nips off the corners of the football field's dead ball line. Turf, grown in triangular timber trays, is used to artificially fill in these corners for matches. I could see the triangles stacked at one end being watered by groundsmen. Under fire safety regulations Odsal, with two small grandstands, and concrete terraces, now holds about 29,000. But in 1954 roads to the ground were blocked for miles, even onto the Pennine highway where drivers simply pulled over and listened to the match on their car radios. Estimates put the true attendance at nearer 120,000 as spectators broke down the turnstiles, poured in and found space on the bare shale ground. Permissable then, not today.

The Kangaroos' second last club match and the last for the mid-week, non-Test, players was against Hull, league leaders, undefeated at home for a year and coached by one of the most respected men in English or Australian rugby league, Brian Smith. The personable ex-Illawarra coach took over Hull in 1988 and lost his first match, a friendly, "by 40 or 50 points, I don't think my mind wants to remember it," said Smith. By season's end he had taken Hull to the league premiership final and the club has since grown stronger. Under Smith's tutelage such youngsters as Eastwood, Jackson and Harrison bloomed to Lions status. Smith wrote a thoughtful column for *Open Rugby* magazine and his quick wit on Granada television's commentary team made John Monie's sensible comments for the BBC sound leaden. In January 1991, after his last match as coach, with Hull still league leaders, the players lifted him shoulder high for Hull's supporters to give him an emotional farewell.

The main road into Hull, 160 kms east of Manchester via the M62, is the Clive Sullivan Way, named after the Welsh-born winger who captained Great Britain in the 1970s. He scored over 100 tries for both Hull and Hull Kingston Rovers, the city's two great rival rugby league clubs. I am not aware of the Gasnier Drive in St George or the Lewis Highway in Brisbane. But then Hull is hooked on rugby league.

It's a tightly knit city, divided by the River Hull and the friendly antagonism of the two clubs. Hull's colours are black and white, Hull KR's red and white, and legend goes that each club's supporters won't touch anything bearing the other's colours — Hull fans won't eat streaky bacon, because it's red and white, Hull KR fans won't touch black pudding, because that's black and white. The two clubs dominated English rugby league for much of the decade when, from 1980 to 1986, one or the other contested six out of seven Wembley Cup finals. But nothing matters to either side quite as much as winning the local derby. Traditionally English clubs, to save travelling on Boxing Day, play the club nearest them. Former Test referee Billy Thompson, who refereed the first State of Origin match in Brisbane in 1980, described one of these annual clashes to me. It's also one of his favourite after-dinner yarns, which goes:

> I always love doing the Boxing Day match. What an appropriate day. There we are, Craven Park, Hull KR home match, against Hull, 20,000 in the ground, kick off 11 am. Three minutes past eleven only me and the two touch judges not fighting! Grand isn't it. Perhaps we were too far away from each other. I quelled it with the help of the touch judges, called the two fullbacks, George Fairbairn and Gary Kemble, up from their far corners and said, 'You two, off! Early bath!' And George says, 'Nay Billy, we were only two not fightin', what's off for?' And I said, 'Cowardice!'

Such a city must have character and Hull's impact begins with the magnificent Humber Bridge, the world's longest single-span suspension bridge. From that entrance Hull effortlessly ranks second to Halifax in my list of attractive cities of the north. For centuries a fishing port, it suffered a civic blow in 1976 when it lost the "cod wars" with Iceland, a dispute about off-shore fishing rights. Hull's cod fleet was reduced from 90 vessels to nine and the city was hit with a commercial depression from which it is only now recovering. Yet Hull remains very much a North Sea port, passenger and vehicle ferries ply to Rotterdam in Holland and Zeebrugge in Belgium, and Hull's destination signs speak four languages. Walking the city streets — Fish Street, Salthouse, Scale and Dagger Lanes — I was rarely out of sight of a dock or a wharf, never far from the salt-sea smell of fish, fresh or cooking.

At Hull's ground, picturesquely named The Boulevard, dark clouds had become heavy showers. I sought out the men's toilet and became aware it had no roof. Looking up I found myself gazing at several lighted windows of homes which overlook the open-air toilet. I remarked upon this unusual view to BBC television commentator Ray French and he recounted how one day at Hull he said on air, "Huge crowd at The Boulevard today, my word you really do see some big ones here," at which point the cameraman panned right instead of left, smack across the men's toilet. This footage is now a BBC archive gem.

For the Roos match Brian Smith handed over to his successor at Hull, Noel "Crusher" Cleal, pig-shooter, Kangaroo, Manly and then Hull second rower. Though it was Noel's first match as coach he and Smith agreed to let me eavesdrop pre-match in Hull's dressingroom. Cleal, with short cropped hair and full ginger-brown beard, has a gentleness of manner which belies his large physique. Smith, short, blond and youthful has a presence which belies his size. For the occasion Smith was immaculately tailored in a blue double-breasted suit and black shoes — but Smith would look dapper in a boiler suit.

The first thing I notice in the dressingroom, pinned to the wall, are two large sheets of white paper with black felt pen writing. The bottom sheet, Smith's handiwork, is a fascinating run-down of the idiosyncracies and capabilities of the Australian team for that night. It reads:-

Alexander — very fast, big chase needed; Fittler — great step either way, but not confident in speed; Ettingshausen — very fast, plays overs — (that baffled me). Hasler was strong, Johns quick. Langer — big right foot step, chips, grubbers, run at him. For Cartwright they were to watch for his right-hand pass and right-foot step. Sargent and Bella had identical comments, ''Runs straight, rip it off him'', as were the comments for Geyer and Gillespie, ''Hitter, step him.'' They were spot on with Kerrod Walters: ''Stops, starts, passes''. And the counter? ''Run at him, belt him!''

Hull captain, Greg Mackey, from Sydney, arrives and jokes about being listed in the second Test program instead of Brad Mackay. ''My mother said, 'Send that program over,' and a couple of my mates did,'' says Greg. Brian Smith quips, ''He'll win a few bets with that in a few years time.'' Mackey, a boy-ish-faced 29, red hair, whippet in build and speed, spent five years at Illawarra and a year at Canterbury before joining Hull in 1989.

At 7.20 pm — 40 minutes to go — Mackey says the words that signal the beginning of a gradual pysche up: ''Plenty of talk tonight eh? Talk it up.'' Players are stretching on the floor, speed jogging on the spot, bending, doing press-ups. On a massage bench two trainers are soothing thigh muscles with linament. The sweet smell soon pervades the air. Useful? I in-quire. Yeah, nods one masseur, ''It helps here,'' he says, tap-ping his temple. Test winger Paul Eastwood stands throwing the ball against the wall, catching its different rebounded an-gles. I hear an Aussie accent, Brad Webb, a centre, who spent three years with South Sydney. Only been here since July, one of Hull's three Aussie imports. Who was he marking tonight? ''ET,'' he says. What does ''plays overs'' mean? ''Backs up well, comes inside,'' says Webb.

Everyone is starting to get a bit toey. Suddenly I spot an Australian tracksuit — jolly Shaun McRae standing a little un-comfortably in the epi-centre of the rising tension in the change room. ''Alfie's bought two left boots, trying to get a right one to fit him,'' he explains. Cleal, rummaging in a shoe room, tells

Shaun he'll send it around, don't wait. A relieved McRae departs.

Test players, winger Paul Eastwood and hooker Lee Jackson pull on their shoulder and chest pads. Eastwood is enormously built for a winger. I can see now how he bullocked over for his try at Wembley. Jackson, his ears bound with surgical tape, has a long, lean upper body but strong legs. His pads are Perseus Maxi — in ancient Greek myth Perseus slew the hideous Gorgon Medusa whose trick was to turn to stone all who gazed upon her. Perseus is now lashed to Jackson's shoulders to protect him against the ancient, many-headed marsupial called the Kangaroos.

7.45 pm. "Five minutes" comes the call. All are fully dressed, walking from one dressingroom to the next, snorting and sniffing, scuffing and shuffling. "Two minutes," just like on the stage. The theatre or battle, or perhaps the theatre of battle. Just then an incongruous interlude. Hull chairman, David Kirkwood, addresses the nervous air, "Lads, you'd like to change your shirts with the Australians . . . or would you?" Yah, yuh, yeah, come the replies. One moment it's the blood and thunder of the challenge, the next it's mementoes of the game, even before it's played.

7.58 pm. The Hull lads return from their on-field warm up, throw on tracksuit tops or wrap towels around shoulders. The match won't start until 8.07 because the live television coverage has to fit in commercials. They are all walking about now, milling like horses in a yard, tossing their limbs and heads, back and forth. Lee Jackson calls out, "Defence has to be solid today." Prop Andy Dannatt shouts, "They're only bluidy men. C'mon, we're not goin' to be intimidairted lark Wigan. Let's intimidairt THEM! For airty minutes!"

Cleal suddenly commands attention. "Come on, you've got seven minutes yet, just sit down, think about what you have to do. Let's not spend it all before we get there, eh." Reluctantly, grudgingly the lads slow their toiling and moiling and find seats on the bench against the wall. Sniff, snort, hiss, exhale, hands on knees, deep breaths and they all steady. Without the heel and toe tapdance of 17 pairs of boot studs on the concrete floor, a comparative quiet falls. "When it's on, it's on," says Mackey, like the last bellow of a herd settling. This sets off a new spate of positive reinforcement shouts. The referee David Campbell, of Widnes, passes around the players, checking hands for rings, patting shoulder pads for hard edges and running his palm over soles for sharp studs.

"Time!" The herd is galvanised. Noel Cleal stays their concerted movement to rise with an outstretched hand, palm down. This is the commander's final address. "Let's not forget, they all get up in the morning and have a piss like the rest of us," he begins graphically. "They're all human, so let's jam it right into them from the word go. They thrive on other sides making mistakes. That's when they're most dangerous. We can be the same way, pressure them to make mistakes." Noel glances from one player to another, shifting his feet, body language urgent. "How do you feel? You all feel all right?" Muffled yuhs, and nods. "Right get up and start walking around. Bluey, it's all yours now." Bluey is captain Mackey. The clatter of the sprig dance begins again. Noel walks slowly around shaking each player's hand. The ritual is so pre-combat they may as well be Athenians preparing to defend the pass at Thermopylae against Xerxes and his Persians. As the Athenians combed their hair and anointed their limbs, so the Humbermen have oiled their thighs and gelatined their knees.

"C'mon lads, we're top of the bluidy league," shouts Andy Dannatt. "Let's do this for our wives, our families and our friends! We dream about winning games like this, now we've got our chance!" One of the trainers smears his palms with linament and cups them so that players can take a deep sniff. They shake their heads as it penetrates their sinuses and waters their eyes.

At 8.03 Cleal walks dramatically out of the room. A new level of tension overtakes the room. They are now masters of their own destiny but so edgy, so turned in upon their task my fly-on-the-wall role is easy. They simply don't see me. With the referee's whistle, Hull are ready to defend the pass.

The crowd of 13,000 has been treated to a stirring rendition of Tchaikovsky's *1812 Overture* followed by fireworks and sky-rockets. Minutes after kickoff Kerrod Walters rockets into a gap to send twin brother Kevin over for the first try. Hull respond with a copybook try after Greg Mackey throws a cut-out pass to give winger Neil Turner an overlap in the corner. 4-4. The next 20 minutes are as intense as any club match on tour, the penalty count helping Hull maintain pressure. Then the Wigan syndrome overtakes Hull and the Roos put three tries on them in just 12 minutes. In the count-down in the Hull rooms I had forgotten that this Australian team contains several discontented Test rejects. An observer in the Kangaroo rooms might have noted Kerrod Walters, Allan Langer and Martin Bella ready to make a point at Hull's expense. The scorers are Ettingshausen and Hasler, twice, for a half-time lead of 20-4.

Benny Elias, standing near the change room entrance, says players still competing for Test spots are producing five-star performances. Benny looks a little wan, fresh out of hospital after a 24-hour tussle with a kidney stone. "Terrible, eh?" I sympathised. "You had one?" he asked. I nodded and he silently acknowledged me as among those who knew ultimate pain.

Hull troop in at half-time, dejected. Some grab water, others simply slump on the benches, heads bowed. Hardly a word is exchanged, or eye contact. Trainers move quietly around checking minor injuries. But the unseen injury is to their egos and this is beyond the red remedy of iodine. Cleal pours himself a Gatorade, confers with Brian Smith and the statistics keeper and then, like an actor making an entrance, hits his unseen mark centre room and confronts the team.

"You're playing too proper," he begins earnestly. "You're playing out of the textbook. Nobody's got any mongrel in them." He's genuinely baffled. Aggression is so endemic to rugby league that its absence is like having to explain to a swimmer how to float. "No one's prepared to put their body on the line," he says. "We're just hitting it up, putting them on the ground. Got to have bit of mongrel in us fellas . . . " He warms to his speech, gauging his impact. "That's one of our problems," he says. "The penalty rate is 2-1 to us, and I reckon that if we put a bit of shit in our game, the penalties will still be 2 to 1 our way, so don't be frightened, without being stupid, to put a bit extra into your tackle." Having pushed that as far as need be, he returns to technicalities. "The last two tries they've scored they've come this side of the pitch," he says, showing which side with his hands. "Then they started rattling it back the other way. At one stage we had four blokes here marking no bastard on this side and Des Hasler has scored two tries the other." He addresses Lee Jackson encouragingly, "Got to adjust Jacko, call them across, take them all across."

After more tactical talk Cleal rounds to his original theme, but this time with more vehemence. "Bluey had to hit it up inside their quarter with five minutes to go because we were running out of volunteers," he says. "If we don't go out there in the second half and have some aggression about us you know what these bastards are like — they'll wipe the floor with you. So, have we got it within us?" General mumbles, yeah, they have, but they are still down.

"Another thing," says Crusher, and now he is pseudo-angry, a formidable sight, this large, bearded pig-shooter who has swapped his skinning knife for a stats pencil. "We're letting them up to play the ball like they're got a bloody God-given right to do it," he says aggrieved. "Yet when we're tackled we lie on the ground and they're all over us like they're rootin' us! So let's turn it around!"

Just then Brian Smith emerges from the backround, seeks and receives permission from Cleal to speak. "For 40 minutes we've played a very good side out there," he says slowly. "Make no mistake about that, they're good." He pauses. "But how good are you? Not you, the team," he explains, and sweeps his arm around the room. "How good are you, singular? That's what matters in any game you play. Do you give up? Or when the pressure's on do you find something extra? You got a bit of pride?" Again Smith waits because private indignation is starting to raise a few eyes from the floor. "Does it matter to you?" he asks. "It matters to me."

Something has happened. The players are all up before it's really time, starting to talk again. Whether it's Noel, Brian, both, or the fact that every second half holds the hope of revival for losing teams, Smith rides the rising crest. "They'll be gloating in there, I tell you, sitting back gloating," he goads, cackling humourlessly, cocking a thumb towards the Aussies' door. "You've got a great chance to go out there now and do something straight away. If you want it badly."

The players' cries of self encouragement reach a crescendo almost equal to the pre-match level. Noel picks up on the sense of intra-team competition. "There's three more changes to be made fellas, let's let it not be you eh?" he says. The herd is up and milling again. Clatter, clatter, the studs rattle like a snare drum, and then in comes the vocal, the staccato mantra, " 'eads oop, 'ead's oop, let's bluidy go, plair f'y' mairts, c'mon, we can do it."

One of the trainers halts them and adds the creme d'insults. "Coomin' back from t' last try," he says. "Cartwrigh' stood in middle and said, 'Let's poot the biggest score yet on t'em.' Eh, the biggest score yet. Let's shoov thart rart down his bluidy throort!"

Hull give it their best in the second half but can't impress the scoreboard. Kevin Walters runs in for his second try and Kerrod reciprocates. Three tries for the twins. Ettingshausen finally scorches 50-metres to score and its all over, 34-4. Somewhere a *Daily Star* sub-editor is composing the next morning's page headline, "Oz Twins Peak".

Hull rattle back into their dressingroom hoping that posterity would prove they were not so much bad as Australia insuperable. Cleal catches them in the weary minutes it takes them to unlace boots and strip off the bindings of battle. "I thought you showed a lot of character even though the game had been lost," he says, "You didn't turn up your toes, you fought right to the death so . . . they're a bloody great side . . . the lot of you can hold your head up high regardless of the score. Orright?'' A few glance up gratefully, for it confirms what they sensed. Wally Lewis's 1986 Roos beat Hull 48-0 but they could not have been more impressive than this evening.

Lee Jackson is subdued, admits to still being down from that draining Test four days ago. ''It's hard to get going when a team's putting 30 points against you,'' he says, ''You think you're crawling back, start playing better and they lay a try against you and that puts you back to square one. Just fighting a losing battle. It's hard to put it together against world class players.''

Shouts from the shower reveal repairing spirits, if not muscles. Greg Mackey groans, ''Oh mate, sore! I've just discovered how hard they tackle in Sydney. I've been away too long. They put a bit of venom in and really hit to hurt. They hurt me, they hurt us with their full on shoulder tackles.'' Mackey examines his wounds. ''At the end I thought, 'God, were they so good or were we poor?' And I didn't know, so I asked one of our coaching staff and he said everyone had tried, but they played some super stuff.'' Mackey threw his boots into a bag. ''The fact they turned in one of their best performances all tour, I hate that,'' he says. ''But I just feel honoured, like proud to have played in the game. Mate it was like a dream.''

14 ONE IN THE EYE FOR WIDNES

Wally Lewis had arrived in England for two testimonial dinners both of which fell through even though, as his biographer, everywhere I travelled English fans couldn't hear enough about him. Just one more setback in the blackest year of Lewis's career. While in the North Lewis attended a Wakefield Trinity past players' dinner at which he and Ray Price were the star guests. Lewis and Price, though they respected each other's ability, were never great mates and after sharing a pre-dinner drink they were seated at opposite ends of the top table. A large audience enjoyed a question and answer session during which Wally announced he wanted his last playing season — whenever that was — to be in England. ''Give 'im cheque now Rordnai,'' a diner called to Wakefield chairman Rodney Walker, amid much laughter.

Wally revealed that when the Broncos did not renew his contract he made a last-minute attempt to join Balmain for 1991, attracted by the best pack of forwards in the world. He even offered to halve his contract fee but Balmain secretary Keith Barnes could not fit him in under the club's salary cap. Only then did Lewis opt for the Gold Coast. Asked to name the best player he had encountered Lewis did not hesitate. ''Brett Kenny by a country mile, he's first and daylight second, not even a comparison,'' he said.

During the evening one of Lewis's State of Origin jerseys was auctioned as part of his testimonial year and bidding closed at $625. Wally thanked the dinner guests but it scarcely made up for the thousands he could have expected from his cancelled testimonial dinners. One brave questioner asked how Wally felt about missing the 1990 Kangaroo tour. The huge dining hall fell silent. ''Are there any women present?'' asked Wally. ''To be perfectly frank I was filthy about it. I believed I was fit, but I just didn't manage to convince the bloke that counted and he believed that I wasn't.''

Having left for England well before the Kangaroo selection I missed that particular saga. All I knew was that English RFL public affairs executive David Howes was shocked when I rang him with the news. ''Oh bloody hell!'' he exclaimed. ''We've been using him as our major promotional drawcard.'' So, throughout the tour, there was Wally head-to-head with Ellery Hanley in advertisements the RFL could not cancel. Every English newspaper, even the parochial Fleet Street ''soccer sections'', carried the story and for one day I felt I was back in Queensland where Lewis's activities provide daily headlines. Sitting beside Wally at the Wakefield top table I heard piecemeal the details of his omission. I decided to track the story to the source, to the ''bloke that counted'', the person Wally couldn't convince, ARL medico and Kangaroo tour doctor Dr Nathan Gibbs.

Rugby league players with medical degrees are a rarity, former Australian captain Dr George Peponis being one exception. Nathan Gibbs captained South Sydney in 1980 and the following season was selected for City firsts. He was then a medical student but once he graduated chose medicine ahead of football and by 1985 was South's club doctor. Gibbs opened his own sports medicine practice in Pagewood, South Sydney and gained experience working with Dr Merv Cross, who Gibbs described as Australia's leading sports orthopaedic surgeon. Gibbs is not an orthopaedic specialist but wants to become a sports medicine specialist. He is a member of the Australian College of Sports Physicians whose aim is to gain government recognition of sports medicine as a field of specialist practice. As the ARL doctor who ruled Lewis out of the tour, Gibbs agreed to talk about his role, and the following is an edited transcript of our conversation.

Gibbs: ''Wally Lewis had hardly played any football but because he is such a great player and such a great Australian captain, he would have been picked automatically by the selectors, sight unseen if you like, with regard to football in 1990, if he could be proven fit with his arm. The selectors said that to make things easy, give Wally a medical a week before, find out if he's fit. If he is they pick him, if he's not they don't. Then they can organise the team structure. Because he had a broken arm and it occurred three months prior, one week either way wasn't going to be of major importance.

"ARL general manager Bob Abbott picked him up from the airport and they went to an x-ray centre in Maroubra Junction where I do most of my work. I met them there and we went on to Sydney Football Stadium to conduct the physical part of the medical."

Q: You'd know almost instantly upon looking at the x-rays whether the fracture had healed?

Gibbs: "Yes. Well not always. Some x-rays are hard. In Wally's case the radius bone had been broken and had a rod put through the centre. The bones were still far from being joined together. If you look at a fracture healing, first the bones glue together with scar tissue, so the bones no longer move independently. However it's still very sore, very weak. Over a period of weeks — a forearm bone can take anywhere from six weeks to six months to heal — the scar tissue actually becomes bone, so it transforms from scar tissue to calcium to bone.

"That's called callus formation, the bone actually unites, then it consolidates. In Wally's case the bone was united, but there was still a quite obvious gap between the bones. It had very fine callus but it was a long way from being consolidated. The problem is that if you have a weak point in the bone, it becomes a stress concentrator, as soon as you land on the arm all the stress goes to the weak point. In Wally's case I was under the impression from what I had heard from his own doctors that the bone had healed."

Q: You spoke with Wally's doctor?

Gibbs: "With Wally's permission I spoke to his orthopaedic surgeon (Dr Peter Myers) the day before the tests. He told me that Wally's arm was still quite stiff because he had only been out of plaster for six weeks at that stage. He did say to me that the bone was good. By that he meant it wasn't fully healed but it was good enough to play with. We didn't go into detail about consolidation union. He obviously passed him fit to play for the Broncos. So that was his decision. Whereas from my point of view it was far from being good enough to play with so that's where we differ in opinion. The bottom line was there was no way that the fracture had completely healed. Long way from it.''

Q: How else did you test Lewis?

Gibbs: ''We put Wally through a three-part medical — the x-ray examination, examination of the arm itself and looking at the function of the arm. With Wally's permission all the Press were watching. His elbow and wrist were restricted in movement, and he couldn't rotate the wrist very well. He had weakness when he punched the boxing bag, he could still throw a punch but it was obviously weaker. Nowhere near as strong as the other arm. He had weakness doing wheelbarrow walks, he quite obviously favoured the arm.

''His mobility was restricted and his strength was weaker and his muscle size had been wasted away. Function is important so you get them doing things that they would have to do in a game. Landing on your hands and pushing off your hands is quite important. If you can't wheelbarrow walk you're not much good to anyone. Some will argue that it will get better in a few more weeks, which it may well have. But what won't get better in a few more weeks was the obvious fact that the bone was a long way from consolidation.''

Q: The role of Dr Merv Cross?

Gibbs: ''I contacted him because of the importance of the decision I suppose, and because I knew he was an orthopaedic surgeon and I'm a pseudo-specialist if you like. I thought I should get an orthopaedic guy down with some pull, to give an opinion.''

Q: When did you first ring Dr Cross?

Gibbs: ''I saw him the day before and said basically be ready

I may need a second opinion. He was quite happy to be involved. After the medical I rang him and he came over to the Football Stadium. He didn't see Wally, didn't see the reporters, he examined the x-rays, he agreed the bone was a long way from being healed and that therefore he wouldn't have advised playing or going on tour. After that I rang Ken Arthurson to tell him the decision, and then told Wally.''

Dr Gibbs was deeply offended at criticism of him for omitting Lewis, but offended also was Lewis's orthopaedic surgeon, Dr Peter Myers, at criticism of his interpretation of the condition of Lewis's arm. Dr Myers had successfully repaired Lewis's right arm when he broke it in a Test against New Zealand in 1988. As with that fracture, he had used a stainless-steel nail through the centre of the bone to stabilise the fracture, a different method from the steel plate and screws used for Mal Meninga's arm fractures. Dr Myers is consultant to the Brisbane Broncos and has a practice in the Brisbane Orthopaedic and Sports Medicine Centre in Brisbane. In defence of himself and Lewis, he agreed to a discussion, of which this is an edited transcript.

Q: Did you OK Lewis to play from the bench for the Broncos against Canberra?

Myers: ''I like the way you worded that — yes. I didn't clear him to play for Australia. I only cleared him to play head-bin reserve for the Broncos. The understanding I had with Wayne Bennett and Wally was that he wouldn't go on in the first half, but if something happened in the second half, depending how far into the game, he'd go on. Otherwise, as occurred, he went on in the last 10 minutes. A gesture more than anything else.''

Q: Did you feel under pressure to pass Lewis fit prematurely?

Myers: ''I felt enormous pressure to pass him fit for a full game which is why I didn't. He knew he wasn't ready for a full game. I was quite happy with the pressure to pass him for head-bin reserve. Wally's type of fracture can really only occur with a specific mechanism of injury, that is a direct blow straight to the middle of the inner forearm, such as you get with a swinging arm when the person suddenly brings their head down, or knee up. You don't do it by landing in a tackle or, if you've got a big protection on your forearm, by taking the ball up. I'm the first to agree the fracture was not fully healed, still isn't, that will take many months. But he was fit to play with the fracture provided he wore a protection. Mal Meninga had several of those breaks and still wears an arm guard, so his is still not at full strength. It remains susceptible for ages.''

Q: So you passed him fit for only 10 minutes?

Myers: ''There's more to it than just the fracture. There's his fitness, his range of movement and his strength, all of which were terrible. It just struck me that he'd only last 10 minutes, though being Wally he could probably get away with a little longer.''

Q: Was there callus formation showing on x-rays before Lewis played for the Broncos?

Myers: ''There was callus across the fracture gap but I think we're getting a bit pedantic. What I think is really unfair is to base a person's fitness to play solely on the appearance of an x-ray. If it's a major problem, if it's a leg fracture and you just can't run, that's fair enough. But when it's a person with Lewis's skills, qualities and abilities, and if at training he can do the push-ups, the wheelbarrows and can clearly use the arm, to say that on the basis of an x-ray he is unfit to play, isn't fair.''

Q: Did you do wheelbarrow walks with him?

Myers: ''No I didn't. That wasn't my role. I'd cleared Wally for head-bin reserve the week before Canberra, for the Penrith game. But he was canned by the Broncos trainer, Kelvin Giles, on fitness grounds. Even the week he did play Kelvin told me he didn't think Wally was fit.''

Q: What did Giles mean by fit?

Myers: ''Fit enough to play a game. If he had to go on for 20 minutes could he keep up with the others. And the short answer is he went on for 10 minutes and still didn't keep up with the others. So when someone a week later tests him for full fitness to play for Australia it doesn't surprise me they find him lacking. The only thing that irked me was that it appeared the only reason for him failing was on two medicos' difference of opinion on the x-rays, which is garbage. It's unfair.''

Q: To you or Wally?

Myers: ''To both of us. Because, as I said, the mechanism of injury to do that fracture is very specific and you can protect against it by wearing a Mal Meninga arm guard.''

Q: Dr Gibbs said that you said the bone was all right?

Myers: ''My comment was that the fracture had healed but was not at full strength. One of the problems with this type of fracture is wrist stiffness, it's universal for about six months afterwards. My concern was not so much with him landing on the bone as with him hurting his wrist, because he couldn't bend it back to land. He couldn't wheelbarrow walk well because he couldn't extend his wrist. By the same token, you don't see lots of players wheelbarrow walking across the tryline do you?''

Q: What would you have done if you'd been in Dr Gibbs's position?

Myers: ''I probably would have failed him, but for different reasons. Lack of movement, lack of strength, lack of fitness, not for the appearance of an x-ray. This was a non-orthopaedic surgeon talking about a fracture and its horses for courses.''

Q: Did you speak to Dr Merv Cross about this?

Myers: ''Yes. He said he thought the fact that the fracture wasn't fully healed constituted what is called a stress riser — that any stress taken on the forearm would be concentrated in one area. That's probably fair comment except that the bone was healing, he had a nail up the middle of it so it was reinforced to some degree, and it would be protected by an arm guard. Dr Cross was toeing the pure textbook line and the textbook line says you don't play. End of story, I don't blame him for that.''

Q: Did you show Lewis's x-rays to other specialists?

Myers: ''I did show it to several colleagues and they were quite happy with my decision. The comment from one chap was that this was good enough to play with but it depended on Lewis's other fitness factors and that's what it boils down to.''

Q: Given the time factors do you think Lewis could have played in the first Test?

Myers: ''I honestly believe he could have played a very good role. If they had been prepared to take him and given him that time to get fit he would have worked hard through it and been ready for the Test. But if they had to take him away fully fit, he wasn't.''

The important element of Dr Gibbs's statement is that Dr Merv Cross did not physically examine Lewis and, therefore, his empirical support for Dr Gibbs's opinion was based only on his examination of Lewis's x-ray. Dr Gibbs accepted that the physical strength and mobility of Lewis's arm would get stronger with passing weeks, but said that Lewis's bone consolidation wouldn't improve quickly. Dr Myers argued that the consolidation of the fracture was adequate for Lewis to play, provided it was well protected, and that the x-ray evidence, by itself, should not have constituted a reason to omit Lewis. On that question the doctors clearly differed. But Dr Myers agreed that, at the time of the ARL test, Lewis could not have passed a full fitness examination which was the yardstick rigidly applied by the ARL for recent Kangaroo tour selections.

Ignoring all extraneous issues — that Lewis should have been given special consideration as Australia's greatest captain, or the conspiracy theory that he had fallen out of favour with the ARL hierarchy — on medical evidence alone, the ARL seemed on solid ground in dropping Lewis from the tour.

Such was the public's perception of antipathy between Lewis and the ARL that rumours were rife in England that Lewis had accepted a large offer to play a one-off game for Widnes against the Kangaroos in their last club match of the tour. Not that Widnes needed any help with their all-international backline. Besides Martin Offiah it included former Welsh rugby union captain Jonathan Davies, Welsh rugby union winger John Devereux, Scottish rugby union centre Alan Tait and British Lions Andy Currier, Tony Myler, David Hulme and Darren Wright. Australia needed no reminding of Widnes's speed, especially the Canberra players humiliated 30-18 at Old

Trafford in 1989 in the first offical World Club Championship. Widnes proudly display that trophy on their clubhouse front counter and the local council advertises the win in tourist brochures. Australia has no idea of the importance England attaches to the championship. If Australian clubs are to continue to play in the challenge, the ARL should get serious, recognise the English clubs' advantage of playing at home, and alternate the match between the countries.

Widnes, just 22 kms from Liverpool, is rugby league's most westerly first division club and its population, 60,000 — much smaller than near neighbours Warrington and St Helens — belies its club's success. Widnes was the birthplace of the UK chemical industry when, in the 1840s, manufacturers were forced out of Liverpool by their obnoxious smells, gases, vapours and residues. Up until the 1960s over half of Widnes's employment was in the chemical industry, hence the football club's nickname, the Chemics. Their major sponsors, ICI, are the reason Widnes could afford a 1989 world record price for Jonathan Davies.

The first feature to greet the tourist in Widnes is their replica Sydney Harbour Bridge across the River Mersey, opened in 1961, 29 years after Sydney's and designed by the same firm. Though it is the longest steel arch bridge in Europe, its main span is nearly 200 metres shorter than Sydney's. The second feature is the omnipresent chemical industry, best viewed from the observation platform of the industry-funded Catalyst chemical museum. A recorded message cheerfully describes the landmarks of Widnes — not church steeples and city halls — but the Fiddler's Ferry power station, to its right ICI's weed-killer works, Lever Bros soap factory and . . . ''on a clear day you may be able to see the flame stack at Shell's chemical plant''. According to the North West River Authority, these three companies are among the top 20 chemical polluters of the River Mersey, one of Europe's filthiest waterways.

Another landmark was an animal rendering factory whose licence was recently endangered when a physically sickening smell wafted from the works across the nearby Spike Island showground where 30,000 visitors were enjoying the annual Widnes fair. Driving along Widnes's main ring road I suddenly smelled sweet lemon and lime fragrances drifting from the Bush Boake and Allen essence plant. Motorists often smell different flavours on their way to work each day. Widnes is not ugly but it is such a town of effluents, residues, toxins and smells that after a while I grew suspicious of them all. I pulled in for tea and scones in a small cafe and immediately was hit by another strong perfume from the town. "Gees, you can't escape smells here can you?" I complained to the waitress. She drew near to me and whispered, "Actually it's that lady's perfume," nodding at a woman at a nearby table. "Awful isn't it!" she said wrinkling her nose.

Local nightclub comedians can always draw laughs with gags about Widnes's smells, and if that fails there's always Big Jim Mills. "Aye, 'twere a proud dare for Jimmy when 'e coom 'orm to play f'Wales, 1975 World Coop, steppin' on t' green gruss — except thut were name of a New Zealand forward! True! Coom buck to 'is awld stampin' ground did Jim, but 'e forgort abart player oonderneath!"

John Greengrass was a New Zealand prop now renowned for an incident which prompted New Zealand rugby league to ban Mills for life. As Greengrass dived over to score against Wales in their World Cup match in Swansea, Mills followed through and stepped on the Kiwi's face, gashing his eyebrow and cheek. It was blatant, brutal and unforgettable — no joke. Mills was sent off, another in the 27 or 28 times he was marched in his career, probably a world record in any code of football. But that day as he trudged to the dressingroom, he was genuinely ashamed. "Stupid y'know. They say the old blue mist used to come over me eyes," he said. "A moment of madness. When I looked at it in the cool of the day I couldn't believe what I'd done. One thing in me rugby career I'm always a bit sad about."

Mills — ex-Widnes, ex-North Sydney, bigger than any of the Kangaroos, hair thinning, ears caullied, eyebrows thick like a boxer's — sat on his nightclub stool with arms folded, rather like an apologetic bear. Football was good to Mills. Three times he walked Wembley's turf with Widnes, once scoring a winning try and a medal from Princess Alexandra. He spent two years with North Sydney, toured the Antipodes with the Lions and retired in 1980 with $125,000 saved from football. He invested in a down-and-out nightclub in Widnes, and Big Jim's made him such a fortune he has just spent $1.25 million renovating and renaming it Top of the Town. Mills is now a respected director of Widnes football club but there are those to whom Mills was and still remains a thug, a menace on the field and a disgrace to the game. Others though maintain that his was a true Jekyll and Hyde personality — wicked on field, but once departed the lockers a gentle giant, with a quick, dry humour and ready laugh.

One who vouches for him is retired Test referee Billy Thompson. "He were last of the big 'ard luds," Thompson told me one day. "But narce as pah off t'field." Thompson recalled sending Mills off during a Widnes-Warrington derby. "Jim stretchered the Warrington prop," said Thompson. "Ah told 'im, 'Another dressingroom job Jim.' He says to me, all innocence-lark, 'I never tooched the bustard!' and I says to 'im, 'Well Jim, thar's only you and me 'ere and I've not laid a finger on the mun!' " Another time Mills protested hopefully, "Wha' for?" Said Thompson, "Lairt tuckle." Said Mills, "Aye Billy, but ah got there as soon as ah could."

Mills's minority partner in Top of the Town is Widnes captain and sometime Cronulla bad boy, Kurt Sorensen. Sorensen learnt at the feet of the master. He was only 18, playing his first international for New Zealand, the day Mills did for Greengrass in 1975. Kurt laughed at his partner's match misfortunes, but as Sydney props will aver Kurt, 34, is no virginal "Boon" to Mills. Kurt mused that many of his partner's sendoffs would be mere sin-bins today. Mills agreed. "Ah've been sent off just on me reputation," he said. "Ah've 'ud crowds send me off. Playin' away from 'ome, crowd's gone up, ref starts panicking and me next tuckle, off! Some were mistaken identity. If there were a bit of feeling I knew ah'd be first to go."

Some were ambitious referees. Behind their whistles Jim could hear them boast, ''I sent off Jim Mills.''

But his reputation worked for him as well. He came from Cardiff rugby union, aged 19, a big, raw-boned farm labourer. ''Me first season everyone's 'avin' a go at me,'' he said. ''Every week a battle and I thought, 'What a gairm this rugby league is!' I used to lose me temper a bit. Then I slowly got on top, got a reputation and found the gairm easier as the years went by.'' In 1970 Mills joined North Sydney and had to assert himself all over again. Third game, off and up before the NSW judiciary. ''Mr Mills you've only been playing a couple of weeks and here you are before us,'' quoth the panel. Replied Mills, ''Right, and it's sorry I am, ah'll do me best not t' see you again.'' A small suspension, but first match back, off and . . . ''Aye, I'm sorry again,'' he told them.

Widnes, with a pack containing Sorensen, huge Tongan signing Emosi Koloto and Australian hooker Phil McKenzie, were a formidable side and, unlike Wigan, fit. Australia was at near full strength, Fulton using the second Test side minus Daley, still nursing his broken hand. Daley's replacement in effect was Alexander, playing his eleventh tour match, five of them as a substitute. Had he left the substitutes' bench in the second Test this would have been his twelfth consecutive match. Fulton acknowledged Alexander as one of the form players on tour. ''We want to see what Brandy can do on the wing,'' he said. How quick was Alexander? ''Toss up between Brandy, ET and Shearer,'' said Fulton. ''Brandy could be the fastest but we don't put them down in a footrace so we don't know.'' At training one day I put that question to Michael Hancock, who might have qualified as the team speedster himself but for his torn ankle ligaments. ''Rowdy over the full distance, Brandy over 50 metres,'' he declared. Shearer was trounced by Martin Offiah in a footrace in Sydney in 1988, but Offiah's second Test injury ruled him out of the Widnes side.

Since Hull, Fulton had trained the squad only once a day, embarking on a 10-day taper to peak for the third Test. ''Not that they were flat, but I had a long talk to McRae and Lewis about it and they figure that's the way to go,'' said Fulton. ''It's a mental thing as well as physical. The problem has been players training three times a day — morning, afternoon and they'd be going down to the gym themselves after that. They weren't overdoing it but this is just our way of saying, 'Hey, we've got these 10 pretty important days coming up.' '' That news disappointed British assistant coach Phil Larder who considered Australia were overtrained and tired at Wembley. ''I had a spot on Granada television where I was going to say I didn't think Australia were fit enough, because I knew Fulton would be watching the show,'' said Larder. ''I hoped he might work them even harder. But when I saw the Aussies again they looked far fresher.''

Sunday, 18 November at Widnes was the coldest day on tour. My photograph on the back cover of this book was taken sitting in the Widnes grandstand as sleet and hail swept the ground. Several times during the match I noticed players half-turn their backs to the wind, like farm animals to a storm. Widnes were the last club to defeat the Kangaroos, in 1978, and were all that stood in the way of the 1990 Kangaroos recording Australia's 33rd consecutive win over English clubs. Just three minutes after kick-off Steve Roach arrowed a superb spiralling pass to Lyons who turned the ball back inside for Belcher to score. In 1982 when Wally Lewis threw long passes it was a revelation, now Blocker Roach was flinging them. With a fierce wind at their backs the Roos might have done better than score one more try, just before the change. Lindner brushed past halfback David Hulme and then shed Andy Currier like an unwanted towel. A short pass sent Shearer the necessary five metres to score.

In between those two tries Cliff Lyons was sin-binned for backchatting the referee and when Roach followed him eight minutes later, after a scrum brawl, a controversy was brewing. Kurt Sorensen and Roach were opposed, nearside to the referee. Roach charged legitimately into the scrum with his head, Sorensen's free arm at first grasped Roach's jersey and then disappeared for a split second in a half swinging motion to

Roach's head. Roach came up hammering at Sorensen and when sin-binned Roach looked accusingly at Sorensen and said, "Send him off!" Roach then made an allegation against Sorensen which Sorensen denied to the referee. "He f . . . . . . did," said Roach departing, giving as good as he got from the 15,000 spectators as he trudged down the sideline.

A few minutes into the second half Sironen took the ball up, Sorensen went high and Sironen's head jerked back as Sorensen's finger poked Sironen in the eye. Sironen was helped from the field and all else in the match became over-shadowed by this incident. Which was a shame because Meninga soon took off on one those long surges of his which we saw in their most pure form only three times on tour. Al-though unable to lift weights for several years because of his arm fractures, Mal is so naturally strong he simply dusted sturdy second rower Richard Eyres and accelerated 40 metres down the touchline. Although he does not have a sprinter's staccato leg speed, Mal possesses the strength of a 400 metre runner and once he's into stride it's one long glorious power glide. When Jonathan Davies's courageous tackle compelled Meninga to find support, Greg Alexander accepted a superb floating pass on his fingertips and flew the last 15 metres for a magnificent try, second only in quality to Stuart and Meninga's at Old Trafford. Nearing the final whistle Sorensen was named Widnes sponsors' man-of-the-match although I would have given it to Jonathan Davies whose all-round talents were re-warded with a last-minute try to make the final score 15-8, the closest club margin of the tour. A fine match was about to be overtaken by recriminations.

Bob Fulton emerged from the dressingroom more angry than I had seen him on tour. In a crowded corridor he an-nounced, "Sironen has a scratched eyeball and he's in doubt for the Test. I don't have to be a medical person to tell you how he got that. There was a lot of gouging going on out there today. It's absolutely disgraceful and all the players know who it is. He's a senior player and the coach should take action against him." Fulton said he thought five or six players had been gouged, one of whom was Steve Roach. I spoke to Meninga as he shaved and he reluctantly confirmed he had complained to the referee about gouging. "We didn't know who the culprit was and the ref said he'd watch out for it," he said. "Then I complained again when Glenn Lazarus was eye gouged and we thought we knew who the guy was. But there's not much you can do unless you catch him in the act." On that evidence Roach and Lazarus were eye gouged but their allegations should not be related to the Sironen incident involving Kurt Sorensen.

Sironen was sitting disconsolately in a corner with a large white gauze pad over his eye. "I don't know whether it was intentional or not but the same guy was going around my head all day mate," said Sironen. "The chances are a lot better you'll get hit in the eye if he's going around your head isn't it? I can cop a punch on the chin or nose but when a bloke's going around your head and your face I can't cop that." Dr Nathan Gibbs confirmed Sironen had a scratch across one half of his cornea and another across the upper part of the white of his eye. "He has blurred vision on one half of his visual field from the scratch across the cornea," he said. "That usually heals fairly quickly. We like to think within three to four days it should be OK. The treatment is antibiotic drops and rest."

I approached Kurt Sorensen in the Widnes clubhouse afterwards and asked about the allegations. He looked hurt and angry. "I was the tackler on Sironen but it was pure accident," he said. "How could it be a gouge? It was first contact in a tackle, out in the open. Tell them all to have a look at the video, see for themselves. That's not my go anyway."

The Widnes match was over but the eye gouging controversy was just beginning. Fulton would normally not enter into such a row without first studying a match video but said he felt compelled to speak out because of Sironen's injury and Meninga's complaints to the referee. "You can't mention the guy's name publicly for fear of litigation," warned Fulton. The next day RFL public affairs officer David Howes, in the *Man-*

chester Evening News, challenged Fulton to produce evidence in support of his remarks.

Fulton had emphasised at Widnes that gouging, "because it's done in traffic", was very hard to find on video. At a press conference on Monday evening Keith Barnes said to Fulton, "Nothing came up on video, did it?" Fulton looked hard at Barnes and said, "Oh mate, I haven't had a look at that." Yet Channel 10 had been providing Fulton with a match video every evening after afternoon matches and first thing in the morning following night matches. To support a point, Fulton was fond of reminding journalists that they had not had a chance to study match videos as he had.

Widnes coach Doug Laughton, every bit as irrascible as Fulton, wrote to the RFL demanding an apology from Fulton for his gouging accusations. By then, midweek, Fulton had examined the tape. "We have irrefutable evidence of gouging," he said dramatically. "If the evidence we've got was given to the Winfield Cup judiciary, it would be thank you linesmen, thank you ballboys." That same Wednesday, RFL Controller of Referees Fred Lindop also studied a tape of the Widnes match. "There's nothing conclusive," he told me. "If it's the same video tape, Fulton's skating on thin ice. It's mischievous of him to make out that he can see anything because it's emotive stuff, gouging. It's a staggering allegation." But Lindop did not publish his views.

And so it raged, back and forth. Ex-Lion Laughton, as he had shown by his undercover agent's role before the second Test, probably hoped he was undermining morale in the Australian camp by prolonging the dispute into the Test week. But provoking Fulton is like quarreling with John McEnroe. All Laughton achieved was to heighten Fulton's sense of injustice and sharpen his combative senses. Thank you Howes, thank you Laughton.

It was an unhappy, wearying end to the club rounds on tour and my mind went back to the Widnes railway station where I had pulled in en route to the match. Opposite the ticket office a bronze plaque declares: "It was whilst waiting for the milk

train at Widnes railway station after a local folk gig in 1965 that
Paul Simon — yearning to be back in London in the arms of his
beloved Kathy — began writing Homeward Bound.''

I wondered how the Kangaroos were feeling, seven weeks
in a hotel, 12 matches gone and only the third and deciding
Test to play. I'd already heard Mark Geyer tell Greater Manchester Radio how the players were starting to miss home. ''All
you can do is write letters and talk on the telephone,'' he said.
''The people here have been very friendly but obviously English weather is not as good as Australian weather. I can't wait
to get back to some sun.'' Perhaps the Roos felt, like Paul
Simon, that each town looked the same, ''the movies and the
factories'', each stranger's face reminding them that they
longed to be, ''Homeward bound . . .''

15 THIRD TEST — SIMPLY THE BEST

Despite the Bozo-baiting, Bob Fulton never let outside tensions interfere with his friendship with Malcolm Reilly, his old Manly buddy. Several times on tour — including during this Test week — Fulton had dinner with Reilly, sometimes with their wives and with another former Manly team-mate, Phil Lowe. "Malcolm's the same as me, obviously fierce competitors but you can't deny your mateship and the camaraderie that you've built up," Fulton told me one evening. "There's probably never been an Australian and a Great Britain coach as close as we are," he said. "I mean it's not a physical confrontation between him and me." He said he and Reilly talked about some of the individual players from both sides, but nothing in relation to the Tests. "We just have a laugh and a joke about some of the things we did when we were younger, rehashing old stuff," he said.

Like the night Fulton, Reilly and Jim Mills emerged merry from a North Sydney pub and decided to test their strength by lifting a huge sidewalk flower tub. Jim Mills told me neither Fulton nor Reilly could budge it but massive Mills did, and then found, to his comrades' hilarity, he couldn't put it back down. Mills staggered across to a car and dumped it on the bonnet which promptly sagged. I said to Fulton, "Mills says he paid the $100 repair bill and never got the money from you two." Fulton guffawed. "Bullshit! I paid for it, there were five of us and it was $20 each," he said. "And I never got my money!" At a Great Britain press conference I asked Reilly, "You've had a couple of meals with Bobby, any tips exchanged over the red wine?" Reilly smiled and said, "No, we didn't talk football." *Sun-Herald* sportswriter Alan Clarkson, who has known Fulton for many years, joked, "I'll bet I know who paid!" Reilly laughed and said, "No, actually he has mellowed, has Bobby."

Reilly had just named his Test squad, unchanged from the second Test, and the chosen players were available for interview before training. Except Hanley of course, sitting enigmatically by himself in all blue: t-shirt, tracksuit top, shorts and long elasticised tights — like a brooding jazz ballet dancer. I heard British manager Maurice Lindsay apologising for Hanley on a portable telephone, "I know this is the biggest Test in 100 years but I can't help you . . ." I knew Offiah had been timed at 10.8 for 100 metres but not that he once opened the bowling for Essex county's Second XI and actually bowled England captain Graham Gooch in the nets. His run-up, he said grinning, was "at speed". Andy Gregory was in his fifth Test series against Australia but he couldn't stay to chat too long. "I'd better go," said the tough little halfback looking over his shoulder. "I don't want Malcolm to give me a bollicking."

Jonathan Davies, the Wales-to-Widnes wonder boy, selected as a substitute, was disappointed not to make the 13. "But the way the lads have played over the two games I wasn't expecting it," he said. Earlier in the season, when I visited Malcolm Reilly at Ledsham, his home village, he told me Davies's physical strength was not what it should be. "I'm sure from speaking to him he'll be making efforts," Reilly had said. But Davies, who weighs 12 stone, told me his Widnes coach, Doug Laughton, was not encouraging it. "Doug said he'd bought me for what I am and didn't want me to put on two stone and lose my speed," said Davies. "So I've put on about 10 lbs in the upper body and haven't lost any pace."

I can vouch for his speed having seen him demoralise Wigan in Widnes's first match of the season. The game was a charity match played in Swansea to once more exhibit rugby league in Wales, the heartland of British rugby union. It was a miserable venue, two stands empty, condemned under stadium safety rules, yet over 11,000 were crammed on to terraces, pens and bare benches. Widnes won 24-8 and as luck would have it all 32 points were scored by rugby union converts, Davies, Offiah, Devereux for Widnes and ex-All Black Frano Botica for Wigan.

At half-time I chatted with a fellow spectator, John Evans, a dairy farmer who hadn't missed a rugby union international at Cardiff Arms Park for 12 years. This was his first live rugby league match. Why are you here? I asked. ''Came to see the rugby contingent,'' he replied. But he was enjoying it all. ''They've changed the rules haven't they?'' he said. ''The scrums are no better but the ball is in play a lot more. There's no dead periods like in our game.''

Rugby league is once more seeking to bring the Northern game to the Welsh valleys but the English RFL has finally grasped that the game must be built from the ground up. All previous attempts failed through seeking to impose ready-made professional clubs, seeded with ex-Welsh internationals, on to resentful Welsh districts. Today amateur rugby league, at colleges and universities, is the thin edge being driven into the tightly knit Welsh rugby union communities. New Zealand may well rue the loss of recent All Blacks to rugby league, but Welsh rugby union has long endured its predations. In 80 years Wales has lost 150 internationals — 13 in the last five years — not including mere club players like the great Billy Boston. By comparison England has lost only 50.

In past years such poaching led to rugby league scouts, if rumbled in a Welsh pub, ending up in a river or at least being escorted to the nearest railway station. A piece of doggerel penned at the turn of the century in a Yorkshire paper went:

> There was a three-quarters from Wales,
> This is true — it's not one of my tales,
> He was sought by each club,
> But we bought him a pub,
> And took the wind out of their sails.

Nearly a century on, Jonathan Davies became the most valuable jewel prised from the Welsh rugby union crown yet no Welshman begrudged him a penny of his signing fee. Davies spoke out against the corruption of privileges at official level in

Welsh rugby union and these days up to 200 Welsh rugby union fans regularly trek 400 kms to the north of England on weekends to see "Jiffy" play for Widnes. Davies rewarded their loyalty by returning to Swansea and scoring three tries, kicking two goals and being voted man-of-the-match.

Afterwards, in a nearby rowdy pub, farmer Evans conceded it had been a good game and he would be happy to watch another. "But for most of these lads," he said, indicating the packed bar, "it'll be first and last. They'd have come out of curiosity." Just then we both heard another group discussing their first experience of rugby league. "You know," mused one. "I've been a fool every Saturday afternoon for the past 15 years. Do you realise that?"

Taffy would not have had to wait so long had it not been for the split between the professional and amateur rugby league organisations in England. One quiet morning of this Test week I drove over the Pennines to Huddersfield, the grand Victorian town where rugby league was born in 1895 and where the amateurs and professionals split in 1973. First I visited the four-storey George Hotel which forms part of the classical St George's Square. All the square's buildings are crowned by stone ornaments — one with elaborate balustrades, another with a massive sculpture of a prowling lion and a third has proud Britannia with her own lion guard. I suppose Huddersfield was chosen as a meeting place by the rebel clubs because it was almost equidistant from the two rugby strongholds in Lancashire and Yorkshire — and The George because it is right beside Huddersfield railway station. The name, George Hotel, is in large gilded letters across the front, above a portico which invites passersby to enter for morning coffee. I accepted and sat in the foyer beside a log fire, and saw on the foyer wall a plaque and relief sculpture, which records:

> In this hotel at an historic meeting on August 29th, 1895, was founded the Northern Rugby Football Union known since 1923 as the Rugby Football League.

I was shown the Tudor Room where the momentous meetings took place but the hotel shows no great pride in its history and I departed disappointed, my visit having conjured up nothing of one of sport's great social revolutions. I walked up past the classic colonnades of the railway station to the head-quarters of BARLA, the British Amateur Rugby League Association, to meet the rebels within the rebels — "the bastard sons of the bastard son" as BARLA national administrator Maurice Olroyd put it.

BARLA was begun at a time when rugby league was known as the "dying game" in England. The RFL — the professional clubs — ran amateur (junior) rugby league but because they were so straitened themselves they neglected the lifeblood of the game. Amateur numbers had so declined that they didn't have sufficient players to field age teams for the annual York-shire-Lancashire county challenge. Maurice Olroyd, then president of the Huddersfield Referees Society, plotted with other sympathisers to escape the RFL's dead hand. "They could have crushed us overnight if they'd manoeuvred sensibly," said Olroyd. "Instead they dug their heels in and cut off money to the amateur game. That bonded us together because we'd scarcely any money before." They began with 155 teams, 25 pounds in the bank and a pure love of rugby league.

Olroyd had read in the British Sports Council journal how English folk dancers had received a large government grant and mused to himself, "Fancy the Council grantin' that much for prattin' about dancin', why can't we get some?" In 1976 the Sports Council recognised BARLA and by 1991 the grant had risen to $400,000 annually. The growth of BARLA is the success story of modern British sport. Over 1100 teams now play amateur rugby league in Britain and the game had spread through universities, colleges and schools. First BARLA broke out of the North and then took the amateur game overseas. Rugby league, which was once played only in the five countries who play it professionally, (England, Australia, France, New Zealand and Papua New Guinea), is now played in 16 countries. Today Phil Larder, national director of coaching and assistant to Malcolm Reilly, is paid by BARLA, not the professional clubs of the RFL. In 1987 BARLA even took on and vanquished the oldest foe of all — rugby union's 92-year-old ban on its members playing rugby league. BARLA beat the RFU at the Sports Council by arguing that government grants required recipients, including rugby union, to open their membership to all sportspeople.

Ideally BARLA acts as a breeding ground for the professional clubs and indeed Garry Schofield and Mike Gregory captained BARLA's Great Britain youth teams, Andy Gregory was former BARLA player-of-the-year and Ellery Hanley a BARLA youth international. But these very youth internationals are in direct conflict with the professional clubs who seek to sign players to contracts at an early age.

BARLA has also become a law unto itself, sending senior amateur rugby league teams on tours to Tonga, the Cook Islands and Western Samoa. Australia's policy is that international tours are reserved for the national professional team as an incentive for juniors and as the pinnacle of achievement in rugby league. I asked Olroyd, light-heartedly, if BARLA had some secret agenda to take over rugby league in England? "Good god, no!" he exclaimed. "It's a lovely compliment and the clubs are absolutely paranoid about it. But it's crazy. We've enough work administering the amateurs without taking on the professionals." At the Rugby League Writers' Association dinner, journalists awarded Maurice Olroyd their 1990 special memorial trophy for services to the game. The 1983 recipient was the RFL's David Howes. Both working for the game, but not together.

It depressed me to hear of such damaging internal wrangling but my mood lightened when I drove back to the Ramada to find the Australian camp buzzing with the remarkable recovery of Paul Sironen's eye injury. Just 48 hours after the Widnes match Sironen declared vision in his scratched eye to be perfect. When Dr Nathan Gibbs checked with an eyedrop stain which reveals corneal abrasions, he was astounded to see the eye was indeed clear. Of the other injury worries Gibbs said he would use a local anaesthetic to deaden pain in Laurie Daley's hand and Benny Elias's damaged rib cartilage. Except for Chris

Johns and Kerrod Walters, retained as emergencies, the rest of the non-Test squad were given leave-of-absence and scattered on trips to Scotland, Ireland and Amsterdam. Even Fulton took a day off for a business trip to London. Their laid back mood contrasted starkly with the dramatic events we watched on television that week as hour by hour Margaret Thatcher lost her battle to remain Prime Minister. Could this be an omen, the end of a long reign?

With all quiet on the Ramada front I accepted a spare ticket from the *Australian*'s John Hogan to a Manchester United-Celtic testimonial friendly at Old Trafford. Friendly? Celtic's fans had arrived in force, 15,000 of them, over a third of the 40,000 crowd and their fervour made me wonder at the wisdom of rugby league seeking to expand nationally. Never have I seen such blind loyalty as exhibited that evening. Celtic fans kept up such a non-stop barrage that the Manchester crowd, normally as vociferous as any, were all but silenced. All the Celtic fans were cooped into one end of the ground, guarded by a thin blue line of helmeted bobbies. Manchester fans adjacent became increasingly incensed at the truculence of the Glasgow lot. The two groups sang songs, leapt up from their seats, shouted abuse and pointed at each other in scary scenes of mass menace. As luck would have it Celtic won 3-1 which probably saved Manchester, the city, from a right royal riot that night. Unforgettable, after Celtic's third goal, were 15,000 fans singing at the top of their voices, to the inevitable tune of Guantanamera: "SO FOOKIN' EASY, OH THIS IS SO FOOKIN' EASY, SO FOOKIN' EEA-SYY, OH THIS IS SO FOOKIN' EEA-SYY!" It took me days to rid my mind of that melody but I will never forget the hostile temper of that soccer crowd. When retired rugby league referee Billy Thompson received his MBE from the Queen at Buckingham Palace, Her Majesty inquired, "Tell me, has anything changed in that wonderful game of yours?" Thompson replied, "No ma'am, the players still respect referees and the spectators go out to enjoy themselves and don't cause any problem." To which the Queen said, "Quite apparent, when you watch the game."

Escaping the soccer we returned to the Ramada to find an animated card game in progress at a bar table. Ricky Stuart, Chris Johns, Benny Elias, Cliff Lyons, the Walters twins and David Gillespie were playing stud poker, a $10 limit so nobody was going to win or lose a fortune. Chris Johns made enough noise to be winning, Ricky Stuart had a losing chair and soon departed. Benny Elias was breaking square and enjoying himself. "You'll take a lot longer to do your dough here than at a casino," he offered knowledgably. As in their football, Kerrod played with more flourish than Kevin while quiet Cliffy passed prudently and showed great joy from occasional wins. The players were all in multi-hued tracksuits, a madhatters tea-party dressed up as footballers, while around them a variety of camp followers arrived from evening's outings and stayed to barrack or sidewalk superintend. The school was still joyfully upping the ante at midnight, the third Test momentarily far from their minds.

On Friday morning I poured luke-warm water over my car windscreen to melt the ice and drove into the Ramada where players were drifting downstairs for breakfast. Kerrod Walters picked up a copy of the latest *Rugby League Week* which had Meninga photos on the front and back pages. "What is this, a Mal Meningathon?" he joked. Others were a little late down and just as Dale Shearer was served his tomatoes and eggs on toast the call came to board the bus for training. "Rowdy" picked up his plate, knife and fork and continued his breakfast on the bus.

The training was at Leigh, in a wind so icy all the players wore thigh-length windjackets and tracksuit pants. Steve Roach shouted "They made the seven wonders of the world and then came Benny Elias," because Elias emerged wearing only shorts and a t-shirt. When Fulton arrived Paul Sironen and the forwards began full speed side-stretches, Fulton's favourite exercise which he does even when in earnest conversation with training staff. "The latest dance craze sweeping England," called Sirro, "the Bozo shake!" For the cameras, Greg Alexander then performed a 20-metre sprint followed by a cartwheel and a backward somersault. "I did gymnastics at school," he said, puffing as he returned. "I was going to do that after I scored that try at Widnes." You should have, I encouraged him. "I will if I score a try in a Test," he said, and did, in France in the second Test.

Late that afternoon I saw imposing Steve Roach and scarred Glenn Lazarus sitting together in the hotel foyer sipping tea and eating dainty petit fours from a fine set of china. Blocker and Lazza were the engine-room of the Australian pack yet looked as poised as two Parisians in a sidewalk cafe. Paul Sironen, wearing the classy Hull jersey, approached them. "Nice jumper, pity they can't play," said Lazza. Everyone seemed to have a stack of footballs for the team to sign. Only when I saw heavy team baggage being brought downstairs by hotel porters did I grasp the reason for the apparent lack of tension. Though building for the final Test, the Kangaroos were also winding down to the end of their English tour. The Test was tomorrow, Saturday, and they would be out of the Ramada by midday Sunday. In a sense the players felt released from further responsibilities in England. Nothing more could be done to prepare for Ashes day at Elland Road.

Came that hour and the Kangaroos ran onto a freezing rainswept ground under a drenched, slate-grey sky, the sulphur-yellow streetlights of Leeds glowing along rows of terrace houses on surrounding hills. Nothing could be more English, nothing less Australian. Eminent interlopers from other ball sports, the *Guardian*'s Frank Keating and Hugh McIlvanney from the *Independent*, had arrived from London drawn by that rarity, the promise of a genuine contest. I was gratified that my own small patriotic suggestion had now escalated into "Waltzing Matilda" being sung by the 150-strong Leeds Philharmonic Chorus. But neither team needed inspiration today.

The 1990 Kangaroos lifted rugby league onto a new plain of professionalism at Elland Road. They had to because Great Britain would have defeated anything less. The Test was decided by inspired moments during 80 gruelling minutes when, out of the perpetual motion that is modern rugby league, Australia contrived tries of sublime simplicity. The first came after nine minutes when Ricky Stuart, undeterred by memories of intercepts, the driving rain or the slippery ball, spiralled a long pass into space, aiming for an appointment which Andrew Ettingshausen duly kept, to slide over in the corner. "Some days you get intercepted, some days you don't," said Ricky, the fatalist, later. The space Stuart identified had been left by centre Carl Gibson who had walked from the field after a knock to the head. Jonathan Davies had not had time to replace him.

Yet Gibson was injured, concussed no less — requiring hospitalisation — nearly two minutes before he was finally taken off. Britain's medicos chose to lead him off just as a penalty had brought Australia to the British 22-metre line. In the previous two minutes Britain twice had possession, when Gibson could have been safely replaced. Why wasn't he? Because the British management didn't trust "Jiffy" — Jonathan Davies — to contain Meninga and wanted to be certain Gibson could not continue. But if Reilly didn't trust Davies's defence, why was he a sub at all?

ET's try gave Australia a 4-0 lead — Meninga's miss gave him an abysmal 14 goals from 31 attempts on tour — yet it is to rugby league's credit that goals rarely determine victories in internationals as they continue to do in rugby union. Britain muffed several chances to peg back that lead before half-time. Instead I have several images of the trend of play — Benny Elias so hounding and harrying Schofield that he quashed Britain's kicking game. Another image was of Ellery Hanley stepping swiftly inside Lazarus and suddenly rocking backwards from a tremendous rib-jarring hit by Sironen. Sironen outweighs Hanley by 20 kgs so even Hanley's tensile strength waned as Sirro clattered him again and again. Yet after each hit Hanley gamely got up and referee Billy Thompson's words came back to me. "People say, 'So-and-so is dead soft', and I say, 'Oh no mairt, there's nobody soft playin' rugby league. There's just them that's 'arder than others.' " And no one harder than Hanley.

Australia's play assumed the pattern of Winfield Cup finals

— intense, disciplined, chancing attacks but leaving nothing to chance in defence. Indeed they entered the realms of a near perfect game, performing to the very limits of their talents and never toppling beyond into ego. As British prop Denis Betts said later, "They were relentless and calculating, they waited and waited, they built pressure and the moment we made a mistake they struck."

Ten minutes into the second half and the Test, the series, the Ashes were there for the taking, by the daring and the bold, or the determined and the patient. Garry Schofield elected for the former. On the British quarterline Elias sent a 15-metre pass to Stuart who lofted a 20-metre pass to Lyons. As Stuart prepared to pass, Malcolm Reilly and Phil Larder on the British bench saw a sudden movement out of the British defensive line and caught their breath in anguish — Garry Schofield had set out for an intercept.

Schofield's attributes are that he reads plays very early and makes lightning decisions, in attack and defence. He made his reputation with his uncanny anticipation but as a strategem for close-hauled defence in a Test match, intuition should never outrank policy. In the dressingroom, five minutes before the match, Phil Larder had taken Schofield aside. "Schoey, if you spot things out wide early, don't move up in front of the defensive line," said Larder. "Take your centres with you. They're pretty astute, a quick word and they'll be with you." When Larder finished, Reilly had the last word to the team and one final word to Schofield, "Schoey, let me underline what Phil said, stay in the defensive line."

Schofield darted out of the defensive line in search of Stuart's pass, in search of one decisive blow, in search of Ashes victory and, just maybe, glory. But he underestimated the deep angle of the Australian backline and though he sprinted 20 metres the ball beat him to Cliff Lyons by a clear metre. He didn't even bother to stretch out his arms. "We couldn't believe it," said Larder. "We saw his first step and put our hands to our heads." In the stands, Schofield's Leeds coach David Ward had winced too. "I could have cried for you," Ward told Larder later. "We've been trying to get him to give up the habit but we can't break him of it." Schofield turned in time to watch unfold the results of his impetuous run. He might have hoped little harm was done but at this elevated standard of rugby league his error was as terminal as if it had been chess — it simply required the inevitable moves to be executed. Lyons intelligently faded across field exposing Schofield's absence and shovelled the ball over his shoulder to Meninga who cut clinically inside three cover defenders to score untouched under the posts. Or as Larder put it, "Cliff went straight across and dropped Mal through a bloody great big hole you could have driven a bus through."

At 10-0 the Roos had reason to be elated. Roach and Lazarus were among the first to their captain and they leapt upon him like a pair of Jumbos practising the mating game. Only a man of Meninga's tremendous stature could have withstood the assault. Mal's try in each Test matched Sam Backo's 3 against the 1988 Lions and Ken Irvine's feat 25 years ago. Laurie Daley completed formalities by taking off from a ruck his side of half-way and weaving his way downfield to set up an Elias try in the corner. Elias's speed to the touchdown made light of his torn rib cartilages now stabbing through ebbing pain-killing injections. With the lead 14-0 the shout went up among the Roos, "Don't let them score!" and nor did they, inflicting the Lions' first ever nil defeat on home soil. There was no justice, or mercy, for Reilly's lads on that cold wintry afternoon.

Five minutes to go and Fulton sent on his four subs, Alexander, Sargent, Gillespie and Hasler for their moment in history. Two minutes to go and it wouldn't have been a Test if "Blocker" hadn't been sin-binned. And then Mal was giving a victory salute and calling his players over to where a mass of green and gold terraces were chanting "Aussie, Aussie". Castlemaine's Nick Potter thrust a garish yellow Fourex cap at Meninga who dutifully put it on. Just for once I wished Potter had stayed his sponsors' hand. A more sensitive eye might have recognised that this moment transcended commercialism. But then again Fourex had supplied the 12,000 cans of beer consumed by the 35 tour members, friends and fellow travellers over two months. Schofield swapped jerseys with Daley, Sironen with Betts, and Lazarus with Platt. "I thought I better grab one while I could," said Glenn. "You never know when you'll get another chance." No worries Lazza. Nothing is surer than that he is the future of Australia's Test pack. Benny Elias was bowing to the Aussie crowd and curling his palm like a bullfighter but for once he was lost for words. He told John Harker of Channel Seven, "It's a great, it's great . . . ummm, it's great for your side, Oh I don't know! It's a great . . . what can I say!" and broke up laughing. Stuart was man-of-the-match but as he said, "They must have picked my name out of a hat, they could have picked anybody."

"TR-ASHED" was to be the *Daily Mirror*'s headline, "Mighty Aussies Leave British Hopes in Roo-ins". Not quite the first, but certainly the second. Australia had retained the Ashes, held since 1973 and stretched their run of unbeaten Test series in England to 31 years, enough reason for their dressing-room to be overrun. Police at the door let the media through in shifts so once I found a corner near Mal Meninga I stayed put. He was a proud, relieved man, Mal. "I've had a fairly long career but taking the Ashes back home, I'll cherish this moment for a long, long time." The future? "It all depends on Wally Lewis but if they want me to captain Australia again I'd gladly do the job." Steve Roach interjected, "Mate, put in that if they pick me I'd like to play too."

After two months in dressingrooms beside the massive biceps, triceps and quadriceps of half-naked Kangaroos, I had gained an insight into why Australia overcame such a determined British side. Mal Meninga could have been an Olympic decathlete, Paul Sironen and Glenn Lazarus possess shot-putters' shoulders, Steve Roach could have been a title contender. For two months the unfortunates of English rugby league had been hammered by footballers with muscular physiques sculpted by modern power weightlifting and cardio-vascular supervision. It was the Australians' body strength, sheer Schwarzenegger muscle-power, which underpinned the

Kangaroos' retention of the Ashes. English rugby league grew out of black coal pits but its future now had to be in the bright lights of sports institutes, exercise testing laboratories and clockwork physiology. Bob Fulton was in no doubt. "Unyielding defence won the day," he said. "When we didn't have the ball we tackled and didn't we tackle! Our defence was so strong that in the end I think the Poms were hiding. They didn't have people to take the ball up. Their gun players were terrorised."

Great Britain manager, Maurice Lindsay, summed it up. "We have to develop our upper body strength so we have big men like Meninga and your forwards," he said. "With defence as strong as Australia's, our attack has to be 100 per cent effective. We might get away with 98 per cent. If we slip to 95 per cent, we need Australia to make an enormous mistake. If we slip to 90 per cent we're no chance at all." Paul Sironen sat quietly, satisfied he had completed a personal mission on Ellery Hanley. "I missed him a couple of times in the first two Tests," said Sironen. "They scored a try in the first Test because I missed him. But we did a bit of work on him and Bozo made me aware I was going too low so today I made sure I aimed at his ribs." They were clubmates together at Balmain in 1988 but as Sironen said, "Who gives a stuff about club bloody friendships, this is an international."

The British dressingroom emptied quickly. Gallant defeats don't make for long conversations. Phil Larder put Australia's winning edge down to the speed of the Kangaroo rucks which enabled the backs to set up attacks. "We have to improve the speed of our play-the-balls by 10 to 20 per cent," he said. Maurice Lindsay endured questions to the last until finally only Lindsay, myself and the baggage man remained. Maurice remembered me from our interview in Wigan's cherry-red members' suite. He was down, but saw the series clearly. "We've gone from being no-hopers before Wembley to having every chance at Old Trafford and here," he said. "We just lack your awe-inspiring confidence," he mused. "We still need to lose our self-doubt, to know we can hold you, get in front and stay there. Only comes with time. We've got two years now to see what we can do in Sydney and Brisbane."

I caught up with Fulton and recognised once more that on the other side of his Aussie abrasiveness is a genuine sensitivity to the feelings of others. "My mate Malcolm has done a Maggie Thatcher-type job in lifting Great Britain," he said. The Iron Lady had actually been forced to resign two days earlier, but I got Bozo's drift. "You could have been in the room next door Adrian, talking to Malcolm, same as you are to me, and I would have been down in the dumps," he said. "That's what sport's all about. In a two-horse race there's got to be a winner and a loser and fortunately for us we're the winners." Fulton had brought the Roos back from the edge of defeat, steeled their nerves and lifted them to this near flawless performance at Elland Road. If you applied the old cricket cliche — who would you have bat for you life? — to rugby league, I'd nominate Bozo. Whatever your fate you'd know he'd have dealt out heaps on your behalf. At the Ashes ceremonies Fulton spent the evening consoling Malcolm Reilly. The pit-face, the trenches, rugby league — all make for powerful mateship. Hanley was declared Britain's man-of-the-series and Bob Lindner Australia's — worthily so, for beyond even Meninga, Lindner exemplified the implacable spirit of the Kangaroos.

I left Leeds for the Ramada and joined in the celebrations in the ground floor bar, catching little snippets from groups here and there. How Hanley fouled Brad Mackay and lost his cool when Brad taunted him, "Mate, you've lost it!" How Meninga spotted the Brits wiping petroleum jelly over the ball to make it greasy before the second half kick-off. "You learn something every day don't you," said Mal. "I'll go home and try that now." Benny Elias commandeered the hotel reception intercom and said mock-seriously, "I have an announcement to make — Australia won the Ashes today, three cheers, you little bloody beauty!" Andrew Ettingshausen had a fat lip which spoilt his male model looks. His Cronulla team-mate Mark McGaw gladly posed beside ET for photographs. "Brings him back to the field," joked Sparkles. As the night wore on a chorus of Kangaroos broke into song — "Waltzing Matilda", "Advance Australia Fair" and "You'll Never Walk Alone", and they all knew the words. The chorus personnel changed constantly but into the early morning the stayers were Rowdy, ET, Badge, Blocker, MG and Lazza. I took my leave and drove home to Delph.

The next day the Kangaroos were gone. When I entered the Ramada, staff glanced curiously at me, as though I was a guest who had forgotten to go home after a long party. And so it was, an adventure party where footballers from all over NSW and Queensland, from the baked clay plains of Penrith, the beaches of Manly and Cronulla, the high cold air of Canberra and the humid sub-tropics of Brisbane, gathered to challenge the only other nation in the world which plays their game at their level of professionalism. Along the way the Kangaroos, almost by osmosis, learned a little about the roots of rugby league and its diverse history in the gritty North. They learned that a Kangaroo tour is much more than the honour of being selected for your country, it is a privileged journey through the towns and cities whose clubs ring with names Australians know by legend. And they learned that the Ashes are only worth the fight necessary to win them, and Great Britain had ensured the prize was well worth the winning.

A week after the Roos left for France — who they duly trounced 60-4 and 34-10 in two Tests — I drove back to Huddersfield to witness the Queen opening BARLA's headquarters. After the ceremony Her Majesty was presented with Great Britain youth jerseys for her grandchildren — Prince Charles's two sons, Harry and William. As the Queen drove off in her massive, 1960 Canberra model, Phantom V Rolls Royce, in the boot lay the four rugby league sweaters, like illicit seeds being secreted out of the North to the South. As the Rolls disappeared I said to Phil Larder, "You've found the perfect rugby league smuggler. No one will think to check the Queen's boot."

My own journey ended early in the new year, after snow turned the Pennines into white alps and transformed the little village of Delph into scenes of Christmas card beauty. The Kangaroos were well and truly home when, one evening, as I watched the BBC's 1990 Television Sports awards, the program suddenly crossed to an interview with Mal Meninga and named him BBC Overseas Personality of the Year. For the soccer-oriented BBC to so honour rugby league nationally was extraordinary. The 1990 Kangaroos weren't Invincible or Unbeatable, but they displayed a strength of character far beyond anything required of their immediate predecessors. As ambassadors for all that is commendable in rugby league, they were simply the best.

TOUR STATISTICS

(Courtesy of *Rugby League Week* and *Rothmans Rugby League Yearbook*)

GAMES PLAYED

Date	Opponent	Result	Score	Crowd
October 7	St Helens	Won	34-4	15,219
October 10	Wakefield	Won	36-18	7,724
October 14	Wigan	Won	34-6	24,814
October 17	Cumbria	Won	42-10	6,750
October 21	Leeds	Won	22-10	16,037
OCTOBER 27	GREAT BRITAIN	LOST	12-19	54,569
October 31	Warrington	Won	26-6	10,200
November 4	Castleford	Won	28-8	9,033
November 6	Halifax	Won	36-18	8,730
NOVEMBER 10	GREAT BRITAIN	WON	14-10	46,615
November 14	Hull	Won	34-4	13,081
November 18	Widnes	Won	15-8	14,666
NOVEMBER 24	GREAT BRITAIN	WON	14-0	32,500

Total crowds: 259,938. Average: 19,995

AUSTRALIAN TOTALS

Played: 13   Won: 12   Lost: 1
For: Tries 68   Goals 38 (1fg)   Points 347
Against: Tries 21   Goals 20 (3fg)   Points 121

INDIVIDUAL PLAYERS

PLAYER	Games played	As replacement	Tries	Goals	Field goals	Points
Greg ALEXANDER	6	6	2	21	—	50
Gary BELCHER	8	—	2	1	1	11
Martin BELLA	5	3	—	—	—	0
Mark CARROLL	2	1	1	—	—	4
John CARTWRIGHT	5	2	—	—	—	0
Laurie DALEY	5	—	—	—	—	0
Ben ELIAS	7	1	2	—	—	8
Andrew ETTINGSHAUSEN	9	—	11	—	—	44
Brad FITTLER	5	—	2	—	—	8
Mark GEYER	4	1	3	—	—	12
David GILLESPIE	5	3	—	—	—	0
Michael HANCOCK	5	1	4	—	—	16
Des HASLER	4	4	2	—	—	8
Chris JOHNS	5	2	3	—	—	12
Allan LANGER	7	1	1	—	—	4
Glenn LAZARUS	6	5	1	—	—	4
Bob LINDNER	8	1	2	—	—	8
Cliff LYONS	6	—	3	—	—	12
Brad MACKAY	7	3	2	—	—	8
Mark McGAW	5	1	1	—	—	4
Mal MENINGA	9	—	7	15	—	58
Steve ROACH	8	—	1	—	—	4
Mark SARGENT	5	1	3	—	—	12
Dale SHEARER	8	1	6	—	—	24
Paul SIRONEN	8	—	2	—	—	8
Ricky STUART	6	1	1	—	—	4
Kerrod WALTERS	6	—	2	—	—	8
Kevin WALTERS	5	—	4	—	—	16
Totals	—	—	68	37	1	347

CAPTAINS: Meninga (9), Elias (2), Langer (2)

LEADING TOUR SCORERS

Andrew Ettingshausen finished as the Kangaroos' top tryscorer with 11, including two hat-tricks. Dale Shearer scored the only other hat-trick.

Greg Alexander headed the goalscoring list with 21, including the tour's best match tally of six.

Mal Meninga was top point scorer with 58 from seven tries and 15 goals.

TOUR CROWD RECORDS

The Kangaroos attracted a record average crowd for a tour of England of 19,995 at 13 matches, beating the 16,732 at 27 matches in 1948.

The tour aggregate of 259,938 was the biggest since 22 matches drew 286,729 in 1963.

The Test series also produced a record aggregate of 133,684, beating the 114,883 in 1948 when Britain won all three Tests.

Receipts for the three-match series were a world record. Wembley produced £560,000, Old Trafford £381,000 and Elland Road £239,000 adding up to the first ever £1 million series with total receipts of £1,180,000.

The top tour crowd was 54,569 for the First Test at Wembley with the biggest at a club game being 24,814 at Wigan.

12-YEAR KANGAROO COMPARISON

	1978	1982	1986	1990
Matches played	16	15	13	13
Tries	79	97	85	68
Goals (fg)	68 (2)	66	56	38 (1)
Points for	375	423	452	347
Points against	117	80	105	121
Average pts for	23.4*	28.2*	34.7	26.6
Average pts agst	7.3	5.3	8.0	9.3

* (In 1983 the value of a try rose from 3pts to 4pts. Adjusting the average points scored by Australia in 1978 and 1982 increases the figures to 28.3 and 34.6 respectively. On converted figures, the 1986 side narrowly retained the best attacking record, the 1982 side easily the best defensive.)